DEVELOPMENT CENTRE SEMINARS

085334

THE FUTURE OF ASIA
IN THE WORLD ECONOMY

Edited by

Colm Foy, Francis Harrigan *and* David O'Connor

ASIAN DEVELOPMENT BANK
DEVELOPMENT CENTRE
OF THE ORGANISATION FOR ECONOMIC CO-OPERATION AND DEVELOPMENT

ORGANISATION FOR ECONOMIC CO-OPERATION AND DEVELOPMENT

Pursuant to Article 1 of the Convention signed in Paris on 14th December 1960, and which came into force on 30th September 1961, the Organisation for Economic Co-operation and Development (OECD) shall promote policies designed:

- to achieve the highest sustainable economic growth and employment and a rising standard of living in Member countries, while maintaining financial stability, and thus to contribute to the development of the world economy;
- to contribute to sound economic expansion in Member as well as non-member countries in the process of economic development; and
- to contribute to the expansion of world trade on a multilateral, non-discriminatory basis in accordance with international obligations.

The original Member countries of the OECD are Austria, Belgium, Canada, Denmark, France, Germany, Greece, Iceland, Ireland, Italy, Luxembourg, the Netherlands, Norway, Portugal, Spain, Sweden, Switzerland, Turkey, the United Kingdom and the United States. The following countries became Members subsequently through accession at the dates indicated hereafter: Japan (28th April 1964), Finland (28th January 1969), Australia (7th June 1971), New Zealand (29th May 1973), Mexico (18th May 1994), the Czech Republic (21st December 1995), Hungary (7th May 1996), Poland (22nd November 1996) and the Republic of Korea (12th December 1996). The Commission of the European Communities takes part in the work of the OECD (Article 13 of the OECD Convention).

The Development Centre of the Organisation for Economic Co-operation and Development was established by decision of the OECD Council on 23rd October 1962 and comprises twenty-three Member countries of the OECD: Austria, Belgium, Canada, the Czech Republic, Denmark, Finland, France, Germany, Greece, Iceland, Ireland, Italy, Japan, Korea, Luxembourg, Mexico, the Netherlands, Norway, Poland, Portugal, Spain, Sweden and Switzerland, as well as Argentina and Brazil from March 1994. The Commission of the European Communities also takes part in the Centre's Advisory Board.

The purpose of the Centre is to bring together the knowledge and experience available in Member countries of both economic development and the formulation and execution of general economic policies; to adapt such knowledge and experience to the actual needs of countries or regions in the process of development and to put the results at the disposal of the countries by appropriate means.

The Centre has a special and autonomous position within the OECD which enables it to enjoy scientific independence in the execution of its task. Nevertheless, the Centre can draw upon the experience and knowledge available in the OECD in the development field.

Publié en français sous le titre :

L'AVENIR DE L'ASIE DANS L'ÉCONOMIE MONDIALE

Foreword

This volume contains contributions from participants in the third conference of the International Forum on Asian Perspectives. The conference, entitled "The Future of Asia in the World Economy", was held in Paris on 23 and 24 June 1997, in the context of the Development Centre's research programme on Global Interdependence and as part of its External Co-operation activities. It was jointly organised by the Forum's co-sponsors, the Asian Development Bank and the OECD Development Centre.

Table of Contents

Part Two

Asian Growth in an International Context

Preface

This book is based on the third annual Asian Development Bank and OECD Development Centre joint Forum on Asian Perspectives. The forum brought together policy makers, advisors and scholars to discuss recent research on the growth prospects and policy challenges facing developing Asia, the OECD and other regions. As the meeting predated the onset of the traumatic financial turmoil that has since affected several economies in the region, the papers do not directly address the implications of that crisis for Asia's growth performance in the years ahead. Nonetheless, both the long-run sustainability of the region's rapid growth and the critical importance of sound national and international policies to ensure sustainability are recurrent themes throughout this publication.

The setbacks in some of the most dynamic economies of the region due to the 1997 financial crisis, notably in Southeast Asia, will require urgent structural reform. However, the long-run growth potential of the region as a whole remains strong, nowhere more so than in the two largest countries, China and India. Realising that potential will depend in the first instance on continued regional and global progress towards trade and investment liberalisation. Beyond that, governments will need to continue to upgrade human capital and to take stronger measures to avoid worsening environmental degradation that threatens to undermine growth.

Asia's difficulties will certainly have an impact on the way other regions view that part of the world. This publication may serve as a reminder that, despite the concern created by the financial crisis, the economic fundamentals throughout Asia are basically sound.

Jean Bonvin   Mitsuo Sato
President   President
OECD Development Centre   Asian Development Bank
Paris   Manila

January, 1998

Opening Address

Francis Mayer

On behalf of Mr. Dominique Strauss-Kahn, the Minister of the Economy, Finance and Industry, I am happy to welcome you to the Pierre Mendès France Conference Centre at the Ministry of Finance.

In particular, I would like to greet Mr. Bonvin, President of the OECD Development Centre and Mr. Bong-Suh Lee, Vice-President of the Asian Development Bank, and to pay tribute to the highly symbolic co-operation between an institution of the industrialised countries and one that is deeply rooted in the Asian continent. This conference's theme largely follows the thinking of the G7 on the stakes of globalisation and the need to be able to deal with its new challenges.

Allow me to make some introductory comments from a financial standpoint.

Besides the trade flows and portfolio investments, foreign direct investments by the OECD countries are indicative of a trend.

Confirming a tendency observed for several years, in 1993 the rapidly developing Asian countries were the leading regional destination of net foreign direct investment, accounting for almost $63 billion out of a world total of $110 billion, excluding the OECD countries. Asia seems to have considerable financial needs, and the World Bank estimates that it will require $1.5 trillion for infrastructure alone during the next ten years.

Naturally this rise of Asia's importance is a great advantage for the world economy and a great opportunity for countries and enterprises of the OECD. Nonetheless, a rapid rise in importance can signify increased financial fragility, at least initially. For that reason, there should be international financial solidarity. That phrase expresses the full meaning of the "international financial community", of which I provide two examples.

1)   The volatility of some short-term capital movements, especially foreign portfolio investments.

The Mexican crisis has demonstrated the major consequences of sudden capital movements. The international financial community has learned a basic lesson and has set up new loan agreements — with which, incidentally, some emerging economies of Asia [Korea, Malaysia, Singapore, Thailand, and Hong Kong (China)] are associated — to increase the resources available to the IMF for intervening in case of a serious financial crisis to $50 billion. Parenthetically, this is not the only way emerging economies of Asia are associated with international financial stability, since five of them [China, Hong Kong (China), India, Korea and Singapore] recently participated in the enlargement of the capital of the Bank for International Settlements.

2)   The solidity of local banking and financial systems.

A rapid expansion of bank credit without accompanying strengthened prudential monitoring and supervision can carry risks when there are large, sudden downturns.

That of course holds true for all countries, including the industrialised ones, but these questions are especially serious insofar as banks are the main means of financing Asian economies, disintermediation's being relatively limited in Asian developing countries. The embryonic local bond markets and the narrowness of stock markets, despite their takeoff, leaves a large place for the banking system. That has led international financial circles to consider how to strengthen supervision and prudential measures for banking and financial systems in emerging countries. In particular, a G10 working group, representing ministries of finance and central banks, is actively studying the question with the help of the IMF and OECD. This G10 working group, a body exclusively representing industrialised countries, for the first time has incorporated representatives of emerging countries, especially those in Asia.

These two examples show that it is possible to control this exceptional economic growth of Asia financially, and thus safeguard it from risks, if the instruments of international financial co-operation are used together.

PART ONE

GROWTH AND DEVELOPMENT IN ASIA

Introduction

Colm Foy and David O'Connor

The third edition of the annual joint Asian Development Bank (ADB)–OECD Development Centre *International Forum on Asian Perspectives* was held in Paris on 23-24 June 1997, on the theme, "The Future of Asia in the World Economy". It provided an occasion for participants to discuss the findings of the sponsors' respective "futures" studies on the growth prospects and policy challenges facing developing Asia, the OECD and the rest of the world in the coming quarter of a century

Sustainability was a recurrent theme in the presentations, and the critical importance of sound policies to ensuring sustainability a recurrent message. What the turmoil which began in 1997 in Southeast Asian markets has demonstrated is that sustained high growth may itself loosen the constraints that normally keep governments from deviating too far from strict policy discipline. Moreover, with ever-greater goods and financial market liberalisation in the region, the economic role of governments is changing and some have been slow to adapt.

The financial instability which struck Southeast Asian markets needs to be viewed in perspective. First, the countries of the region still possess a number of fundamental strengths, such as high savings rates, industrious and increasingly well-educated populations, and outward-oriented and liberal policy regimes. Second, important as the Southeast Asian economies are collectively, their combined population is still only about half India's and one-third China's (though, because as a group they are richer than the two regional giants, their combined economic weight is proportionally larger than their population), and by the end of 1997 these two large countries were only modestly affected by the crisis (despite the difficulties faced by Hong Kong). Third, for many countries in Asia, demographic factors are likely to remain favourable to high savings and rapid labour force expansion at least through the first quarter of the next century. More specifically, fertility rates have been falling, reducing young-age dependency and expanding the ranks of prime earners and savers, but (with the important exception of China) not yet significantly raising old-age dependency.

Quite apart from the slowing of growth that normally accompanies income convergence towards levels of the advanced industrialised countries, there is a real risk of a protracted growth slowdown in those economies most adversely affected by the crisis, possibly aggravating social and political strains. On the other hand, the large, low-income economies of the region still have enormous long-term growth potential, and their strong growth should have a positive impact on their neighbours. They represent rapidly growing — and increasingly open — markets for regional exports. They can also exert strong competitive pressure on their high-wage neighbours to boost productivity and restructure towards more skill- and technology-intensive activities (though, as in the OECD countries, the adjustments also carry costs). On balance, Asia is likely to remain one of the most dynamic regions of the world economy in the next few decades, though its centre of dynamism may well shift further towards the larger, low-income countries.

Growing Links between Developing Asia and the OECD Countries

As the large Asian countries open their markets to foreign trade and investment, the region as a whole has become increasingly integrated with the OECD area. In the 1990s, developing Asia came to account for some 10 per cent of European trade (excluding intra-EU trade), for between one-fifth and one-fourth of total US trade, and for around 40 per cent of total Japanese trade. (For Australia the share is around 35 per cent.) Overall, towards the end of the 20th century developing Asia accounts for 15-20 per cent of world trade. In a scenario of rapid economic growth, that share could increase to 30 per cent by 2020. Developing Asia is likely to remain a major market for OECD capital goods exports, while rising regional food and feedgrain consumption, combined with declining trade barriers, should boost North American and Australian agricultural exports. Similarly, as trade in services is liberalised, the OECD countries' strong experience in financial and other services should be a source of comparative advantage in developing Asian markets.

A sizeable share of OECD outward foreign investment has gone to developing Asia. The region is by far the largest developing-country destination for foreign direct investment (FDI), accounting for two-thirds of all inflows to developing countries (and roughly one-fifth of total FDI inflows) in 1995. China alone accounted for roughly 12.5 per cent of world FDI inflows in that year and, while FDI to India is still small, it is likely to increase rapidly in coming years as foreign companies capitalise on the more open economic environment and large potential market. The promotion of private sector participation in infrastructure projects and the deregulation of the service sector should both provide a strong impetus to OECD foreign investment throughout the region.

Trade and Labour Markets

With the rapid integration of Asia's labour-abundant, low-income economies into global markets, concerns have arisen about the potential impact on OECD labour markets. Unskilled workers in the OECD area have for some time been suffering a decline in their position compared to that of skilled workers. This is reflected in a widening wage gap and, in most of Europe, particularly high unemployment rates. While economists disagree about which factors — skill-biased technical change; trade; migration; or institutional change, including the declining influence of trade unions — are most important in explaining past wage and employment trends, fuller integration of large countries like China and India into world markets might, if anything, exacerbate the problems facing unskilled workers in OECD countries. These countries have large reserves of underemployed, unskilled, cheap labour, mostly in peasant agriculture, which will eventually transfer to more productive jobs in industry (making goods both for domestic markets and for export). Quite apart from any future trade-related pressures, the rapid diffusion of advanced technologies in OECD countries is likely to continue to favour skilled over unskilled workers. This explains the imperative facing OECD governments to accelerate skill upgrading so as to enable their labour forces to participate more fully in the benefits of a global economy.

Human Capital and Technological Requirements

The Asian developing countries need to improve the quality of their labour forces if they are to sustain growth and rising living standards into the future. For the more advanced countries of the region, the emphasis will need to be on producing more highly educated scientists, engineers and other professionals, while in some of the less advanced ones the number and quality of secondary school graduates remains a matter of concern. In a number of low-income countries in Asia, universal primary education of acceptable quality has yet to be achieved. Extending and upgrading formal education is only part of the challenge, however. Raising the capacity for effective utilisation of technology and know-how by productive enterprises is also crucial. While a competitive market environment encourages strong technological effort, the East Asian experience suggests that a variety of other institutions — R&D institutes, venture capital funds, technology consulting services — can facilitate rapid uptake and adaptation of new technologies. At an early stage of development, the government may play a catalytic role in technology diffusion, but as an economy matures private-sector competition should sustain vigorous innovation.

In their quest for both knowledge and technology, the emerging economies of Asia look predominantly to OECD countries as suppliers. The higher education industry is one of the OECD's largest export earners, and Asian students are major consumers. Similarly, OECD firms earn substantial revenue from the sale or licensing of their intellectual property to Asian firms, including their own affiliates in developing Asia. There is no reason to expect this to change radically in the next few decades.

Global Saving-Investment Balance

Emerging Asian capital markets may not look very attractive to OECD investors at the moment, but in a longer-term perspective they offer valuable opportunities —as do other emerging markets — for portfolio diversification by OECD pension funds and other institutional investors. It is well known that OECD pay-as-you-go pension schemes will face solvency problems in coming decades as the support ratio (i.e. the ratio of working age people to those above 60 years of age) falls steeply in country after country. Even fully funded schemes, however, could be plagued by financing problems when large numbers of "baby boomers" start drawing down their pension assets to finance retirement. Partial diversification into emerging markets, while not a panacea for this problem, could offer the prospect of somewhat higher long-term returns for a given level of risk. With young and growing labour forces contributing to a strong growth potential, these countries should continue to enjoy relatively high returns on investment for many years.

To sustain rapid growth, investment will need to remain high in developing Asia. Many countries face serious infrastructure bottlenecks that must be relieved, and addressing environmental problems will also require sizeable investments. As in the past, so in the future a portion of that investment financing will be provided by OECD investors — whether multinational corporations, banks or institutional investors — but the bulk will come from high domestic savings. The experience of East and South-East Asia suggests that rapid growth induces high rates of savings, which in turn permits higher investment and sustained growth. While some large countries in the region — notably in South Asia — still have relatively low savings rates, as their reform efforts pay off in faster growth they could well complete this virtuous growth-savings-investment-growth circle. In any case, it seems clear in the wake of the Southeast Asian currency crisis that in the future countries will need to maintain fairly strict limits on the size of their current account deficits in relation to GDP or, in other words, on the extent of their reliance on foreign savings to finance domestic investment.

Natural Capital and the Environment

The environmental toll of rapid, unregulated growth has become glaringly apparent to those living in the Asian region. Even with the best of intentions, governments have found the enforcement of environmental regulations difficult if not impossible in the face of strong pressures to "go for growth". While preserving environmental quality is not costless, governments have often neglected to calculate the alternative costs, i.e., the health, productivity and other losses associated with severe environmental degradation. Increasingly, those costs are coming to be recognised, with the 1997 regional "haze" episode serving as an unavoidable reminder. It may be true that growth and higher incomes bring with them a stronger effective demand for environmental improvements, but it is not the case that poor people attach little or no value to environmental quality. A growing number of empirical studies have demonstrated how willing poor people in Asia's crowded cities are to pay for such environmental amenities as clean drinking water, improved sanitation and solid waste disposal.

For much of developing Asia, domestic environmental problems remain the predominant preoccupation, even as the region as a whole becomes a rather significant contributor to global environmental problems (e.g. through rapidly rising greenhouse gas emissions). The OECD countries need to be sensitive to these priorities, while at the same time recognising that there are significant "win-win" opportunities — e.g. through energy efficiency improvement and renewable energy development — for addressing domestic and global pollution problems simultaneously. Governments in the region can no doubt benefit from both technical co-operation with and environmental policy advice shared by OECD countries.

Welcoming Remarks

Jean Bonvin

It is now three years since the Asian Development Bank and the OECD Development Centre decided to establish the International Forum on Asian Perspectives.

The theme adopted for this year's Forum, "The Future of Asia in the World Economy", is of special interest at the dawn of the third millennium. More than ever, optimism is appropriate in the Asian region: there are encouraging prospects for economic development, as well as for eliminating the poverty which is still the fate of hundreds of millions of Asians. The striking results in this domain obtained by a good number of Southeast and East Asian countries have prompted other countries to follow their example and open their economies, thereby benefiting from closer foreign trade and investment links. At times, governments needed considerable political courage to stand up to the opponents of change, but personal convictions no longer determine decisions to adopt liberalisation measures: their benefits have been widely demonstrated by the success of the region's most dynamic and open economies.

Asia's integration in the world economy has been a determining factor of rapid growth over several decades. The rise of manufactured exports from the Asian developing countries has been largely a result of their access to the markets of the developed countries of Europe, Japan and North America. Political leaders of the OECD countries have also had to be courageous in resolutely defending the continued liberalisation of world trade against sometimes strong domestic resistance. While it is true that access to markets is not yet free in some sectors such as textiles, clothing and agriculture, the general trend is towards increasing liberalisation, a process which culminated in the signing of the Uruguay Round agreement in Marrakesh.

The Asian developing countries greatly contributed to the favourable outcome of that negotiating cycle. Moreover, their support will be vital for advancing the timetable of the post-Uruguay Round trade reforms, in particular in the complex domain of services.

The development of Asian markets has attracted an increasing number of exporters from the OECD countries. European multinational firms recognise that the European market is too small to fulfil their international aims. While Europe has certainly not exhausted its potential for growth, in particular with the planned integration of central and eastern European countries into the European Union, still prospects of growth are now more promising in Asia and other developing regions. European exporters are increasingly entering the emerging markets of Asia, which absorb a growing proportion of their exports. For example, the proportion of European telecommunications products exported to Asia increased from 9 to 15 per cent during a five-year period from 1989 to 1993. Exports of specialised machinery increased from 10 to 19 per cent. This trend should continue and even accelerate in coming decades, since India and other large countries of the region now have growth rates approaching those experienced by China and Southeast Asia over the past 20 years.

Moreover, European countries with large accumulations of wealth are attracted by the high returns from investments in rapidly growing Asian countries. Some of the region's countries, with China in the lead, have become favoured destinations for foreign investors. Thus far, India has attracted much less investment than China, but its potential to attract such investment is high. Other countries, which have been neglected by foreign investors, could also receive a wave of investment. However, that will necessitate political stability, the creation of a favourable policy framework, and investment in physical infrastructure, education and labour training.

Besides direct investment, the emerging Asian markets should attract a growing proportion of portfolio investment from the OECD countries. With large young populations and increasingly abundant labour, Asian countries will be in good position to make productive use of financial assets in the OECD countries. Just as trade has mutual advantages for countries having different resources, so the growing integration of financial markets should benefit both the OECD countries and Asian developing countries, where the capital and labour endowments differ. By helping Asia to finance rapid growth, savers and investors of the OECD countries participate in the benefits of this growth. That should lead to improving their standards of living and their future pensions.

The 21st century could well be the Pacific century. The incomes of Asian developing countries will probably grow faster than those of the industrialised economies of Europe, North America and Japan, which have reached maturity. The standard of living in the former countries will converge towards that of the developed world.

This prospect should provide satisfaction for the OECD countries. When the productivity of Europe and Japan caught up with that of the United States after World War II, exports, foreign investment and economic growth rose considerably. Consequently, there is good reason for expecting that the process of catching up begun by Asian developing countries will stimulate exports, foreign investment and economic growth in Europe, North America and Japan. Of course those who benefit the most will be those who are the quickest to fill the needs created by Asia's rapid growth.

In that respect, it must be admitted that Europe is lagging behind somewhat in relation to North America and Japan. The decision makers and heads of enterprises of the "old world" are conscious of the challenge facing them. They must now rise to the challenge so that the European economy and society can also obtain benefits from globalisation and the emergence of Asia.

The Asian Development Bank's Contribution to the Consolidation of Asian Growth

Bong-Suh Lee

It is my pleasure to join Mr. Bonvin in welcoming you on behalf of the Asian Development Bank to this Third Joint ADB/OECD International Forum. The purpose of this series of meetings is to help forge a greater understanding of Asia among the OECD countries. In Asia, there is a strong sense of mutuality of interest between our developing member countries and the economies of OECD countries. The process of globalisation is bringing our respective constituents ever closer together. Indeed, it is a source of great satisfaction that the economic achievements of Korea, one of our member developing countries, has led to its membership in the OECD.

In a sense, globalisation is not new. Prior to World War I, there was relatively free trade and large capital flows from Europe to the then developing economies of America and Australia. There was also comparatively free migration at that time. The collapse of the world economy that followed World War I occurred despite a widespread view that the process of globalisation was irreversible. It is also a sharp reminder of the economic havoc that isolationist policies can produce. Today, once again, integration of the world goods and capital markets is proceeding apace. Now a much larger number of countries are involved. Information, people and commodities travel at much less cost and much more quickly than ever before. Globalisation has certainly been helped by technological advances that have made the world smaller, but it has also been an outcome of conscious policy choices made in a large number of countries.

Since World War II, tariff barriers have tumbled and quantitative restrictions on trade have been dismantled in developed and developing countries alike. Much of the impetus for these developments has come from the General Agreement on Tariffs and Trade and the various rounds of multilateral negotiations that have been held under its aegis. But it is also true that many countries, including those in East and Southeast Asia, recognised the benefits of openness early on and took significant unilateral action to become integrated more fully in the world economy.

In the developing countries of Asia, there is certainly a sense of optimism afoot. The mistakes of the past have been recognised. The success of policies based on openness of markets has been amply demonstrated, and there is a determination to make up for lost opportunities.

There are very few people who now believe that economic development is best promoted behind protectionist barricades. It is widely appreciated that statist policies have resoundingly failed to raise incomes and reduce poverty. While there is now a general recognition of the benefits of free trade, the process of opening up markets is far from easy. Problems beset market liberalisation at both the domestic and the international level. In the international arena, liberalisation is best carried out and problems best solved in a multilateral spirit in a framework of mutually binding rules.

The orderly and equitable functioning of these arrangements requires that the voices of all can be heard. Against this background, the first WTO Ministerial Conference in Singapore in December of 1996 was a particularly welcome event. Along the road between Marrakesh and Singapore the world trading system has become more open and multilateral arrangements have been strengthened. Important initial agreements were made in Singapore on the extent of the WTO's mandate and the further steps that are envisaged to ensure that the Uruguay Round is fully and successfully implemented.

Nevertheless, despite these very real achievements, there remains much to be done. The process of trade liberalisation and harmonisation is far from over. Liberalisation of trade in services and agriculture has only just started and the Asian countries remain concerned about a number of issues of which three seem particularly relevant here.

First, while the Ministerial Conference agreed that the ILO is the competent body for dealing with labour standards, there is still apprehension among many in the developing world that issues about labour standards may yet resurface. In Asia, labour standards are typically seen as a developmental issue rather than a trade or legislative issue.

Second, Asian developing countries are also concerned by the prospect of the loss of autonomy that may follow from the adoption of multilateral investment rules that some countries are pressing for. The adoption of such rules, it is feared, might weaken the ability of a government to negotiate with powerful foreign investors on an equal footing.

Third, Asian developing nations are anxious that pressure groups within industrial countries may begin to push for restrictions on exports from low-wage Asian countries. The maintenance of fair and effective arrangements for settling disputes will be essential to support fair competition in international markets. There remains a danger that industrialised countries may use anti-dumping duties or other countervailing measures to protect uncompetitive sectors.

As trade flows have burgeoned in recent years, there has been a growth of capital flows from developed to developing countries. Attracted by market liberalisation and better governance in many developing countries, investors are now looking much more closely at what emerging markets have to offer. If Asia continues to grow, as many expect, its future capital needs will be massive. To meet these needs, first and foremost, there will have to be a sustained effort at mobilising domestic savings. The experience of both East and Southeast Asia suggests that without high domestic savings rates it will not be possible to finance capital investment. There are a few countries which have been unable to sustain large resource gaps for long, partly because large resource gaps imperil creditworthiness.

Increasing domestic savings requires, among other things, a fiscally prudent government and the broadest support for the development of a market-based financial system. Also, to attract responsible long-term investors, such as pension funds, to Asian markets, a high priority has to be given to the development of domestic capital markets. Despite a massive surge in the capitalisation of Asian securities markets in recent decades, its debt markets are still comparatively underdeveloped. In some economies, the supervisory prudential and economic standards required by investors are lacking. Often, legal codes have failed to keep pace with technological and financial innovations. While progress is coming, much more needs to be done.

The Asian Development Bank places a high priority on assisting its developing member countries in their efforts to develop their capital markets. The ADB's technical advice on sectoral policy reform, its private sector and co-financing operations and its support for the development of a capital market infrastructure are notable in this regard.

Asia and World Trade to 2020:
An Evaluation of the Situation
after the Singapore Ministerial Meeting

Arthur Dunkel

Our title links the year 2020 with the first ministerial meeting of the World Trade Organization which, significantly, was held in Asia. The linking of a date and meeting of the World Trade Organization are worth a comment. 2020 is the year that the members of APEC adopted for the goal of liberalisation of trade and investment. What is especially significant is that it planned to continue pursuing this objective in a non-discriminatory manner. That is, to adopt these measures not only for APEC members but also for third parties. In other words, the APEC members intend to put into practice what has been called "open regionalism", which is a remarkable innovation. Linking this date and its objective with an evaluation of the first ministerial meeting of the WTO amounts to asking a key question. Are APEC's partners in the drive towards globalisation of the world economy following in its footsteps, or still better, are they inclined to rise to the challenge? If the answer is "yes", what will be the World Trade Organization's role? Will the WTO be the centre for new global negotiations leading to worldwide free trade?

The history of the last 50 years proves that there is always a relationship between progress in trade liberalisation at the regional level, in particular in Europe, and the opening of markets at the global level through the well-known GATT negotiations. Was not the Kennedy Round, whose aim was a 50 per cent reduction of customs tariffs, initiated because of a concern that common tariffs of the original European Economic Community could become too high? The Tokyo Round was also motivated, in part, by the European Community's increased membership, while the inclusion of services in the Uruguay Round (to cite only this example) was inspired, at least in part, by extension of European integration to this sector. The four freedoms, free movement of goods, services, capital and labour have not yet been taken up, as such, under the framework of the World Trade Organization, but it is also true that measures of liberalisation or integration at the regional level have sometimes been used or presented as a fallback position or a threat when there has been no prospect of progress at the global level. To prevent regional agreements from contravening the rules and principles of the multilateral trading system, GATT and the WTO, there are specific provisions defining the "conditions of cohabitation between the two approaches", the regional and multilateral approach (cf. Article 24). But it must be recognised that after almost 50 years of the GATT's existence, the signatories of the agreements for the WTO who met in Singapore considered it essential to examine in depth the compatibility of regional arrangements that are expanding around the world with the multilateral system. In making this decision, the WTO members recognised that it is advisable to prevent a trend in which persistent protectionist forces would be embodied in regional groups rather than national policies. The possibility that the world could be divided between a number of "hostile" trading blocs has been envisaged for some time. In that respect the decision of the APEC members to establish open regionalism sets an example whose true value should be appreciated. There is another point which should be emphasized with respect to APEC's initiatives: they mark the entrance of new partners into the management of international economic and trade relations.

The world economy of a large part of the 20th century has been dominated by Europe and the United States. Today that is neither possible nor desirable. The economic power located around the Atlantic is in the course of being extended to the Pacific, which means that the prosperity of Europe and North America is going to depend increasingly on interactions between the different regions of the world of which Asia is one of the great new poles. In only a few years the bipolar world has been transformed into a multipolar world and this trend will be strengthened as the 30-odd countries, among them China and Russia, which are negotiating to enter the WTO become members.

As much as these prospects for potential economic growth, job creation and human development provide satisfaction at the global level, they give rise to fears and a sense of insecurity among people in the United States and, especially, in Europe who tend to consider that economic globalisation calls into question their institutions, jobs and markets. These fears and sense of insecurity should be taken seriously because they strengthen forces which could challenge the extraordinary progress achieved in recent years towards establishing a world market whose operations are governed by common rules. An awareness of the challenges to these trends is necessary for seeking, and putting into effect, the solutions that are indispensable to preventing backward steps.

The first of these challenges is to overcome the lack of information. For the greater part of public opinion world trade is considered as a sum to be divided among an increasingly large number of participants, and thus is an exercise with winners and losers. It is forgotten that the "cake" expands as trade increases, and consequently there can only be winners, but to be a winner, one must participate in the "race".

A second information problem is the widespread belief that globalisation is a sort of inevitability imposed by an invisible hand. Who are the masters: governments, international institutions, multinationals or the market? Many questions require clear answers and basic information. It should be clearly understood that the structural reforms confronting all countries are not caused by the process of globalisation but by technological progress. The engine is not the opening of markets but the astronomical rate of technological change which is occurring. Thus the World Trade Organization, International Monetary Fund, World Bank, European and regional agreements are not responsible in themselves for making structural reforms necessary; technological change is the real culprit.

The second challenge is one facing the founders of the existing system, namely the great "old" industrial nations. The United States and Europe have given lessons to the rest of the world. Despite their having preached the values of a market economy and liberalism, there is tendency for them not to practice what they preach though the lesson has been adopted by others. Look at the policies still practiced by the industrialised countries in domains such as textiles and clothing, agriculture and automobiles. How can Indonesia be criticised for wanting to create a protected automobile industry when it has the example of the industrialised world's past behaviour. Thus the industrialised world must also put its house in order.

The third great challenge arises from the fact that more than a third of international trade consists of trade between enterprises, but enterprises were not participants in the international negotiations since they were entirely intergovernmental. It is time to take this reality into account in international negotiations so that all interests at stake can be taken into consideration and responsibilities will be shared better.

The fourth challenge can be called the challenge of the marginalised. When we talk about globalisation, it is generally assumed that the major concerns are Asia and Latin America. But there remains a fringe of countries which the international community must be concerned with because they are excluded from prosperity. In a few months the WTO is going to hold an important conference on the problems of the less developed countries to try to find better ways and means of integrating them into the process. The north-south and east-west barriers have fallen, but there remains a fundamental barrier between a number of the less developed countries and the rest of humanity.

There has already been an allusion to one of the challenges which results from a highly encouraging phenomenon but which has a counterpart that is cause for concern. The encouraging phenomenon is that humanity has entered a period of relative peace — without of course neglecting the sometimes dramatic local conflicts whose importance should not be minimised. The cause for concern is that while the armies are staying in their barracks, governments are trying to use other instruments of pressure and coercion to assert or impose their national positions, by the simple instrument of trade policies. The trade weapon is used to impose policies on workers' rights and the trade weapon is used to advance policies to defend the environment, leading to completely inexplicable situations. For example, the international press recently published an advertisement financed by the WWF making known the death of turtles caught in the nets used to catch shrimp. The WWF proposes to establish an embargo on import of shrimp from countries which do not fish with nets that protect turtles. It would be more useful to spend the resources used for this type of advertisement to buy appropriate nets for fishermen of developing countries who cannot always afford the fishing equipment used in industrialised countries. A similar problem has arisen out of concern for protecting dolphins. There has been an attempt to use an embargo on tuna to force investment in equipment providing greater protection for dolphins. It is possible to like dolphins and doubt that trade policies are the most appropriate way to resolve this sort of problem.

Finally, the traditional domains of trade policies affecting trade in goods where there are still major obstacles should not be forgotten in the haste to deal with new categories like services and intellectual property rights. Progress should continue on all fronts to take into account the realities of the market and needs of traders on international markets,

The multilateral trading system now represented by the WTO will be 50 years old in 1998. Renato Ruggiero, Director General of the WTO, would like to highlight this anniversary, not by negotiations on a particular point, but by a gathering at the highest level (if possible Heads of State) whose main task would be to address world public opinion to emphasize, once again, the great advantages of an open trading system for the people of this planet.

Asia and World Trade to 2020 (An Outline)

Long Yongtu

The following factors, in differing degrees, will decide whether or not the trade of developing countries and economies in Asia will continue to grow at the forecast level of 15 per cent per annum (double their GDP growth rate), as it has during the 1990s.

A) The trade policies pursued by these economies, i.e. how fast and how consistent the domestic trade and investment liberalisation process in the countries remains.

Even though most of the countries and economies have adopted increasingly liberalised trade and investment policies, the inherent resistance to liberalisation and, therefore, a protectionist tendency in the countries is still very strong. To overcome these protectionist tendencies, important considerations are:

a) how developed economies treat these fast-growing economies, whether they are treated as constructive trading partners or as threats to their own development;

b) the example set by some more successful developing economies would have more impact on the other developing economies. Therefore, co-operation among developing economies in general, and co-operation in the Asian region in particular, will be important;

c) international organisations such as the WTO and APEC must play a positive role and function on a fair and balanced basis; and

d) most crucially, how the developed economies make their industries more internationally competitive.

B) Direction of the trade and investment process of APEC, i.e. whether or not APEC pursues real open regionalism.

Even though it is a declared policy of APEC to pursue a policy of open regionalism, there is still a strong political and economic incentive to move towards some kind of regional bloc. To ensure APEC pursues open regionalism, it is imperative that:

a) the composition of APEC be enlarged gradually, and the current stringent restrictions on the membership should be lifted;

b) the subregional groupings within APEC not become de facto trading blocs, and if that is the principle, the concept of EAEC should be encouraged to develop further in order to ensure the diversity of APEC;

c) ASEAN be considered a welcome development, especially considering its role of encouraging APEC to pursue open regionalism;

d) the rules and disciplines of the WTO on regional economic and trading arrangements be strengthened.

C) The balance of new rules to be formulated by the WTO, i.e. whether or not these new rules, especially the rules in the context of increasing globalisation, will be fair to the newly developing and fast-growing economies.

The WTO's role is being strengthened and its impact, and especially the impact on Asian economies of the new rules being formulated for the 21st century, will be much more direct and important than before. However, the WTO, for all its changes since the Uruguay Round, is still an institution influenced by its past. In order to make sure that the new rules are formulated on a fair basis, it is important that:

a) the WTO should change its image as a "club for the rich" and make greater efforts to win the trust of the developing economies. The domination of the decision making process by a few major players is something that should be addressed;

b) the WTO should achieve its goal of universality as soon as possible; the rule-making process will be ineffective without the participation of some players; and

c) the WTO's rule-making process should be more receptive to different voices in order to formulate balanced rules that are fair to the newly developed and fast-growing economies. In this connection, the WTO should establish a closer relationship with organisations oriented towards developing countries, such as UNCTAD, the Asian Development Bank, etc.

Asia's Contribution to Prosperity in the 21st Century: Liberalisation and Development Co-operation

Rak-Yong Uhm

This conference provides an excellent opportunity for strengthening co-operation between OECD Member countries and Asian Developing Countries (ADCs). As is well known, Korea is the only country which belongs to both groups. I would like to take this opportunity to share Korea's experience with others.

The world economy has changed considerably in the last decade. These changes are due to the efforts of many countries to establish a new world economic order. It is likely that this new economic order will be firmly established in the 21st century.

In 1994, the participants in the APEC Bogor Leaders' Meeting made a commitment to complete the achievement of free and open trade and investment in the Asia-Pacific area no later than the year 2020, the industrialised economies by 2010. The developing economies reach this target by 2020. By that time, integration of the world economy should be nearly complete.

According to the OECD's recent document *Towards a New Global Age: Challenges and Opportunities*, which contains the OECD's forecast of the world economy in the year 2020, the abolition of trade barriers and liberalisation of capital flows will increase the growth rate of world output by more than 1 per cent. The share of the output of non-OECD countries (mainly developing countries) will be greatly increased.

Among the developing countries, the Asian developing countries which are making serious efforts to adjust to globalisation will play the pivotal role in the next century. The rapid integration of the world market makes it necessary to reconsider the relationship between the developing and developed countries.

Liberalisation has been promoted through unilateral, bilateral, regional and multilateral means. Many countries have liberalised their economies unilaterally in order to strengthen their competitiveness and increase consumer surplus.

Bilateral talks have accelerated the liberalisation process. Regional approaches by the EU, NAFTA, APEC and other integrated bodies have also stimulated liberalisation. Multilateral negotiations in the Uruguay Round resulted in the formation of the WTO. All these developments have had one core purpose, that of establishing global free trade and investment.

Meanwhile, development co-operation has been discussed in various forums. The importance of development co-operation is already universally acknowledged, although there is lack of agreement on how it should be carried out.

For the new world economic order of the 21st century, the two pillars of liberalisation should be firmly established. In addition, an efficient way to harmonize their requirements should be examined.

During the Uruguay Round negotiations, global free trade and investment was extended and strengthened. However, completely free trade and investment is very difficult to attain.

Many developing countries are reserved about liberalising their markets because of the difficulties of economic restructuring. Generally speaking, they accept liberalisation under pressure from developed countries. They would prefer more gradual liberalisation, managed by their own policies, because sometimes the situation does not allow enough time for adjustment.

Even some developed countries have a tendency to protect their sensitive sectors, since their governments are under pressure from interest groups, generally representing less competitive industries. These protectionist attitudes hinder the movement towards total free trade and investment. In addition, regional approaches, which became a worldwide phenomenon after the formation of the European Union, do not always have a positive effect on multilateral free trade and investment.

Development co-operation is not promoted effectively because of generally reserved attitudes of developed countries. They agree on the importance of development co-operation, but their financial commitment is relatively low. Moreover, they are tending to reduce their commitment to development co-operation.

During the cold war era, some developing countries benefited from the bipolar political system. The superpowers competed in aiding some developing countries. In other words, the East-West problem mitigated the North-South problem. However, this phenomenon disappeared with the end of the cold war, and many countries in the South have lost substantial aid.

If we agree on the need for a new world economic order which promotes prosperity for all countries, we must deal with these problems. First, there has to be a greater commitment to liberalisation. Liberalisation by one country benefits exporters in other countries, but it benefits the liberalising country even more. Every country works to strengthen the competitiveness of its industry. Without dynamic competitive pressure from foreign sources, increased competitiveness is difficult to achieve. Also, liberalisation can increase the welfare level through the consumer surplus.

Even if the adjustment process seems painful in the short term, developing countries need to undertake structural adjustment to increase their economic growth. Liberalisation is also an effective way to achieve structural adjustment.

Developing countries need to maintain sound macroeconomic policies for liberalisation, with the help and co-operation of developed countries and international institutions when they cannot be achieved solely by their own efforts. For example, the raising of interest rates in OECD countries can cause serious instabilities in the financial markets of developing countries by stimulating outflows of invested funds. In this regard, the OECD countries and ADB need to play an active role.

Views on development co-operation also have to change. It is not only for the economic growth of developing countries, but also for the economic growth of developed countries. When developing countries achieve a certain level of economic growth, imports will be stimulated, thereby resulting in the expansion of world exports. Moreover, the economic growth of developing countries increases investment opportunities for investors from developed countries.

To be sure, the economic growth of developing countries can create a more competitive environment which will require structural adjustment in developed countries. This situation may also cause political difficulties in these countries. In the long run, however, structural adjustment is essential for achieving sustainable economic growth in developed countries.

Development co-operation can be promoted more effectively by market forces than by government action. Thus developing countries should actively participate in the integration of the world economy in co-operation with developed countries.

The priority between liberalisation and development co-operation has long been debated. We do not believe that these objectives need to be ranked against each other. Both objectives should be promoted simultaneously and harmoniously.

Let me use Korea as an example. Just a few decades ago, Korea ranked amongst the poorest countries in the world. However, by maintaining a relentless effort to open its economy, Korea has experienced rapid growth as well as enhanced international status. In light of the experience of other countries, especially of the ADCs, it should be evident that open economic policies have demonstrated their effectiveness.

In order to sustain economic growth in the future, Korea needs to pursue liberalisation of the economy further in order to increase foreign capital inflows and to obtain more technological know-how, as well as to carry out a fundamental reform of the economic system.

Korea's accession to the OECD is no doubt an important step in this direction. It will provide the opportunity to learn from the experiences of the developed economies, while at the same time enabling Korea to cultivate closer co-operative relationships with them.

As the economies of ADCs mature, quantitative accumulation of capital and labour will not be sufficient to maintain growth. Therefore, they will have to shift their growth path to one supported mainly by technological progress and increased productivity. Many factors are necessary for such an approach, but the majority of them can be acquired by mutual co-operation with OECD countries. Thus liberalisation and deregulation are inevitable. Many ADCs are now reaching this stage of economic maturity.

To give an example, beginning in the 1990s the rapid economic growth of Korea has been slowing down, as indicated by a decline in the annual growth rate. In order to sustain growth while maintaining macroeconomic stability, Korea now needs to concentrate more on technological innovation and structural adjustment in industry, along with a drastic reform of the regulatory system, including the financial sector.

The ADCs have experienced rapid economic growth in recent decades, comprising the most dynamic economic region. They have liberalised their economies with a view to enhancing their competitive edge. Furthermore, the ADCs are supposed to join the countries leading the movement for global free trade and investment. In particular, they should implement the decisions of the Uruguay Round. They should also actively participate in the efforts to resolve new international issues, such as those related to the environment and labour. These things cannot be accomplished unilaterally. Rather, they need to be addressed at a multilateral level by means such as a strengthening of the role of the WTO.

The short-term difficulties experienced in developing countries should not lead to backtracking on market liberalisation and deregulation. Moreover, they need to accelerate liberalisation, considering that it is inevitable for achieving high growth. However, maintaining macroeconomic stability is very important during economic liberalisation. In particular, a road map for appropriate pacing and sequencing of financial sector liberalisation will be very helpful to the developing countries.

OECD countries, as leaders of the world economy, are expected to put more emphasis on development co-operation. The OECD should develop detailed plans for effective development co-operation that can be mutually beneficial for both the developed and developing countries, since user-driven development co-operation is actually a necessity.

Both developed and developing countries should also reject inward-looking regionalism. The regional approach should complement global free trade and investment. Achieving real open regionalism is essential for global liberalisation.

The OECD and ADCs face many other challenges which require closer co-operation. One of the main problems, which most OECD Member countries are now experiencing and will continue to face in the future, is the decline in the working population. The population's ageing can make sustainable economic growth increasingly difficult.

In order to meet rising social security costs, the funds will search for increasingly attractive investment opportunities in the developing countries where there is higher growth and higher rates of return. As such, higher growth rates, based on sound macroeconomic management in the developing economies, are very important for the developed countries.

On the other hand, the developing countries should become more closely integrated into the world economy. They also have to meet increasing demands for capital, skilled labour and new technologies. Furthermore, the ADCs have to cope with problems such as industrial restructuring to enhance competitiveness and environmental protection. These challenges will require greater foreign investment and transfer of technology.

In this regard, the 1997 Council Meeting at the Ministerial Level stated that the OECD will increase co-operation with non-member countries through official and non-official activities. In addition, the OECD will endeavour to take part in other international forums to enable ADCs to participate in discussions regarding issues such as MAI, Bribery and Regulatory Reform.

Korea is eager to participate in both of these processes. As one of the largest beneficiaries of development assistance, Korea now wants to extend the benefits to other developing countries. Finally, Korea will accelerate its market liberalisation for its prosperity as well as for world prosperity.

The Results of the Singapore Conference and the Prospects it Opened

Jacques de Lajugie

On the whole we can be satisfied by the Singapore Conference. The programme of work adopted at Marrakesh has been consolidated. New studies have been undertaken on investment, competition and public markets. At the European Union's initiative we adopted a plan of action for the less advanced countries, whose importance was underlined by the G7 Denver Summit after being at the centre of discussion at the 1996 Lyon meeting.

Nonetheless, we would have wished for greater progress concerning the environment and a more genuine, intense and exhaustive dialogue on the most sensitive subjects like basic social standards, which should not be a pretext for calling into question the comparative advantages of developing countries in Asia or elsewhere, and should be clearly limited to fundamental labour rights.

The Singapore conference showed the strength of the multilateral trading system and proved that the WTO is an institution which functions satisfactorily. Its work has been increased and widened by the sectoral agreements negotiated since the beginning of 1997 on information technologies and basic telecommunications. An agreement on financial services could be concluded by the end of 1997. We should make the necessary effort to achieve this.

With the consolidation of the gains of the Uruguay Round and the adoption of this enlarged programme of work a first stage has been completed. Significantly, this happened in Singapore.

The convergence of economies in a globalising economy necessarily leads to increasing trade problems and a strengthening of the rules governing them. In particular that assumes shifting the emphasis from tariffs to non-tariff measures, being ambitious for the multilateral framework and tackling all the problems linked to facilitating trade and market access.

Of course this process is only just beginning in a number of areas. Doubtless it will be necessary to wait until the 1999 ministerial conference of the WTO to learn more about the progress of work begun after Marrakesh and Singapore, as well as the trends shaping the multilateral agenda at the beginning of the 21st century.

This time for reflection should enable us to begin thinking about what is needed and what concerted action is required for the economy of the 21st century.

Some projections provide the background for these reflections, but they should also take into account Asia's increasing place in the world economy.

Some Projections of Asia's Place in the World Economy Around 2020-2030

All the projections indicate that Asia will be the major pole of the world economy around 2010-2030.

Thirty years ago the OECD countries accounted for about 70 per cent of the growth of global GDP, compared to 10 per cent for the developing Asian countries. By 2020-2030 Asia should account for more than 50 per cent of the world's growth, while the OECD countries will recede from 40 per cent to less than 20 per cent. At 55 per cent of the world's GDP, Asia's economic strength will almost be equivalent to the weight of its population.

The Asian region already ranks second in trade, accounting for 30 per cent of world commerce. Its rise has been very rapid from only 15 per cent in 1980 and it is now the most dynamic region of world trade. The proportion of manufactured products in exports of Asian developing countries has increased from 7 per cent in 1960 to more than 50 per cent in 1990.

Tomorrow, even more so than today, Asia will be a region of growth and prosperity, a pole of attraction and an essential outlet for all dealers, in other words, an essential trading, economic and financial partner.

This also means that the triangular relationship of Europe, America and Asia which concentrates 70 per cent of world trade, will continue to be the major axis, but will undergo changes corresponding to the relative weight of the partners and the strengthening of regional integration.

The consequences of this observation and these projections are clear:

First of all, Asia has to become a more integrated part of the multilateral system.

In the short term, China should become a member of the World Trade Organization on suitable conditions for assuring equilibrium between its rights and obligations. China is destined to become a major partner in the world economy (in 2030 it will represent one-fourth of the world economy with a growth rate greater than 8 per cent until 2005) and China's membership will establish the WTO's universality.

Negotiations leading to accession should concentrate on the essential points, particularly on commitments concerning market access, tariffs and services.

The mutual opening of economies should also continue. First, differences in customs duties of Europe and Asian countries remain too large and slow the growth of trade. Second, the rise of Asian economies will lead to greater reciprocal investment flows between the two regions. Under the auspices of the WTO, achieving common rules for protecting and liberalising these flows is urgent. Third, the multilateral framework should involve substantial progress on competition and intellectual property policies, and access to markets for goods and services.

Secondly, Asia's ability to influence the multilateral agenda will increase.

An active partnership signifies greater ability to shape the multilateral agenda. If the interests of all partners are not taken into account on their merits, there will be a tendency towards withdrawal which would be harmful to the whole system.

Globalisation means strengthening the rules of the game, but progress will be much more difficult to achieve when levels of development become comparable. Lack of comparable openness of economies, even a tendency to withdraw, will make it impossible to achieve "critical masses", which alone can meet the basic principle of a multilateral system, namely mutual liberalisation based on mutual benefit. That was clearly shown in the WTO negotiations on telecommunications, and there is good reason to think that the stakes will be similar in the negotiations on financial services which should be concluded by December 1997.

Lack of respect for the fundamental rules, discriminatory practices contrary to the principle of national treatment, or non-reciprocity will give rise to a revival of protectionist attitudes in the public opinion of industrialised countries.

Finally, the relationship between the multilateral rules and agreements of regional groups must be clarified.

No one doubts that economic and trade integration will continue. That means that commitments for liberalisation which could be implemented by ASEAN — or, between 2005 and 2010, in the framework of APEC — should be based on open regionalism. In this respect, it will be essential that regional liberalisation should be fully compatible with the World Trade Organization and its principles — its standards, customs procedures or rules of origin.

In the growing triangular relationship of America, Asia and Europe, Europeans and Asians have a particular interest in making sure that the relationships between the three poles is, and remains, balanced. The dialogue of the Asia-Europe Meetings (ASEM) between Asia and the European Union provides this framework, and France is very active in the process.

The adoption of action plans to facilitate trade and investment by the ASEM ministers of commerce in September 1997 should lead to progress in facilitating and liberalising trade and investment at the same time.

Only by developing this long-term perspective will it be possible to assure a balance between the regional and multilateral dimensions and, more generally, strengthen the multilateral trading system.

Investment by Pension Funds in Emerging Markets in Asia with Special Reference to India

P.G. Kakodkar

This presentation will reflect my experience as a banker for about 40 years in India's largest commercial bank, the State Bank of India.

The two prime requisites for investment by any fund manager are:

i)   the security of the investment, and

ii)   the rate of return.

Depending upon the security of the investment, the rate of return varies. Generally, the higher the security, the less will be the rate of return and vice versa. While this is true for all investments and fund managers, fund managers of pension funds have a higher responsibility to fulfil. They are in charge of the funds which represent the lifelong savings of people who have saved assiduously, month after month, to provide for themselves and their dependants, when they become old or infirm, and no longer in a position to work.

Bearing in mind this human aspect of these ultimate beneficiaries of pension funds — our own elders — the responsibility of the fund manager is naturally high. Populations are ageing in the industrial world, and birth rates are already below replacement levels. Thus, the number of retirees each worker must support is increasing. To some extent, this can be mitigated by immigration. This, however, has its limitations. Hence, to maintain living standards of pensioners, the workers' contributions must go up. As the proportion of retired people to workers increases, this will become increasingly difficult. Hence the need for any good and prudent fund manager to be consistently on the lookout for investment opportunities which will combine safety, security and liquidity, with higher and higher returns.

Pension Funds are Long-term Cautious Market Players

Pension funds are all long-term players. They are less adventurous and are cautious and conservative, as they represent a segment of society which looks for a steady flow of returns — insurance for retired life. It is therefore natural that they were conspicuous by their absence during the early phases of liberalisation in the emerging markets, when there were some investment opportunities, but when both the returns and the risks were also high. However, with the adoption of reforms, especially in India, and development of a market-friendly institutional and regulatory framework, the risks are manageable and the returns have remained relatively high. Hence, since 1989, fund flows from the developed countries have diversified to the emerging markets. Furthermore, the share of portfolio flows (including pension funds) in total capital flows has been rising, relative to both bank lending and foreign direct investment.

Economies are Privatising and Globalising to Attain Faster Growth

Winds of change are sweeping over the world's economies. The developing economies are moving away from a highly centralised system of decision making to a decentralised allocation system led by market forces. In the process, many barriers preventing free flow of goods and money are being dismantled. Globalisation, leading to freer flows of technology and capital across political boundaries, and privatisation, which has given economic decision-making power to a large number of competent entrepreneurs, have become the most favoured means of achieving faster economic growth.

Developing countries are endeavouring to catch up fast with developed countries by carrying out economic reforms covering, *inter alia*, industrial restructuring, investments in infrastructure projects, and reform of financial institutions. Now that these markets have experienced an initial round of reforms, which in India have been going on for five years, the degree of risks for investors has been reduced. To illustrate this, in India there has been growth on all fronts: self-sufficiency in food, all-round growth in industries, and hitherto undreamed of growth in exports. The traditional 3.5 per cent growth rate has nearly doubled. Foreign exchange reserves are increasing. Funds continue to pour into India through foreign institutional investors and foreign direct investment. Some pension funds are already investing in India. Others may feel the time is ripe to do so.

Emerging Markets

The emerging markets have certain common characteristics:

i) they cater to the financial needs of relatively weak economies which are trying to overcome the constraints from structural rigidities with respect to land, labour and capital, as well as from poor infrastructure, low productivity and low rates of investment.

ii) they lack depth and use, in the absence of a large number of big investors, scrips and a variety of instruments. Large investors such as pension funds are conspicuously absent. However, the momentum of growth fuelled by new political initiatives is changing all this; and

iii) being in the initial phase of liberalisation, they may lack an adequate regulatory framework and judicial system. India, however, has a strong and independent judiciary as is evident from several recent judgements which have gone against the government and in favour of business, and the regulatory framework is being constantly brought in line with the requirements of a healthy market. The trading systems, settlement processes and title transfer mechanism are all being streamlined. In India, all big stock exchanges have computer-based trading and now even a scripless depository.

The emerging markets are those in which the economic liberalisation process is relatively new and, as such, these economies have large untapped resources; hence the rate of economic growth and returns is very high. In the process of liberalisation, to bridge the capital gap, capital market reforms are undertaken and foreign investment is solicited by reducing entry barriers and taxes and by increasing investment ceilings. In the initial stages, the perception of risk in these countries was extraordinarily high. However, with stabilization of financial reforms, the risk perception has improved, resulting in the entry of a larger number of market players. In the process, while returns have come down relatively, nevertheless, they are still higher than those offered by the mature markets. This is evident from the fact that while the six months and one year DEM interest rates remained at around 3.2 per cent and 3.4 per cent respectively, the rate of interest in Indonesia is 13 per cent and 14 per cent, in the Philippines, 11.2 per cent and 11.5 per cent, and in India, 7.5 per cent and 8.5 per cent respectively.

Emerging Markets *vis-à-vis* Mature Markets

The rate of economic growth and a few selected key statistics indicate the attractiveness of the emerging markets.

Real GDP growth in emerging economies was more than double the US growth rate. Although inflation is high in these economies, these countries have taken concrete steps towards curbing inflation, and the emerging markets in Asia have been successful in containing it to less than 9 per cent, which can be considered no mean achievement in the light of the spiralling inflation rates of the past. Even after making allowances for depreciation in exchange rates, we observe that the average lending rate/bond yield in these economies was higher than that of the United States in 1996, even though the US bond yield was then at its peak level for the 1990s. For example, the rate of return in India works out at around 11 per cent after taking into account about 3 per cent depreciation in the currency value *vis-à-vis* the dollar, whereas the US figure was 6.52 per cent. Incidentally, it might be noted that as the Indian rupee is pegged to the dollar, it has considerably appreciated *vis-à-vis* major European currencies.

Another interesting indicator for higher rates of return in emerging markets was substantially higher compounded annual stock market returns for 1986-96. During the period, the compounded annual stock market return was 17.2 per cent in Malaysia, 22.3 per cent in the Philippines, 19.4 per cent in India and 20 per cent in China. Such ten-year returns are virtually unmatched. However, before taking a position on investing in emerging markets, it would be necessary to take into account major credit risk indicators. Here we find that there are certain weaknesses: external debt as a percentage of GDP is quite high, ranging from 56.2 percent in the Philippines to 9.2 per cent in Korea, with India in between at 31.3 per cent. However, the percentages in Asia compare favourably to other emerging markets like those of Latin America. In any case, this ratio points towards the scarcity of resources rather than weaknesses of those economies. Moreover, these emerging economies in Asia have fairly sound foreign exchange reserves, which is evident from the fact that the reserves in 1996 were as high as $112 billion in China and $11.5 billion in the Philippines. India's foreign exchange reserves were $19.1 billion.

These figures may be comforting for pension funds looking for investment opportunities. Another comforting factor for emerging markets is the country rating given by agencies like Moody's and Standard and Poor's. It may be observed that the credit ratings of the emerging markets have undergone a change for the better and most of the countries in emerging markets in Asia have been rated as creditworthy. This long-term indicator certainly is a noteworthy pointer for pension funds which look for long-term returns on investment.

India: An Investment Opportunity

After having dealt with the emerging Asian markets from a broad perspective, let me discuss conditions in India.

India has an area of 3.3 million square kilometres in southern Asia, with vast natural resources. Among its human resources is a large number of scientifically trained personnel. It has a developed legal and political system, both inherited from the British. English is one of the most widely spoken languages in the country. India has a duly elected democratic government. The GDP in 1996-97 was $346 billion and the average gross domestic savings for the past seven years as a percentage of GDP was 23.11 per cent. Exports in 1995-96 stood at $31.8 billion, while imports were $36.7 billion, resulting in a trade deficit of $4.9 billion.

The future outlook of the Indian economy is bright. The GDP growth rate for India is expected to settle at around 7 per cent per annum for the next few years. Furthermore, with inflation at 6-7 per cent, India is a good bet for medium to long-term investments. The interest rates adjusted for exchange risk are also attractive in the long term. Improved fiscal discipline should bring down the fiscal deficit to 4.75 per cent of GDP by the end of the 1998 financial year and to about 4 per cent by the turn of the century. Corporations are expected to report good profits as the interest burden falls and economic growth improves their profitability. Exports and imports should show healthy growth rates of 20-22 per cent and 22-24 per cent per annum respectively in the next two years. Participation in the WTO will assist in improving the foreign trade of India. Based on the public sector reforms and the reduction in the fiscal deficit, gross domestic savings are expected to be 26-27 per cent of GDP. India hopes to see great improvements in infrastructure as a result of tax incentives for channelling savings to infrastructure projects, clearer policies and increased attractiveness to the international investor.

Since independence in 1947, India has emerged as a stable democracy with the necessary institutions to safeguard and nurture it. It has strong political parties, and an independent press and judiciary. English is well understood by the educated class. It has possibly the third largest pool of scientific and technical human resources in the world. It is well endowed with varied natural resources, a large number of basic and heavy industries, adequate infrastructure and is self-sufficient in food. No wonder the GDP has been growing at a healthy 7 per cent.

Recently, after elections in mid-1996, a multiparty coalition has assumed power. This created political uncertainty, and even though this fear persists, the Union budget for 1998 and the monetary and credit policy of the Reserve Bank of India have clearly shown that the direction of economic reforms is irreversible, even though some specific initiatives may be delayed at times, particularly when they have immediate political implications.

India, with a population of around 900 million people, is almost the size of a continent. It has at least 150 million middle class ("consumers") who, thanks to liberalisation, can now spend their money, which makes India a huge potential market for goods and services.

Positive Features of the Indian Economic, Regulatory and Institutional System

Change in the Role of Government in the Economy

Realising the inadequacies of the past economic growth strategy, India has adopted a new economic approach. It involves:

i)   removing constraints on production and distribution of goods and services by dismantling the regulatory framework;

ii) encouraging competition by lowering protection and tariff and non-tariff entry barriers;

iii) rationalising the tax structure;

iv) reforming the financial sector;

v) facilitating inflows of new technology and foreign capital; and

vi) movement towards current account convertibility.

Throughout the 1980s, India's fiscal deficit remained at a high level, leading to an alarming rise in public debt (union government liabilities). As a part of the fiscal reform, the government is endeavouring to achieve fiscal discipline by gradually bringing down the deficit to 3.5 per cent of GDP from a high of 8.3 per cent in 1991 by, *inter alia*, reduction of subsidies, and PSU disinvestment. The fiscal deficit is now around 5 per cent.

Most Industries Deregulated

Most industries have been deregulated with price, distribution and capacity regulations lifted. A few industries such as fertilizer, oil, coal, mining, sugar, power, telecommunications, etc. are controlled, but entry by the private sector is permitted and encouraged.

Reforming the Financial Sector and Attracting Foreign Capital Investment

In order to make available adequate finance at reasonable rates to the corporate sector, financial sector reforms have been initiated. These include the following measures:

1) restrictions on foreign direct and portfolio investment in India have been relaxed. Indian corporations have been allowed to tap global capital markets more freely. Net foreign exchange inflows increased from $4.1 billion in 1994 to $5.4 billion in 1997;

2) in a bid to improve liquidity of the debt markets, institutions have been established to act as market-makers for government paper and trading is encouraged through exchanges. The FIIs are now allowed to invest in debts as well;

3) to improve transparency and functioning of equity markets, the stock exchanges and regulatory authorities have initiated measures, which include;

a) introduction of screen-based trading at stock exchanges as opposed to the outcry system;

b) carrying out faster settlement of trades by reducing the settlement period (to one week from earlier two-three weeks) and introducing fixed settlement dates (earlier flexible);

c) faster registration. Since India still follows the physical certificate-based system, the transfer of ownership used to consume time besides the risk of "bad delivery" (rejection of request for transfer on technical or substantive grounds). Steps have been taken to reduce these problems by monitoring transfer agents (for time taken) and brokers (for bad deliveries);

d) a law for paperless trading has been passed and a National Securities and Depositories Limited has been set up for the purpose. About 40 companies have already agreed to dematerialise their shares and scripless trading for 32 of these has already commenced. Some of the bigger Indian corporations such as ACC, IPCL, Reliance Petrochemicals and Reliance Capital are among these. Other bigger corporations like SBI are likely to follow soon. The extent of dematerialisation will increase as more companies and investors join the depository system;

e) the change in the regulatory stance focuses more on prudential and organisational controls to protect the integrity of the system without being unduly restrictive for legitimate and sound business practices;

f) computerisation of the stock exchanges. By the end of March 1997, 16 of the 22 stock exchanges had computerised trading systems. This has been achieved over a period of two years. The remaining stock exchanges are expected to go on-line shortly this year. Automation of the systems has definitely improved the transparency of operations and has brought about a reduced number of bad trades. With this step, further improvements could be quickly brought about like prompt settlement systems, regular auctioning of uncovered positions, improved information disclosure, better monitoring of brokers' exposures and capital adequacy norms, surveillance systems to check unusual activity and price rigging, if any;

g) entry of mutual funds. Allowing public sector banks to start mutual funds in 1987 was an important step taken to provide the retail investors with an avenue for participation in financial markets through professional fund managers. Foreign and private sector mutual funds entered in 1993-94. Foreign mutual funds currently operating in India include Morgan Stanley, Threadneedle (with ITC) and Templeton. The mutual fund industry has registered a decent growth rate. Despite a lull for the past two years, the industry appears to be gaining strength, as indicated by the entry of new players in the market. The potential for the mutual funds is immense; and *h)*   establishing a regulatory watchdog. The Securities Exchange Board of India (SEBI), in 1992 was another important step. The SEBI has had its own share of successes and failures, but the presence of the SEBI has definitely reduced malpractices. The SEBI has also instituted several changes including liberalising the investment norms for fund managers, while simultaneously increasing the responsibility and compliance requirements.

Financial sector reforms are continuing. Bold changes are being contemplated to bring the financial system in line with the rest of the world. Only in the insurance sector has progress been agonisingly slow due to resistance by the public sector unions at insurance companies.

Old World Savings for Asian Growth

Norbert Walter

A sabbatical in the United States once gave me reason for thinking about the issues we are dealing with today. During that sabbatical at Johns Hopkins in 1986-87, I studied demography and it proved to be a very good choice, especially for an investment banker. I will discuss some of those long-term issues below, rather than concentrating on the time horizon of an investment banker which is three days or three weeks and, on occasion, even three months.

The question we are addressing here could be defined as "does Southeast Asia need the savings of the Old World?" While there are some interesting projects in Southeast Asia, probably most of the savings required to fund them can be accumulated in the region itself. So it seems Krugman is right, that there are quite extensive resources out there in Southeast Asia, human and financial, and there is not much that we could provide in terms of those resources. But what are the limiting factors for development in Southeast Asia? In some instances, they could be management skills, while in other cases the networks for a larger international market that come with foreign direct investment are much more important. Thus, are we really addressing the question of whether the Old World needs investment opportunities, because we have run out of good ideas with high rates of return in our old economies? We could invest in the vital and dynamic United States, rather than in Southeast Asia. So is this conference irrelevant because Southeast Asia has all the savings it needs and the Old World has all the investment opportunities it needs on the west coast of the United States? Of course that question is a caricature.

When we discuss pension funds, obviously we are talking about something that is different from what many in the Old World still consider the best retirement system, namely a pay-as-you-go system. At least this is true in France and Germany. Our systems have lasted for a good hundred years. They have survived world wars and they have survived currency reforms. So why should we worry about demographic change? Yet the critics of the pay-as-you-go systems are right on the mark, because those who are defending them have little idea of what will occur in the future.

It is really unfortunate that in our old countries, particularly in continental Europe, young people do not participate in the political process. If they did, we would not have the retirement pension systems we have, because the young people would understand right away that they will be the victims of those systems, rather than the beneficiaries. If this is true and if this is understood, then there are good reasons for moving from a pay-as-you-go to a fully funded system, and the savings rate in the Old World would go up.

Of course, the change from a pay-as-you-go system to a private, fully funded system is not simply a matter of having more savings, and, in turn, having a better resource base for more investment. Actually the change from the pay-as-you-go system to a privately funded system is something that greatly enhances capital productivity. That is a much more important factor, because the agents who are taking care of investment will adopt a totally different approach from those who are responsible for investment decisions today.

Japan is already a greying society, and Europe is rapidly following suit. The United States, with a higher fertility rate than either Japan or Western Europe, and with an intelligent (i.e. selective) immigration policy is in better shape than the rest of the G7. Their ageing problem will be less pronounced than in Japan and Europe, but the picture is incomplete if we only look at the First World. The Second World has been neglected because it was behind the Iron Curtain for so long, but the demographic issues facing the G7 not only exist for the eighth member of the club, Russia, but also for all the rest of central and eastern Europe. There was a slight exception for Poland, but since the end of the Cold War Poland has been moving in the same direction as the rest of us.

Now ask again whether the Old World should look for better investment opportunities in Southeast Asia. The answer is "yes", because the demographic trends there are different.

So what will happen if Old World pension money flows to the emerging countries? The big unknown is political risk.

The question is not only about pension funds and emerging markets, it is also about diversification. Since there are political risks — and we have been seeing some of those political risks materialising in Thailand — will there be a contagion effect. After having had a "tequila" effect in Latin America, will there be a comparable effect in Asia? If so it may not be as troublesome, may not be as severe, but there are reasons to be concerned about Malaysia. There are also reasons to be concerned about the political stability of Indonesia. Thus, there will be difficulties for funds going in that direction in the immediate future.

How will the United States respond if not only Thailand, but other Southeast Asian countries also devalue their currencies against the dollar? How will that affect the attitudes of major American pension fund managers towards diversification into Southeast Asian markets? Despite the present price/earnings ratios of equity markets, it is probably unwise to be overly optimistic about other possibilities too soon, because of the political risks and a need for good governance. Good governance is a very important factor, and the Old World and the international institutions should be very supportive, helping to make it understood in Southeast Asia and other emerging markets what pension fund managers require.

Many pension plans are moving away from a defined benefits system to a defined contributions system. This is a trend that will continue and there will be more diversification. Certainly, there is an interest in more diversification, but it is difficult to say whether other "old" countries, like France, Germany and Italy, for example, will move from the one system to the other, and what their policies for investing this money will be.

If there is a change, it will come very slowly because the political will and commitment to change in these countries is rather limited. The issue was addressed in Germany, and resulted in something called a "reform" of the pension system. Then a debate on reform will have to begin again, and none of the political parties now appears ready to accept a structural reform.

At this moment, Italy seems to be the most willing country to address the issue under the pressure of the Maastricht Treaty. On this question the Italians are being more courageous than the French or Germans.

One might have expected that an investment banker would only suggest that we should move towards a privately funded system, that a high proportion of it should be invested in equity, and that we could probably benefit a lot from such changes. That advice alone would be short-sighted.

Since the emerging world will also be ageing by the year 2030, we have to consider investment opportunities further down the road and we have to consider other instruments to take care of our retirement problems. We have to revive the idea of the three-generation family. If we do not develop tax policies based on that principle, we will not be in a position to sustain the elderly. One cannot possibly expect family solidarity to sustain 400 million Chinese who will be 65, or older, after the year 2055. Such an immense task will require a different kind of tax system, one that is based on the family.

It is good to learn that the Chinese government is only subsidising housing for three-generation families. To some extent, therefore, the principle is already understood, and it is good that more fundamental questions, and even ethical questions are being addressed. If we are intelligent we would tailor tax structures accordingly, rather than sticking to pension fund schemes that are invested in equity, preferably in the emerging markets. Of course, this is still a very important instrument, and we should help emerging countries understand that more transparency than now exists is necessary to enable pension fund managers to diversify their funds into such countries. But that will be insufficient for the very long run, for the dramatic problems down the road, unless we address the ethical issue of the family as a major factor for making our world more sustainable. This will be particularly true for the economic and population giants of Asia, China and India.

Pension Fund Diversification and Asia's Emerging Markets

Roberto F. De Ocampo

As we usher in this new century, we are confronted with the realities of global integration at a pace unimaginable just a few decades ago.

Globalisation of Financial Markets

In no other field outside finance is the rapid pace of global integration felt so powerfully. With the aid of new and increasingly sophisticated information and telecommunications technology, billions of dollars may be instantaneously transferred to any part of the globe at a moment's notice. Capital now flows freely in the global market without any heed of formal political boundaries. It does not move seasonally, like birds, but constantly in search of marginally better returns. This globalisation of financial markets has enabled net private capital flows to developing countries to rise from an average level of $10 billion per year in the mid-1970s to over $100 billion per year at present. These inflows have been used to generate more trade and investment.

As we enter a new century, markets, rather than rules or governments, will play a decisive role in shaping economic decisions. Global fund managers, with billions of dollars at their command, are becoming increasingly more important as they expand their portfolios into Asian markets. Mutual funds dedicated to Asian equities are also on the rise. Investment banks and securities subsidiaries of commercial banks are now becoming more dominant. In short, institutional investors are now becoming the driving force behind emerging markets in Asia.

The ascendancy of international capital flows is shaping the development strategies and policies of many emerging market economies. Capital markets have a way of requiring fiscal and monetary discipline that can be more stringent than that of the IMF or a creditor bank advisory committee. This was amply demonstrated in the case of Mexico.

It is significant that the panic touched off by the Mexican crisis in 1995, which threatened to destabilize emerging economies, saw Asian markets riding out the storm. Indeed, after a sober assessment of economic fundamentals, fund managers began to realise that not all emerging markets are the same.

The fundamental changes in market players, instruments, and the volume of capital flows have resulted in the need for a new mindset. This new thinking, which is increasingly being adopted by the emerging markets of Asia, is one which is characterised by the market-driven philosophy of competitiveness, liberalisation, and globalisation. In line with this, the newly industrialising countries as well as those aspiring to that status, are learning to maintain sound policies and avoid capital and foreign exchange controls. Instead, they are now creating investor-friendly climates for both foreign and domestic investors.

In fact, there are already vast sums of homegrown capital at work in Asia. This is perhaps the key to preventing a debacle such as occurred in Mexico. While the demand for foreign capital continues to be high in view of the rapid growth of the Asian economies, what is essential is to strengthen the domestic capital base, and pension funds are a strategic feature of domestic capital market development.

In many Asian economies, including the Philippines, pension funds address the twin but interrelated issues of savings mobilisation and domestic capital-market development. Well-developed capital markets play a crucial role in mobilising savings and making available longer-term capital, especially for investment in infrastructure. It is estimated that the infrastructure requirements of Asia over the next ten years range from a low of $1 trillion to a high of $8 trillion. Pension funds are now being tapped as an alternative source of financing to meet this huge infrastructure gap.

Over the years, the importance of pension funds has gained wide recognition and acceptance in an environment of liberalisation and globalisation. At the APEC finance ministers' meeting in the Philippines in April 1997, the APEC finance ministers agreed to undertake collaborative initiatives to facilitate increased private sector participation in infrastructure, promote the development of the financial and capital markets and support the freer flow of capital.

One of these initiatives is a regional forum on pension fund reform where issues related to pension fund reform in APEC member economies will be discussed, including issues related to sustainability, the relative roles of the private and public sectors in pension fund management, the implications for domestic savings and capital market development, and the prudential regulation of pension fund investments.

The Philippine Economy

The Philippines has erased the image of "the sick man of Asia" to become what many describe as "Asia's emerging tiger".

The international recognition accorded the Philippines over the past few years was earned by dint of sheer determination and the political will to face up to the factors that had inhibited our growth in the past two decades. The need to catch up and get our growth on the fast-track so that we could turn the corner as the new century begins has led us to pursue the less travelled road of discipline. We have adopted a regimen of liberalisation and deregulation in an environment that had grown used to protection, subsidy and misguided nationalism.

So we opened up to foreign investment, lifted virtually all controls on foreign exchange, and welcomed foreign banks into a closely knit domestic banking system. We liberalised foreign trade by removing quantitative restrictions and simplifying our tariff structure.

We have likewise taken positive action to develop our domestic capital market and liberate it from the vestiges of inward-looking, timid and fearful thinking. We put in place reform measures which were anchored to the principles of full disclosure and self-regulation. Full disclosure leads to greater transparency and creates investor confidence as the volume and quality of information become the critical elements in risk assessment and decision making. On the other hand, self-regulation represents a covenant among all parties that they will be true to their commitments.

Pension Funds in the Philippines

Despite the respectable growth performance of the Philippine economy over the past four years, our savings rate remains the lowest in ASEAN. This is the reason why we have taken serious steps to strengthen our fiscal position such that we now have had three consecutive years of budget surpluses. We are also looking at our pension fund system as an important vehicle for mobilising savings.

The pension fund system in the Philippines consists of the social security system (SSS, for the private sector), the government service insurance system (GSIS, for government employees), the armed forces of the Philippines retirement and separation benefits system, private pension funds, and several multi-employer plans. The bulk of the system's assets is accounted for by the SSS and GSIS.

While still relatively young, our pension fund system has already become an important source of retirement benefits for Philippine workers and one of the major sources of long-term capital, particularly for infrastructure projects. Fortunately, the Philippines still has a fairly young population. Thus, actuarially speaking, we have more elbow room compared to other countries where the population is rapidly reaching the point where the demand for pension funds is high.

One of the more recent steps we have taken to improve our pension fund system further are the charter amendments in the social security system which broadened its investment powers. For example, the SSS can now invest 30 per cent of its investment reserve fund in infrastructure projects. In addition to this, the SSS is now allowed to allocate 7.5 per cent of its investment reserve fund for foreign currency denominated investments.

The SSS also now has the power to appoint local and foreign fund managers to manage its reserve fund. The new charter also enables the SSS to change its rate of contribution, where necessary, to assure the actuarial sustainability of the system.

We are also rationalising our tax system to ensure that double taxation, inequities in the tax treatment of the various financial instruments and market discrimination will soon be a thing of the past. We are now in the process of overhauling our tax system so that it will be conducive to capital market development.

Over the long term, we are pursuing plans to develop further our pension fund system in line with current trends in the global arena. We are currently looking at Chile's success in privatising its pension fund system to see if it is applicable in the Philippines and whether privatisation is the answer to promoting greater efficiency in the system.

Diversification

The liberalisation of global markets and the freer flow of capital across borders has necessitated a diversification of portfolio investments. In the case of pension funds, it is really a question of diversifying not only the uses of pension funds but diversifying pension funds themselves in terms of their nature and their sectoral leadership.

The historical experience of most countries has confirmed that equity investments generate much higher risk-adjusted returns over time than other classes of assets, although such assets are more volatile in the short term. Because of this experience, most pension funds should place a higher percentage of their assets in equity investments with internal diversification. With a much larger capital market, we could make a strong case for increasing this allocation as this would be consistent with maximising the risk-adjusted return on the portfolio.

We should also encourage the private sector to participate more actively in the pension fund system. At present, most existing pension funds are owned and managed by the public sector. Thus there are instances where limitations hamper decisions to diversify investment. In addition, we should also encourage the establishment of other funds like mutual funds and provident funds that will make available a larger pool of money in the capital markets.

In the final analysis, fund management decisions, whether by the public or the private sector, should be based on sound criteria for maximising returns consistent with maintaining the safety of principal and liquidity.

In short, the central challenge for us is to strike a balance between conservatism and diversification. While we diversify our portfolio investments, let us make sure that we protect the integrity of our pension funds.

PART TWO

ASIAN GROWTH
IN AN INTERNATIONAL CONTEXT

Asian and Global Economic Growth: Aspects of Structural Interdependence

Frank Harrigan

Introduction

Thirty years ago, the incidence of poverty in East Asia was among the highest in the world. Myrdal (1963) in his celebrated study, *Asian Drama*, painted a rather stark future for the region at the time. But events since have irrevocably changed the economic and social landscape of East Asia. They have also changed thinking about how development can best proceed. Sustained economic growth in East Asia has seen the region's incomes catch up rapidly to levels in the industrialised countries. Many other economies in the developing world are now seeking to emulate this achievement. Southeast Asia has progressed next farthest along this path, perhaps assisted by its proximity to East Asia and Japan, but the People's Republic of China (PRC), the transitional economies of Indochina, and now the economies of South Asia are also pursuing market reforms that they hope will quickly propel their incomes upward. The lessons of East Asia are also being examined in other parts of the developing world, including in Latin America and Africa.

When the East Asian economies embarked on their strategy of manufacturing for export-led growth, the ripples that this created in the pool of world trade were small. These economies were small in absolute size and their output could easily be absorbed in world markets. With many more countries now competing for export markets, there is concern that developing countries may "crowd-out" opportunities for each other. There is also mounting concern in industrialised countries that despite the efficiency and welfare improvements that are identified with free trade, it may have unfavourable (and politically unpalatable) distributional implications. Today, of course, it is much easier for goods from developing countries to enter industrial markets than in earlier decades. Tariff barriers have tumbled and the impediments posed by transport and communications costs are being steadily eroded.

This paper attempts to do two things. First, it paints a possible scenario for future Asian growth and traces its implications for the stature of Asia in the world economy. This part of the paper draws heavily on the *Emerging Asia* study (ADB, 1997). Second, the paper asks what impact Asia's growth might have on patterns of global saving and investment, and industrial structure. Albeit indirectly, we examine some of the issues that have been raised in the debate about international trade and the rise in earnings inequality in industrialised countries. The remainder of the paper divides as follows. We present projections of Asian economic growth. We then go on to describe how we examine the impacts of this growth within a general equilibrium model of the world economy. Finally, we present the main results of this exercise followed by a short conclusion.

Prospects For Growth In Asia

The story of East and now Southeast Asia's remarkable economic growth in the past thirty years is explicable in terms of a reasonably well understood set of structural, policy, and institutional factors. The same framework is also capable of explaining why South Asia and other parts of the developing world have performed less well. In this sense, growth in East Asia has not been miraculous. Its origins are identifiable and the experience of fast economic catch-up is replicable for many who still lag far behind.

These conclusions are based on a careful empirical study of the determinants of growth across nations over the past thirty years (ADB, 1997 and Radelet, Sachs and Lee, 1997). This analysis suggests that fast growth in East Asia was a consequence of an initial potential for fast economic catch-up, which was then ignited by good policy choices and institutions. East Asia's geography and its comparatively fast demographic transition have both assisted income growth but, above all, it has been smart policy and institutional choices that have propelled incomes upwards. East Asia's growth was a consequence of its outward orientation, its success in achieving macroeconomic stability and high levels of domestic saving, and its comparatively good governance structures. By contrast, incomes in South Asia have grown much more slowly. For much of the past thirty years, South Asia has been hobbled by inward-looking policies that provided a fertile breeding ground for favouritism, corruption, and inefficiency. South Asia's late demographic transition has also worked against fast economic growth.

Table 1, reproduced from Asian Development Bank (1997), provides a breakdown of how differences in economic performance within Asia and across the developing world can be attributed to a variety of structural, demographic, policy, and institutional factors. While many of these factors have been identified in other studies, including by the World Bank's *East Asian Miracle* (1993), the relatively large contributions of demographic change and institutional factors to explaining differences in growth have not been widely recognised and are worthy of note.

Table 1. Contribution of Selected Factors to Growth Differentials between East and Southeast Asia and Selected Regions, 1965-90

(per cent)

Factor	Contribution of each variable to the difference in annual per capita growth relative to East and Southeast Asia		
	South Asia	Sub-Saharan Africa	Latin America
Initial conditions	0.3	0.7	-1.2
Initial per person GDP	0.5	1.0	-1.2
Schooling	-0.2	-0.4	-0.1
Policy variables	-2.1	-1.7	-1.8
Government saving rate	-0.4	-0.1	-0.3
Openness	-1.2	-1.2	-1.0
Institutional quality	-0.5	-0.4	-0.5
Demography	-0.9	-1.9	-0.2
Life expectancy	-0.5	-1.3	0.1
Growth in working-age population	-0.3	0.1	-0.2
Growth in total population	-0.2	-0.7	-0.1
Resources and geography	0.2	-1.0	-0.6
Natural resources	0.1	-0.2	-0.2
Landlockedness	0.0	-0.3	-0.1
Location in the tropics	0.5	-0.2	0.0
Ratio of coastline distance to land area	-0.3	-0.3	-0.3

Source: ADB (1997), Table 2.2, p.80.

An important aspect of the results of the ADB study is that they provide support for the notion of "conditional convergence". That is to say, other things being held constant (i.e., geography, resources, policies, institutions, and demography, all of which may influence equilibrium growth and income levels), countries that begin with lower levels of income will tend to grow more quickly. This is because lower income countries, provided they are not "too backward", will typically have greater opportunities for learning, and higher rates of return to investment in physical and human capital. This is what Gerschenkron (1962) referred to as the "advantage of backwardness". But as a country's income level approaches those in the richest economies, then other things being equal, its growth will begin to slow as rates of return fall and opportunities for "catch-up" diminish. This pattern of growth accelerating, remaining high for a while, and then eventually slowing can be seen in the empirical records of Japan, Hong Kong, and Chinese Taipei.

It is important to understand that "conditional convergence" does not mean that poor countries will automatically catch-up with rich countries — quite the reverse. Indeed, most countries that are poor show little tendency to catch up to income levels in the industrialised countries (IMF, 1997). Even within Asia, there has been absolute income divergence. Incomes in South Asia have over the past three decades fallen further behind those in Japan as well as those in East and Southeast Asia (Dowling, Harrigan and Villafuerte, 1995). Broad comparative international experience suggests that income convergence has occurred only where initial conditions have been conducive and good policies and institutional structures have been put in place. Even then, some countries may remain handicapped by their geography or other aspects of structure, and may never catch up.

Table 2. **Growth Performance and Prospects for Selected Asian Economies,**
1965-95 and 1995-2025

(per cent)

Region and economy	Growth rate of per capita GDP	
	1965-95	1995-2025
East Asia	6.6	2.8
Hong Kong	5.6	2.1
Republic of Korea	7.2	3.5
Singapore	7.2	2.5
Chinese Taipei	6.2	3.1
People's Republic of China	5.6	6.0
Southeast Asia	3.9	4.5
Indonesia	4.7	5.0
Malaysia	4.8	3.9
Philippines	1.2	5.3
Thailand	4.8	3.8
South Asia	1.9	4.4
Bangladesh	1.6	3.9
India	2.2	5.5
Pakistan	1.6	4.4
Sri Lanka	2.3	3.9
Papua New Guinea	0.4	1.5

Source: ADB (1997), Table 2.11, p. 80.

There are many hazards in projecting growth into the future. After all, thirty years ago few would have imagined that East Asia would transform itself from an economic backwater into the most dynamic region of the world. Nevertheless, if only as a thought experiment, it is of interest to ask what past experience might suggest for prospects for growth in Asia. One way of looking at this question is to ask what the statistical model on which the results of Table 1 rest imply for future growth. Assuming that economic policy and other conditions remain broadly as they were around 1995, allowing for likely changes in the demographic structure of countries, and the fact that growth slows as (initial) incomes approach the frontier, the results shown in Table 2 are obtained[1]. One particular limitation of these projections is that growth in one country is independent of growth in others. Unfortunately, economic theory has yet made little headway in elucidating cross-country interdependence in growth.

In summary, the results of Table 2 suggest an acceleration in the growth of per capita income in South Asia over the next thirty years. By 1995 there had been significant improvements in policy and institutional conditions in South Asia compared with the previous three decades. Latest indications are that the governments of this region remain highly committed to the reform process. Indeed, further improvement in policy and institutional conditions could mean that growth in South Asia will match what has been achieved historically in East Asia. In Southeast Asia and in the PRC there remains ample opportunity for fast growth, provided these economies continue to follow outward-oriented policies and take measures necessary to support markets. In the first instance, the PRC's success in managing the reform of its state-owned enterprise sector will be crucial. In Southeast Asia, the main challenge will be to prepare for on-going industrial restructuring that their continued engagement with the global economy will necessarily entail. In East Asia, where incomes are already approaching those in the industrialised countries, a slowdown in growth is likely as rates of return on capital fall and opportunities for catch-up growth are exhausted. While growth will slow in East Asia it is not set for a precipitous collapse. The experience of Japan over the 1970s and 1980s is perhaps the best guide we have as to what is likely.

If Asia grows at the rates shown in Table 2, then by 2025 its share of world income, expressed in purchasing power parity terms, will have increased to around 57 per cent from its current share of less than 40 per cent. Also, while there has been (absolute) income divergence among the countries of the region in the past thirty years, there is the prospect of incomes converging over much of Asia in the next thirty. Many countries that are currently poor may soon begin to close the gap with their richer neighbours, and indeed with the industrialised countries.

There is of course nothing preordained about this optimistic scenario. Indeed, the summer of 1997 has seen considerable turmoil in Southeast Asian currency and asset markets. Some have even pronounced the demise of the Asian Miracle. This judgement is too hasty. A hallmark of Asian policy making in the past has been a pragmatism and an ability to adapt. In the mid-1980s the ASEAN economies were afflicted by a dramatic slowing of growth. Their economies proved resilient and they quickly bounced back.

Policy errors and institutional failures, shifts in fundamentals, contagion effects as well as bouts of self-fulfilling panic have all contributed to the current turmoil. Globalisation has magnified the cost of the errors that have been made. But the potential benefits of globalisation far outweigh its downside risks. To seize the benefits of globalisation, and to make good on their long-run promise, the economies of Southeast Asia must develop policies and institutions for the management of their monetary and financial affairs that are better attuned to emerging global realities.

Looking to the longer term, growth within Asia will require cohesion among regional neighbours. Domestically, it will require a commitment to good policies and improved governance structures that can sustain job-creating growth. Countries will also have to learn how to steer their way through the economic turbulence of globalisation. Internationally, a conducive trading and investment environment will be essential. A collapse of the international financial system or some other catastrophic event would set the economic clock back in Asia as it would in other countries of the world.

The prospect of continued economic vigour in Asia is regarded with trepidation among some in the industrialised countries. For example, if fast economic catch-up across much of developing Asia were to imply a need for a massive sectoral reallocation of resources in the industrialised countries, the question would then arise as to whether immobile factors in the declining sectors of these countries would resist economic change and, if so, what the costs of the associated dislocation might be. Some have argued that the increased integration of labour-abundant, low-skilled Asian economies in the world trading system has widened the wage gap in favour of skilled labour in the industrialised countries, and has exacerbated unemployment among the low skilled (Wood, 1994). Wages are usually emphasized in North America, and jobs in Europe.

In the next section we will explore these and other issues that are raised by the prospect of an economically larger and more influential Asia.

Asian Growth and Global Economic Structure: The Framework of Analysis

If Asia manages to grow as we have suggested in the previous section, what impact will this have on global saving and investment balances and global economic structure? Even if our growth scenario were to turn out to be correct these are not questions that are easily answered. Indeed, the possible linkages are so complex and interrelated that it is difficult even to begin to look at these issues without the assistance of some appropriate modelling framework. In this section, we describe in outline the ingredients of one such framework.

The Global Trade Analysis Project (GTAP) model (Hertel and Tsigas, 1996) is a computable general equilibrium model of the world economy. A general equilibrium framework is perhaps best suited to the analysis of the issues that interest us here. Macroeconometric models do not contain the sectoral detail we need, and a partial equilibrium approach would omit many of the secondary interactions that could have a critical bearing on outcomes. For a general introduction to computable general equilibrium models, see Dervis, et al. (1982) or Shoven and Whalley (1992). The version of GTAP used here identifies 17 regions of the world, and 13 activities and commodities. Regions are identified in Table 3 and commodities in Table 4. Of the 17 regions, 11 are in "developing Asia". Our classification omits some small economies including the transitional economies of Indochina and of Central Asia. It also aggregates Bangladesh, Pakistan, and Sri Lanka into a region labeled "The Rest of South Asia".

Table 3. **GTAP-EA Regions**

Region	Comment
Japan	
Hong Kong	
Singapore	
Chinese Taipei	
Republic of Korea	
Malaysia	
Thailand	
Indonesia	
Philippines	
People's Republic of China	
India	
Rest of South Asia	Bangladesh, Bhutan, Nepal, Pakistan, and Sri Lanka
North America	United States and Canada
Western Europe	European Union 12
Latin America	Argentina, Brazil, Mexico, Rest of Latin America
Sub-Saharan Africa	
Rest of the World	includes the Pacific Islands Developing Member countries, Central Asian republics, Vietnam, Lao People's Democratic Republic, Cambodia, Myanmar, as well as North Africa, Middle East, Eastern Europe and the former Soviet Union, Australia, New Zealand, and other countries n.e.c.

Table 4. **GTAP-EA Activities and Commodities**

Activity/Commodity	Comment
Rice	Paddy rice
Other grains	Wheat and grains other than rice
Other agriculture	Non-grain crops, wool, fishing, livestock
Natural resources	Forestry, oil and gas, coal, other minerals
Processed foods	Processed rice, meat, milk, other food, beverages and tobacco
Textiles	Multifibre Arrangement (MFA) sector
Wearing apparel	MFA sector
Light manufacturing	Leather, lumber and wood, other manufacturing
Machinery and equipment	Transport industries, machinery and equipment
Heavy industry	Steel, chemicals, rubber and plastic, primary ferrous metals, non-ferrous metals, fabricated metal products, pulp and paper, petroleum and coal products, and non-metallic minerals
Electricity, gas, and water	
Construction and housing	Construction and ownership of dwellings
Services	Trade and transport, other public services, and other private services

Taken together, around 98 per cent of the total income of Asia is accounted for by the Asian regions identified in the model. The rest of the world is divided into: North America (United States and Canada), Western Europe, Japan, Latin America, Sub-Saharan Africa, and Oceania and the rest of the world. While some greater disaggregation of commodities and regions would have been desirable, computational and data constraints prevented this.

For a detailed description of the structure of GTAP, see Hertel and Tsigas (1996). A full explanation of how this framework was applied in the present exercise is given in Harrigan and Sumulong (1996).

Most critically, it should be understood that we do not use the GTAP model to project rates of per person income growth in Asia or in other regions of the world. We fix these "exogenously" as in Table 2, and then impose them as a constraint on the model's solution. In our exercise we use the baseline projections in ADB (1997). Given exogenous projections of the labour force for each region of the world, regional populations, the effective supply of land, and total factor productivity growth, the GTAP model is then used to solve for the terminal levels of the capital stock needed to support the exogenously projected level of income in each region.

Given capital stocks, endowments of land, and the labour force in each region, the composition of output in GTAP is determined via Rybczynski effects, by our assumptions about technological change (total factor productivity growth) and by tastes (demands). Trade flows are influenced by changes in factor proportions, by assumed changes in the trade policy regime, and by technological advances that reduce transportation and communication costs.

GTAP is a model of the real economy. Real factor prices and relative goods prices adjust to ensure that goods and factor markets clear simultaneously in all regions. Commodity material balances are satisfied at the country and the global level. Commodities produced in different regions are imperfect substitutes for one another. Real wages are determined locally as there is no labour migration allowed between different countries' labour markets. Given technology, the rental on each country's capital stock is determined by the capital stock needed to satisfy the terminal income target. While balanced trade is not imposed, trade balances do not move too far from their baseline shares of GDP.

GTAP has no monetary sector, and no asset markets. An exogenous numeraire anchors nominal prices, incomes, and expenditures. While our focus on the "long run" justifies our neglect of money, the absence of asset markets from the framework is possibly problematic. There is, for example, no requirement that government balance its budget (private and public sector saving are effectively fungible) and, since asset incomes are not fully identified, the model does not provide estimates of regional current account balances nor of private wealth.

In Table 5, we show the assumptions made about population growth, labour force growth, growth of total factor productivity, and per capita income growth. Population growth estimates and labour force growth rates are taken from UN (1994). Estimates of TFP growth are drawn from a variety of sources including Bosworth, Collins, and Chen (1995), and Rao and Lee (1995). Exogenous growth rates of per capita income are, as we have noted, given by the projections in Asian Development Bank (1997). For non-Asian regions, estimates are essentially guesses, based on historical experience. In the next thirty years, we anticipate somewhat faster income growth in Western Europe than in North America, but growth in both is expected to remain far below the Asian average. The assumed North American growth rate of 2 per cent per person is marginally larger than the long-run average of US growth over the past 150 years of 1.7 per cent (Maddison, 1995).

Table 5. **GTAP-EA Baseline Assumptions — Annual Average Compound Growth Rates, 1992-2022**

(per cent)

Region	Population	Labour force	TFP	Per person income
Japan	-0.03	-0.50	1.75	2.53
Hong Kong	0.12	-0.09	1.50	2.10
Singapore	0.61	0.34	2.00	2.50
Chinese Taipei	0.73	0.79	1.75	3.10
Republic of Korea	0.69	0.62	1.75	3.50
Malaysia	1.63	2.17	1.00	3.90
Thailand	0.81	0.97	0.50	3.80
Indonesia	1.19	1.59	1.50	5.00
Philippines	1.58	2.12	1.75	5.30
People's Republic of China	0.81	0.87	2.75	6.00
India	1.43	1.89	2.00	5.50
Rest of South Asia	2.18	2.75	1.50	4.04
North America	0.82	0.69	1.50	2.00
Western Europe	0.03	-0.14	1.50	2.49
Latin America	1.39	1.74	0.50	2.14
Sub-Saharan Africa	2.68	3.06	0.50	1.65
Rest of the world	1.31	1.58	1.25	2.50

Source: Population growth (UN 1994 revised); labour force growth (UN 1994 revised); TFP growth (author estimates, see text); per capita income growth (ADB, 1997).

Assumed TFP growth rates are one of the most problematic parts of this exercise. Our assumption allows reforming economies to be able to attain a maximum value of 2.75 per cent per annum. Economies with comparatively poor institutional structures are assumed to have TFP rates of about 0.5 per cent. As economies mature economically, we assume that their TFP rates approach those in North America. If the story of economic development is indeed about economic catch-up, then, in the long run, it will not be possible for countries to sustain rates of TFP growth quicker than those in the most advanced economies. These conjectures about future rates of TFP growth are of course subject to considerable doubt. Indeed, for some countries (Malaysia and Thailand), we had to revise downward TFP growth rates to avert implausibly low estimates of saving rates. For this and for other reasons, it is probably more meaningful to focus on regional averages rather than on the estimates for specific countries.

Our projections also make a number of assumptions about the emerging trading environment. We assume that the provisions of the Uruguay Round, including the Multi-Fibre Arrangement (MFA), are implemented fully; that there is some future liberalisation of agricultural trade; that both the PRC and Chinese Taipei gain admission to the WTO and that they lower their tariff and non-tariff barriers to the Southeast Asian average; and finally, that there are reductions in trade barriers in services, comparable to the reductions that have been negotiated for manufactured goods in the Uruguay Round.

Results

We begin by outlining some of the broad dimensions of these results. In Table 6, we show the initial (1992) and terminal (2022) values for Asia's share in total global income, population, trade, and investment. Note that these estimates are calculated using GTAP not purchasing power parity conversion factors. GTAP dollar flows and stocks are calculated at historical market exchange rates. As is well known, the use of market rather than purchasing power parity conversion factors will understate the contribution of developing countries, including those in Asia, to world income. All data, except where otherwise noted, are now expressed in 1992 dollars measured at market exchange rates.

We have already remarked that, in purchasing power parity terms, our baseline growth scenario implies that Asia's share in world income will expand from less than 40 per cent today to somewhere around 57 per cent three decades hence. These estimates, however, include the income of Japan. Once Japan is excluded, the increase in the share of Asian income in world total is more dramatic though the level shares are naturally smaller. Our calculations, based on 1992 market exchange rates, suggest that income in developing Asia as a share of world income could increase from around 7 per cent to 15 per cent over the next three decades. Purchasing power parity shares are likely to be approximately double these numbers. It is important to note that it is the growth of developing Asia, not Japan, that will account for the increase in Asia's share of world income in the next thirty years.

Table 6. **Asia in the World, 1992 and 2022**
(per cent)

Asia's share in the world	1992	2022
Income		
including Japan	22.97	27.86
excluding Japan	7.32	14.78
Population		
including Japan	52.56	50.72
excluding Japan	50.28	49.19
Trade		
including Japan	27.02	36.50
excluding Japan	17.05	28.08
Investment[a]		
including Japan	32.91	28.45
excluding Japan	10.19	14.09

a. The investment shares refer to estimates of accumulated investment over the period 1992-2022.
Source: Author calculations.

Trade accounts for a larger share of Asian income than it does for other nations of the world. Indeed, in the GTAP baseline data, developing Asia's share of world trade (17 per cent) is over twice as large as its share of world income[2]. Our calculations suggest that these trade shares will, over the next three decades, remain disproportionately high, and that Asia's trade will grow more quickly than world trade on average[3]. By 2022, developing Asia's share of world trade could be around 28 per cent. The increase in Asia's share of world trade is slightly less than the increase in Asia's share of world income[4].

Asian Investment Demands

Asia's claims on global saving are also set to expand in the next thirty years. In 1992, developing Asia accounted for approximately 10 per cent of global investment. Our baseline income projections suggest that this share could rise to around 14 per cent by 2022. The projected increase in developing Asia's investment share is proportionately less than the increase in its income share. Although investment demands grow significantly in South Asia they are projected to decline in the newly industrialised countries and to a lesser extent in Southeast Asia. While India and the PRC are large **countries** they are not, as yet, large **economies**. Naturally, the weights applied in the calculation of regional investment shares reflect economic not country size. Even with the optimistic assumptions made about growth in this exercise, accumulated income in the PRC over the next three decades will still be comparable in magnitude to accumulated income in the newly industrialised economies (NIEs). Accumulated income in the ASEAN 4 (Indonesia, Malaysia, Thailand, and the Philippines) over the next three decades is still likely to exceed that in India.

In Table 7, we show estimates of developing Asia's accumulated investment needs over the period 1992-2022, and express these as a proportion of accumulated income in each region. To sustain the growth rates set out in Table 5 our calculations suggest that developing Asia would have to invest around $35 trillion in 1992 prices. Of this, somewhere between $6 to $12 trillion would be for infrastructure needs alone. The World Bank (APDB, 1997) has estimated that East Asian economies would require $1.5 trillion (1995 prices) for infrastructure investment between 1995 and 2005 to sustain growth at historical levels[5]. Our "lower" bound estimate might result if infrastructure investment were to remain at its historical Asian level of around 4-5 per cent of GDP. The "upper" bound estimate allows a doubling of this on the assumption that infrastructure investment has been historically neglected in Asia, and that there would be a need to catch up lost ground. Recent estimates of infrastructure investment in East Asia are over 6 per cent of GDP (APDB, 1997).

These projections entail mammoth investment demands in both the PRC and India. Indeed, if India is to attain the growth rates that we impose, its investment rate would have to increase significantly over historical levels. In the PRC, we estimate that rates of investment would have to be sustained at about their current high rates over the next three decades. As income levels in the NIEs approach those in the industrialised countries, GTAP projects that their investment rates will fall to around the OECD average. While the model also projects a decline in Southeast Asia's investment demands (as a share of income), they are projected to remain well above OECD levels. Naturally, were Asia to grow much more slowly than our baseline projections assume then its investment demands would be diminished.

Table 7. **Asia's Investment Needs, 1992-2022**
($ trillion in 1992 prices)

Region	Total	Infrastructure
People's Republic of China	11.7	2.3 to 4.7
India	7.8	1.6 to 3.1
Rest of South Asia	1.6	0.3 to 0.6
Southeast Asia	7.0	1.4 to 2.8
NIEs	6.3	1.3 to 2.5

Source: Author calculations.

These estimates raise the question of whether Asia's appetite for investment is likely to put pressure on global saving (IMF, 1995). If this were to occur, Asia's economic emergence might put upward pressure on long-run real interest rates and dampen global growth. While GTAP does not provide any independent estimates of saving, nor of the likely impact of investment demands on long-run interest rates, it seems unlikely that Asia's growth will result in a global saving "crunch".

There are two broad reasons why Asia's saving is likely to rise with its investment demands. First, evidence from Asia and elsewhere suggests a strong correlation between income growth and saving. Fast income growth seems to be associated not just with high rates of saving but also with rising saving rates. This has been the experience of much of East and Southeast Asia in recent decades. Therefore, to the extent that rising investment demand is reflected in growth, there should be some "automaticity" about its financing. Indeed, our own projections suggest that it is unlikely that Asia's demand for global investment funds will grow by proportionately more than its contribution to global income. Second, large parts of Asia are now primed to enjoy the benefits of rapid declines in young age population dependency. Most of this decline will occur in the first two decades of the next century. There is convincing evidence, that falling young age dependency generates a large saving dividend (*inter alia*, ADB, 1997; Harrigan, 1996; Higgins and Williamson, 1996; Kelley and Schmidt, 1996; Edwards, 1996; Masson, *et al.* 1995). Taken together, quick income growth and fast falling young age dependency should help Asia finance much of its burgeoning investment needs.

Structural Change and Asian Growth

Structural change is a natural concomitant of economic development. In the next thirty years, global economic structures will be influenced by a variety of factors including developments that will allow an increasingly sophisticated international division of labour. Economic structure will also be affected by accumulation and by shifts in the composition of endowments in different regions. In the next thirty years Asia's comparative advantage is likely to shift gradually from low-skilled, labour-intensive processes to higher-skilled, more capital-intensive activities[6]. This will happen within industries as well as among them. The newly industrialised economies of Asia have already moved some way along this path.

GTAP is essentially a real trade model. Therefore, its predictions about the impact of technological change, changes in trade policy, and shifting factor endowments on economic structure and trade accord quite closely with what would be predicted by the classical Hecksher-Ohlin framework. For example, as supplies of capital increase relative to other factors we would expect to see a shift in the composition of economic activity toward more capital-intensive activities. This is the well-known Rybczynski effect. And as trade barriers are lowered, the Stopler-Samuelson theorem suggests that factor returns should move against those factors employed intensively in protected industries.

In Tables 8 and 9, we have projected changes in the composition of real output and employment in "primary", "secondary", and "tertiary" activities for a number of regions of the world. In general, these anticipate that developing countries will move resources from primary into secondary production and tertiary sectors. The industrialised countries will shift resources from secondary into tertiary production. These projected shifts are more pronounced for output than they are for employment.

Table 8. **Change in Real Output Shares, 1992-2022 (Sectorally Neutral TFP Growth)**
(per cent)

Region	Primary	Secondary	Services
Japan	+0.06	-2.83	+2.77
NIEs	-0.03	+0.28	-0.24
Southeast Asia	+0.16	-1.59	+1.43
India	-9.74	+5.54	+4.20
People's Republic of China	-3.99	+7.16	-3.16
Rest of South Asia	-4.58	+3.96	+0.62
North America	-0.21	-1.16	+1.37
Western Europe	-0.16	-3.31	+3.47
Rest of the World	-1.05	-1.02	+2.07

Table 9. **Change in Employment Shares, 1992-2022 (Sectorally Neutral TFP Growth)**
(per cent)

Region	Primary	Secondary	Services
Japan	-0.99	-0.84	+1.83
NIEs	-1.95	+0.94	+1.00
Southeast Asia	-5.93	+2.54	+3.39
India	-14.57	+3.02	+11.55
People's Republic of China	-8.14	+4.57	+3.56
Rest of South Asia	-9.49	+3.00	+6.49
North America	-0.54	-0.63	+1.17
Western Europe	-1.19	+0.11	+1.07
Rest of the World	-2.31	+1.41	+0.90

While some aspects of these results seem plausible enough, they do not quite capture the stylised facts of recent historical shifts in the sectoral allocation of resources. This is much more so for industrialised than for developing economies. While it is true that the share of secondary output in constant-price value added has trended downwards in both Western Europe and in North America (see IMF, 1997), this is not true in Japan. Also, sectoral shifts in employment structure in the industrialised countries have been more pronounced than our calculations would appear to suggest, and have been much more pronounced than shifts in the composition of output[7]. To better replicate these outcomes it is probably necessary to allow for bias in technological progress favouring manufacturing. The results reported in Tables 8 and 9 are generated by a model in which it is assumed that the incidence of technological progress is sectorally neutral. Also, to account for contrasting trends in real output shares across regions, differential income elasticities of demand for manufactured goods and services are also likely to be needed across different regions of the world. Currently the GTAP "default" elasticities are used.

Bearing these features of the results and the underlying model in mind, measuring changes in sectoral shares is one way of looking at the "turbulence" in global economic structure that could occur in the next thirty years. But measured changes in sectoral shares must be sensitive to the level of aggregation in the underlying model. Obviously, in a one sector model there can be no change in sectoral shares! As a more refined sectoral grid is applied, the likelihood of observing sectoral shifts must increase. Accordingly, the sum of absolute changes in output or employment shares will be non-decreasing in the number of sectors identified in a model.

In Table 10, we provide a measure of potential "turbulence" defined as the sum of absolute changes in sectoral employment shares, divided by two. If there were no change in the size of the labour force, this would measure the share of the labour force which would have to migrate inter-sectorally over the period in question. If there are frictions that prevent the instantaneous adjustment of wages and movement of labour then we might expect "turbulence" to be associated with "structural" unemployment. Even if factor prices do adjust quickly, a large value for the "turbulence" index might suggest large underlying income redistributions which could be potentially (politically) problematic. This will be particularly so if factor proportions differ greatly between industries. We show this measure for various disaggregations of GTAP ranging from three sectors to 13 sectors. As anticipated, measured potential "turbulence" is a non-decreasing function of the number of sectors.

Table 10. **Employment Potential "Dislocation" Index, 1992-2022**

(per cent of the labour force)

Region	3 sectors	6 sectors	13 sectors
Japan	2.10	2.12	2.45
NIEs	2.79	4.27	5.12
Southeast Asia	5.42	7.50	9.99
India	12.01	13.67	16.79
People's Republic of China	5.15	9.09	11.63
Rest of South Asia	7.74	8.93	12.12
North America	2.36	3.01	3.01
Western Europe	2.42	3.22	3.74
Rest of the World	1.61	3.62	4.14

Source: Author calculations.

Our calculations suggest that for our baseline growth assumptions a minimum of 3 per cent of the labour force in North America and close to 4 per cent of the labour force in Western Europe would have to migrate between sectors. Further sectoral disaggregation, disaggregation by skill type, or allowance for sectorally biased productivity growth, would increase these numbers. Once these are accounted for it is entirely possible that a much greater percentage of the labour force in North America and Western Europe would have to migrate between sectors, and/or occupations, as a result of on-going changes in global economic structure. It is important to stress that these effects cumulate over a thirty year period, and that they would occur in a context where there would be "natural" turnover in the labour force. They would also occur in a context where the labour force in both North America and Western Europe is growing. To the extent that labour force entrants are sectorally and occupationally more mobile than incumbent workers, the "pain" of structural change would be eased.

These estimates of "turbulence" in economic structure are caused by the interplay of a variety of factors, not just by Asia's emergence in the world economy. Changes in endowments, total factor productivity growth, and trade policy across all regions combine to determine final outcomes. One simple way of trying to disentangle these various effects is to ask what would happen to economic structure if endowments, accumulation and productivity growth are held constant in the industrialised countries (Western Europe, North America and Japan), and the developing world grows as per baseline assumptions. Alternatively, we might "freeze" incomes in the developing world, and let the industrialised economies grow as in the baseline. The results of these two experiments are shown in Table 11.

Table 11. **Change in Employment Shares, Different Scenarios, 1992-2022**

(per cent)

Region	Industrial countries stagnate			Only industrial countries grow		
	1°	2°	3°	1°	2°	3°
North America	-0.45	-1.29	+1.74	-0.36	-0.04	0.35
Western Europe	-0.94	-1.59	+2.53	-0.69	+0.87	-0.17
Japan	-0.93	-1.66	+2.60	-0.52	+0.22	+0.30

Source: Author calculations.

If we hold endowments and total factor productivity fixed in the industrialised regions, and let the developing world grow as in the baseline[8], then we observe larger declines in secondary employment and larger increases in services employment in the industrialised countries than occur in the baseline simulation. It would seem that shifts in endowments, accumulation and productivity growth in the developing countries would encourage a movement of workers from manufacturing into tertiary activity in all of the industrialised countries. This tendency is confirmed by our second experiment in which we fix endowments and productivity in the developing regions and let the industrialised regions grow as in the baseline. Now the share of employment in secondary activities in the industrialised countries increases relative to the baseline results summarised in Table 9.

These results suggest that the net impact of growth in the developing world would be to shift employment out of the manufacturing sector into services and possibly to non-traded good activities in the industrialised countries[9]. By identifying the factor content of these activities we can draw some broad inferences about likely relative factor price movements even though these are not explicitly identified within the GTAP framework. In general, manufacturing activities are low-skill intensive compared to service activities in the industrialised countries. If we disaggregate somewhat further within GTAP, we observe erosion of employment shares in the industrialised economies of the least skill-intensive manufacturing activities such as "Processed Foods", "Textiles" and "Wearing Apparel". Employment shares in the more skill-intensive manufacturing activities such as "Machinery and Transport Equipment" and "Light Manufacturing" increase overall. Taken together, these results suggest a shift in demand for labour towards skill- and human capital-intensive activities. For given factor supplies, this will tend to increase the wage premia on skills and, hence, likely to widen wage dispersion in industrialised countries. If there were resistance to these real wage realignments then unemployment among the unskilled could result. Such effects could be amplified by changes in the composition of demand within industries which favour skilled labour. It should be understood, however, that these shifts in relative wages would be occurring in a context where the real wages of the unskilled would still be increasing. Finally, it is of note that the model suggests that growth in the developing countries raises the return to physical capital in the industrialised countries.

The general direction of these effects comports with the findings of other studies and would seem to support the view that growth of, and trade with, developing countries may widen wage dispersion and/or increase unemployment among the lower skilled in industrialised countries. However, the magnitude of the effects we detect are small. Lejour, Tang and Timmer (1997) also find small impacts.

We have already noted that the sectoral shifts predicted by the model are much smaller than those that have been observed historically in the industrialised countries. In an attempt to better replicate historical experience and to isolate the contribution of developing countries growth to structural change in the industrialised countries, we now allow for sectorally differentiated productivity growth. Specifically, we assume that the rate of productivity growth in manufacturing in industrialised countries is twice as large as that identified in Table 5, and the rate of productivity growth in services activities is only half as big. Accordingly, the rate of technological progress in manufacturing is now four times as large as it is in services. All other assumptions are as before. In Tables 12 and 13, we show the associated changes in real output and employment shares for the industrialised regions.

Table 12. **Change in Real Output Shares, 1992-2022 (Sectorally Biased TFP Growth)**
(per cent)

Region	Primary	Secondary	Services
Japan	+0.07	1.99	-2.06
North America	-0.25	4.31	-4.06
Western Europe	-0.10	1.37	-1.28

Table 13. **Change in Employment Shares, 1992-2022 (Sectorally Biased TFP Growth)**
(per cent)

Region	Primary	Secondary	Services
Japan	-1.01	-9.20	+10.21
North America	-0.79	-5.41	+6.20
Western Europe	-1.19	-5.71	+6.90

While there is very little change in the share of primary output and primary employment from the baseline there are large changes implied in the shares of secondary and services output and employment. Relative goods prices now move sharply in favour of services. Declines in service output shares are now projected in all regions where previously increases were predicted, and manufacturing output shares now rise rather than fall. While this is what has happened in Japan, it does not reflect the historical experience of either Western Europe or North America. Possibly, for Western Europe and North America both the assumed price and income elasticities of demand for manufacturing goods are too large.

The model's projections of employment shares however now look much more "realistic". This is true both of their magnitude and their regional dispersion. Japan, which still has a comparatively large proportion of its labour force employed in manufacturing (compared to its per person income level), experiences the largest shift from manufacturing to services. The employment shift towards services in Western Europe is slightly larger than in North America. While the magnitude of the predicted shifts in North America and Western Europe are smaller than those which have occurred in the past, smaller shifts are not at all implausible. Since there is presumably some floor on manufacturing's share of total employment (and some ceiling on services' share), the rate of decline in manufacturing's share of total employment is likely to taper off. Our estimates imply that in most industrialised countries only one in eight workers may be employed in manufacturing three decades hence, with a slightly greater share being retained in manufacturing in Japan. Of course, these numbers depend on the somewhat arbitrary differentials that we have imposed on sectoral productivity gains. If we were to assume that the manufacturing bias in technological progress were even more pronounced than we have assumed here, then even larger sectoral reallocations of labour would be projected.

It is of interest to try and decompose the underlying "turbulence" in sectoral employment into the different contributory factors that we have identified. To do this we identify the proportion of the absolute changes in employment shares attributable to sectorally biased technological change and to income growth in the industrialised countries. The residual is then attributable to the covariance between the two and to other influences, including growth in the developing countries of the world.

Of the factors we identify, sectorally biased technological change accounts for the overwhelming proportion of employment turbulence. In Western Europe, our simulations suggest 65 per cent of total employment reallocation is attributable to this one factor. In North America the corresponding figure is 62 per cent, and in Japan it is even larger at 79 per cent. By comparison, changes in endowments, given unbiased technological progress, accounts for comparatively little of the projected employment reallocations. In Western Europe and Japan just 5 per cent of the sectoral reallocation results from endowment changes; in North America around 14 per cent is attributable to changes in endowment. Residual factors, including growth in, and increased, trade with the developing countries, account for 30 per cent of employment change in Western Europe, 24 per cent in North America and just 15 per cent in Japan.

Bearing in mind the limitations of the structure of the model on which our results rest, they suggest that while growth in the developing world will require restructuring in the industrialised countries, the magnitude of the required adjustments seems manageable. Our results are more in tune with those of Krugman and Lawrence (1994), Sachs and Shatz (1996) and with the conclusions of IMF (1997) than with the findings of Wood (1994). Even allowing for growth in the share of industrialised countries' imports from developing countries in the next thirty years, trade among developed countries still seems likely to dominate trade with low wage developing countries. The countries that are likely to experience most turbulence in their economic structures are the developing countries themselves.

Conclusion

In this paper, we have explored some aspects of structural interdependence between the industrialised and developing countries of the world. We have conducted this exercise with the assistance of a global general equilibrium model, having applied ADB's (1997) baseline projections of global economic growth. Given the limitations of the modelling apparatus used, and the hazardous nature of projecting so far into the future, the calculations reported in this paper represent only a preliminary attempt to think about, and to illustrate, some of the interdependencies that link different regions of the world. More work needs to be done to test the robustness of our results to alternative conjectures about critical parameter values and to alternative behavioural assumptions.

The principal conclusion of the paper would seem to be that growth in the developing world will entail some restructuring of economic activity in industrialised countries but that this is unlikely to entail massive dislocation. In particular, if Asian growth is export led, as it has been in the past, then inevitably Asian demands for goods produced elsewhere in the world will grow commensurably. This will create opportunities for investment and will create jobs elsewhere in the world[10]. Even if this assessment grossly underestimates the need for restructuring in industrial countries, a protectionist response would be wholly inappropriate. Distributional problems ought to be tackled at the root through a combination of self-limiting safety nets, educational and retraining programmes as well as through market liberalisation.

Notes and References

1. There are a number of critical technical assumptions involved in this exercise. It is assumed for example that all the "explanatory" variables are strictly exogenous. That is to say that they are determined independently of contemporaneous, lagged and future growth, and of its higher order moments.

2. Note here that we are referring to world income in units that are not adjusted for PPP. As is typical for a developing region, unadjusted income is much smaller than PPP adjusted income.

3. Asia's larger trade shares are a function of its geography, resource endowments, country size as well as trade policies and institutions.

4. Historically, the income elasticity of world trade has been greater than one. Our results seem to imply that the income elasticity, though greater than unity, is lower for developing Asia than for other countries of the world. While this is certainly not true historically, the emergence of large economies in Asia and late trade liberalisation in other regions does not make it such an implausible outcome in the future.

5. To the extent that growth might edge down in some East Asian economies in the next decade this figure possibly overestimates actual needs.

6. As a determinant of trade, natural resources are also likely to diminish in importance.

7. The share of manufacturing employment in total employment fell by 12 percentage points in the United States over the period 1965-94. It fell by 10 percentage points in the countries of the European Union between 1970-94 and by just 4 percentage points in Japan over the period 1974-94. In the United States, the real output share of manufacturing fell by around 4 percentage points over the period 1965-94 and by about the same amount in the European Union, but with a later date marking the start of the decline. In Japan, the share of manufacturing output in total employment has increased by about 5 percentage points since the 1970s. (IMF, 1997).

8. Effectively, growth rates in different regions are independent of one another. While this is an obvious limitation of the model, there is as yet no widely accepted theory as to how income growth is linked across countries. Openness and trade, along with other factors, seem to play an empirically important role but the theoretical origins of this relationship are still disputed (ADB 1997).

9. The observations that follow draw on the GTAP database which identifies the "human capital intensity" of different activities in each region. The model does not, however, include human capital as an additional factor of production. These data were kindly made available by Tom Hertel of the GTAP Consortium and Purdue University. We are currently exploring versions of GTAP that include human capital as a fourth primary factor of production.

10. Although not shown here, our calculations suggest that industrial countries should also benefit from an improvement in their terms of trade. Thus it is possible that even if there is downward pressure on real product wages of the low skilled, their real consumption wages might increase.

Bibliography

ASIA PACIFIC DAILY BRIEF (1997), *Oxford Analytica,* 4 June.

ASIAN DEVELOPMENT BANK (1997), *Emerging Asia: Changes and Challenges,* Manila.

BAUMOL, W. (1967), "Macroeconomics of Unbalanced Growth", *American Economic Review,* No. 57, June.

BOSWORTH, B., S. COLLINS AND CHEN (1995), "Accounting for Differences in Economic Growth", *Brookings Discussion Papers in International Economics,* No. 115.

BURTLESS, G. (1995), "International Trade and the Rise in Earnings Inequality", *Journal of Economic Literature* 33(2).

DERVIS, K. *et al.* (1982), *General Equilibrium Models for Development Policy,* Cambridge University Press, Cambridge.

DOWLING, M., F. HARRIGAN AND J. VILLAFUERTE (1995), "Asia: Connections and Convergence", Paper presented at the Eighth Workshop on the Asian Economic Outlook, 23-25 November, Asian Development Bank, Manila.

EDWARDS, S. (1996), "Why are Latin America's Savings Rates So Low? An International Comparative Analysis", *Journal of Development Economics,* 51(1).

GERSCHENKRON, A. (1962), *Economic Backwardness in Historical Perspective,* Harvard University Press, Cambridge, Mass.

HARRIGAN, F. (1996), *Saving Transitions in Southeast Asia.* Asian Development Bank, Manila.

HARRIGAN, F. AND L. SUMULONG (1996), "Aspects of Asian Macroeconomic and Structural Interdependence", Background paper for *Emerging Asia: Changes and Challenges,* Asian Development Bank, Manila.

HERTEL, T. AND M. TSIGAS (1996), "Structure of the GTAP Model", in HERTEL, T. (ed.), *Global Trade Analysis: Modeling and Applications,* Cambridge University Press, Cambridge.

HIGGINS, M. AND J. WILLIAMSON (1996), "Asian Savings, Investment, and Foreign Capital Dependence: The Role of Demography", Background paper for *Emerging Asia: Changes and Challenges,* Asian Development Bank, Manila.

INTERNATIONAL MONETARY FUND (1995), *World Economic Outlook,* Washington, D.C.

INTERNATIONAL MONETARY FUND (1997), *World Economic Outlook,* Washington, D.C.

KELLEY, A. AND R. SCHMIDT (1996), "Saving, Dependency, and Development", *Journal of Population Economics*, 9(4).

KRUGMAN, P. AND R. LAWRENCE (1994), "Trade, Jobs, and Wages", *Scientific American,* 270(4).

LEJOUR, A., P. TANG AND H. TIMMER (1997), *Trade and Wages in an Interdependent World.* Background Study for OECD Linkages II, OECD, Paris.

MADDISON, A. (1995), *Monitoring the World Economy: 1820-1992,* OECD Development Centre, Paris.

MASSON, P. *et al.* (1995), "International Evidence on the Determinants of Private Saving", *Working Paper* WP/95/51, International Monetary Fund, Washington, D.C.

MYRDAL, G. (1963), *Asian Drama: An Inquiry into the Poverty of Nations,* Allen Lane, The Penguin Press.

RADELET, S., J. SACHS AND J.-W. LEE (1996), "Economic Growth in Asia", Background paper for *Emerging Asia: Changes and Challenges,* Asian Development Bank, Manila.

RAO, V. AND C. LEE (1995), "Sources of Growth in the Singapore Economy and its Manufacturing and Service Sectors", paper presented at the 20th Federation of ASEAN Economic Association Conference, 7-8 December, Singapore.

SACHS, J. AND H. SHATZ (1996), "U.S. Trade with Developing Countries and Wage Inequality", *American Economic Review,* 86(2).

SHOVEN, J. AND J. WHALLEY (1992), *Applying General Equilibrium.* Cambridge University Press, Cambridge.

UNITED NATIONS (1994), "World Population Prospects 1950-2050: the 1994 Revision", electronic data, New York.

WOOD, A. (1994), *North-South Trade, Employment, and Inequality: Changing Fortunes in a Skill-Driven World*, Clarendon Press, Oxford.

WORLD BANK (1993), *East Asian Miracle,* Oxford University Press, Oxford.

A Comment

*Philip Turner**

How the rapid rise of Asia will affect the rest of the industrial world is a very important question, politically as well as economically. The author should be congratulated for his systematic approach to the task. It is also very brave to present a paper on growth prospects for the next 30 years, especially at the OECD.

In sheer sophistication, Frank Harrigan's paper is an impressive attempt to provide numbers for issues economists do not agree about. Despite what he says, the remarkable economic growth in Southeast Asia is not easily "explicable in terms of a reasonably well understood set of structural, policy and institutional factors". Quite different policies have been pursued by equally successful countries. The institutional contexts have also varied enormously. Economists have not yet settled the argument about the relative importance of high rates of investment and of increased productivity to the growth process. So the issue addressed *is* difficult to analyse.

Harrigan's paper raises three questions. The first is about the foundations of the medium-term prospects for growth of the selected Asian economies set out in this paper. On what are they mainly based? The second question concerns the role of investment in the "Asian miracle". The final question concerns international linkages, notably real exchange rates and capital flows. All these questions have a bearing on the impact of developments in Asia on the industrial world — which is the central focus of this paper.

First, it is not entirely clear how the many rather diverse factors behind growth differentials listed in Table 1 of Harrigan's paper actually translate into the projections of growth in per capita GDP shown in Table 2. An influence that appears to be dominant is related to Gerschenkron's "advantage of backwardness", that "countries that begin with lower levels of income will tend to grow more quickly". When reading the paper I wondered whether the very recent performance of certain countries (and immediate prospects) had also somehow affected the projections, with those that have performed well recently (India and the Philippines come to mind) getting "marked up". Thus, as a simple experiment, I regressed the projected GDP growth rates for the 12 countries shown in Table 2 (labelled G below) against (a) average growth in 1996, 1997 and 1998 (labelled $G98$), and (b) GNP levels (Y). The result was (t-statistics in parentheses):

$$G = 6.56 + 0.37 \, G98 - 0.56 \, log \, Y$$

$$(7.4) \quad (3.4) \qquad (6.1)$$

$$R^2 = 0.79$$

This suggests that the projections may actually be dominated by the "catch-up" hypothesis, or "convergence", as the author puts it. Recent performance also (i.e. actual growth for 1996 and ADB projections for 1997 and 1998) appears to play a role. Although the "catch-up" hypothesis has a certain intuitive appeal, one should not underestimate the degree to which bad policies and poor conditions can prevent countries from achieving their catch-up potential. Perhaps the estimates of growth in this paper should be interpreted as what countries *could* achieve with the right policies.

For the purposes of the simulations, growth in per capita income in the industrial countries was taken as given. However, there is some discussion about the key issue of how Asian growth would affect real wage growth in Europe, or in North America, and I suspect that fixing per capita income in the industrialised countries for the simulations excludes what could be the key channel for affecting the growth of per capita GDP in Europe.

The second question concerns investment, both the rate of investment and its rate of return. The studies of this question appear to agree that increased physical capital per worker accounts for at least one-half of the growth in real income. One (imperfect) indicator is investment as a percentage of GDP. In Southeast Asia (Indonesia, Malaysia, the Philippines and Thailand), this percentage has risen to 36 per cent in the 1990s from 26 per cent in the late 1970s and the 1980s (see Table 1). But the investment ratio has risen much less in South Asia (Bangladesh, India, Pakistan and Sri Lanka) and is still relatively low. Therefore, is there good reason to assume that the investment ratio will rise substantially in the medium-term in South Asia? Can per capita income gaps be narrowed without such an increase?

The other aspect is the rate of return on investment. An important issue is to what extent the investment boom has depressed the marginal productivity of capital in Asia. It is not possible to know. Nevertheless, there is some not very sophisticated evidence that average returns have indeed declined. The only measure of this that can be readily extracted from national accounts statistics is the incremental capital-output ratio (ICOR)[1]. The reciprocal of the ICOR may be interpreted as an average gross rate of return for investment, although it is a very crude measure, and depends on a number of assumptions. At best, it can be indicative of broad orders of magnitude when computed for a long period of years.

The calculated gross rates of return in Asian countries are shown in the table. As is well known, rates of return in Asia have been high, around 25 per cent on this measure, well above the estimates for most industrial countries. But it appears that returns have generally fallen in the 1990s, with rather sharp declines in some countries. All this is very oversimplified, but it does suggest some questions. Are rates of return on investment declining? The 1997 BIS *Annual Report* looked at the property market in Asia. The construction boom in some countries has gone too far and substantial excess supply has been created. There are also signs of excess capacity in some manufacturing sectors. How do rates of return evolve in the model underlying this paper? What would be implications of declining rates of return? Does it suggest that investment ratios are likely to fall?

An interesting question is how the international implications of growth that is based on total factor productivity differ from growth that is based on a greater accumulation of capital. The former should lead to terms-of-trade improvements for the industrial countries — as relative prices of Asian goods decline as productivity increases — while the latter may drain capital from Europe and the United States. It might be interesting to explore this issue.

The final question concerns the international linkages and the medium-term evolution of current account balances. Several rapidly growing Asian countries have run current account deficits of around 5 per cent annually since 1990. Is this something that can or will be maintained in the medium term? It is natural that foreign capital should be attracted with the high rates of return, but current account deficits would be the natural counterpart of this.

But if rates of return on investment decline, capital inflows will tend to slacken and domestic investment ratios may fall more sharply than domestic saving ratios. Current account *surpluses* may begin to emerge and these countries would then become capital exporters. Japan went through such an evolution when investment ratios fell after the period of high growth.

Let me conclude by referring to an ill-fated OECD exercise in 1970[2]. It is usually overlooked that the *cross-country pattern* of growth that was projected then actually turned out to be quite accurate. In terms of a simple regression, the projection "explains" much of the cross-country variance of actual growth rates in the 1970s; growth rates observed in the previous decade had no significant relationship with actual growth in 1970-80[3]. So the projections did much better than simply extrapolating from the past. There are good reasons to believe that Frank Harrigan's attempt will be more accurate. He is rightly circumspect about drawing conclusions. Such exercises are useful at least in providing a point of departure for highlighting important policy issues.

Table 1. **Gross Fixed Investment and Incremental Capital-Output Ratios**

| | Gross fixed investment as % of GDP | | Gross rates of return* | |
	1975-89	1990-98	1975-89	1990-98
East Asia	29.1	31.4	29.2	21.7
Hong Kong	27.8	30.5	29.7	16.9
Korea	30.1	36.5	28.2	20.4
Singapore	41.3	34.5	17.9	23.9
Chinese Taipei	25.9	23.2	33.8	27.3
China	33.8	39.1	25.8	25.4
Southeast Asia	26.8	36.1	22.8	19.8
Indonesia	26.0	35.8	23.6	20.7
Malaysia	28.9	39.1	21.5	22.3
Philippines	24.7	23.7	13.9	15.0
Thailand	28.5	42.4	26.2	19.0
South Asia	20.7	23.8	25.5	23.0
Bangladesh	10.8	15.3	40.1	31.9
India	22.4	25.8	23.8	21.9
Pakistan	18.4	19.9	32.1	25.5
Sri Lanka	23.6	24.7	11.9	21.9

*   Defined as reciprocal of the incremental capital-output ratio: the ratio of gross investment to GDP divided by average rate of real growth for the period).

Sources: Asian Development Bank, *Asian Development Outlook 1997 and 1998*; IMF, *International Financial Statistics* and national data.

Notes and References

*   The views expressed here are the author's and do not necessarily reflect those of the Bank for International Settlements.

1. If investment I increases real income by DY, then the ICOR can be written as (ignoring depreciation etc.)

$$\frac{\Delta K}{\Delta Y} = \frac{I/Y}{\Delta Y/Y}$$

Where I/Y is the investment/GDP ratio and DY/Y is the rate of GDP growth.

2. OECD (1970), *The Outlook for Economic Growth*, Paris.

3. The equation was run over 19 OECD countries (excluding Iceland and major oil exporters). The result was:

$G = 1.21 + 0.72\ PROJ - 0.27\ PAST$

    (2.6) (4.5) (1.5)

$R^2 = 0.55$

where

G = Actual rate of GDP growth 1970-80

$PROJ$ = Projected rate of GDP growth 1970-80

$PAST$ = Rate of GDP growth 1960-70.

Trade, Employment and Wages: What Impact from 20 More Years of Rapid Asian Growth?

Dominique van der Mensbrugghe

Introduction

Many countries in Asia have seen remarkable growth during the second half of the 20th century, starting with Japan in the 1950s and 1960s, followed by the first wave of Asian tigers — South Korea, Chinese Taipei, Hong Kong and Singapore, and then the second wave — Thailand, Malaysia, Philippines and Indonesia. Perhaps more stunning has been the evolution and success of China which has transformed its economy from almost virtual autarky and a high degree of regulation to an increasingly open and very dynamic economy. The success of the so-called Asian model is catching on in the rest of Asia — notably in India, Bangladesh and Vietnam — accompanied by the introduction of outward looking policies, deregulation, privatisation, and financial market reforms.

The rapid growth in Asia over the last 25 years has already raised the living standards in several countries close to OECD levels, and if current trends continue, the Asian region as a whole will converge significantly towards OECD income levels. Further, given the absolute size of the regional economy, its weight in the world economy and its share in world trade will inevitably increase and shift perceptibly the centre of global economic activity.

High aggregate growth is likely to affect political relations both within the Asian region as well as between Asia and the rest of the world. The economic impact of rapid aggregate growth is not necessarily easily discernible. However, detailed economic analysis provides a richer picture of how economic relations could potentially evolve, and answers some of the following questions:

— What will be the evolution in the structure of production and demand, and hence the impact on trade relations?

—   What are the impacts of changes in labour supply and labour productivity on the composition of production?

—   How do wages evolve with respect to these factors?

This chapter attempts to provide some food for thought on these and related questions. The underlying analysis relies on a global applied general equilibrium model known as LINKAGE[1]. The Annex provides a brief description of the main features of the LINKAGE model including a description of the regional and sectoral coverage. The model is used to project the world economy forward to the year 2020, incorporating dynamic elements such as population and labour growth, capital accumulation (through saving and investment), and productivity improvements. These basic trends, coupled with changes in (trade and fiscal) policies and the underlying natural resources, provide a consistent and plausible picture of the structure of world economic activity including changes in terms of trade, wages, and real exchange rates.

Aggregate Results

This section paints the overall picture of a potential scenario of the evolution of the world economy through the year 2020. The scenario is not a projection. The principle assumption underlying the scenario is one of high growth in all regions of the world, i.e. it is a scenario where all goes right — best practice economic reforms are implemented in all regions, there are no systemic failures, major conflicts or natural catastrophes with global implications, and each region is able to expand to its maximum potential its production possibility frontier[2]. While the likelihood that one or more regions fail to maximise their potential is high, this scenario provides a useful benchmark for assessing the benefits and costs from rapid global growth and further globalisation of the economy. The first part of this section sets out the underlying assumption behind the so-called high growth scenario, and the second part describes the aggregate implications of these assumptions.

The Underlying Assumptions

Exogenous Trends

Attaining the growth rates underlying the High Growth scenario requires a set of (exogenous) trends in productivity, factor availability, and a few other variables. The aggregate GDP growth rates are provided in Table 1. Under this scenario world growth will average 3.7 per cent per annum between 1995 and 2020, with the OECD region growing at a rate of 2.7 per cent, and the non-OECD region growing at a rate of 6.5 per cent[3]. The (five) Asian regions grow at an even faster clip than the aggregate non-OECD region, at a rate of 7.2 per cent.

Table 1. **Average Annual Growth Rate of Real GDP**

(per cent)

	1992 1995	1995 2000	2000 2005	2005 2010	2010 2015	2015 2020	1995 2020
ANZ	4.0	4.3	4.7	4.7	4.3	4.3	4.5
CHN	11.8	9.3	8.2	8.2	7.2	7.2	8.0
DAE	7.0	7.7	7.0	7.0	6.4	6.4	6.9
ECE	1.7	5.5	5.5	5.5	4.0	4.0	4.9
EUR	1.8	2.4	2.8	2.8	2.3	2.3	2.5
IDN	6.9	7.5	7.0	7.0	6.7	6.7	7.0
IND	4.5	6.5	7.2	7.2	6.6	6.6	6.8
JPN	1.3	3.3	2.9	2.9	2.3	2.3	2.7
LAT	3.8	4.3	5.9	5.9	5.1	5.1	5.3
MNA	2.8	5.0	7.1	7.1	6.9	6.9	6.6
NFT	2.6	2.2	2.7	2.7	2.6	2.6	2.6
NIS	-3.8	3.5	6.0	6.0	6.9	6.9	5.9
RAS	6.0	6.5	6.6	6.6	6.5	6.5	6.5
ROW	6.0	6.5	6.6	6.6	6.5	6.5	6.5
SSA	1.8	4.6	5.0	5.0	5.5	6.0	5.2
Total	**2.5**	**3.3**	**3.7**	**3.9**	**3.6**	**3.8**	**3.7**
OECD[a]	*2.0*	*2.6*	*2.9*	*2.9*	*2.5*	*2.5*	*2.7*
Non-OECD	*4.4*	*6.1*	*6.7*	*6.8*	*6.4*	*6.4*	*6.5*
Asia[b]	*7.8*	*7.9*	*7.4*	*7.4*	*6.7*	*6.7*	*7.2*
Non-Asia	*2.0*	*2.8*	*3.3*	*3.4*	*3.1*	*3.2*	*3.2*

a.   OECD includes ANZ, ECE, EUR, JPN and NFT (see Annex for regional abbreviations) but does not include Korea. (Due to data limitations, Turkey is included in the region ROW.)

b.   Asia includes CHN, DAE, IDN IND and RAS. (Due to data limitations, Vietnam is included in the region ROW.)

Note: Aggregate averages are weighted at official 1992 exchange rates.

Source: OECD staff estimates.

The population and labour growth rates are derived from the most recent UN population projections using the Medium Variant. Population growth rates are projected to decline (in all regions), though with significant regional variations[4]. The OECD population growth rate will be cut in half by 2010, with a more modest reduction in the non-OECD region (see Table 2). Asia overall will see a more rapid drop in the population growth rate than the non-Asian region as a whole. The growth rate of labour supply is more rapid than the population growth rates in all non -OECD regions, reflecting a combination of changing demographics and labour force participation rates (see Table 3). After 2010, the OECD region may witness an actual absolute decline in labour supply.

The scenario is calibrated along a so-called balanced-growth path. Under this assumption, labour supply in efficiency terms (i.e. incorporating both the absolute increase in the labour supply, as well as the increase in labour productivity), grows at the same rate as GDP. In essence, this is almost equivalent to assuming that labour productivity growth is the difference between GDP growth and labour supply growth.

Table 2. **Average Annual Population Growth Rate**
(per cent)

	1992-1995	1995-2000	2000-2005	2005-2010	2010-2015	2015-2020	1995-2020
ANZ	1.1	1.1	1.1	1.0	1.0	1.0	1.0
CHN	1.1	0.9	0.7	0.6	0.6	0.6	0.7
DAE	1.5	1.4	1.2	1.1	0.9	0.8	1.1
ECE	-0.1	-0.1	-0.1	-0.1	-0.1	-0.1	-0.1
EUR	0.4	0.2	0.1	0.0	-0.1	-0.1	0.0
IDN	1.6	1.5	1.3	1.1	1.0	0.9	1.2
IND	1.8	1.6	1.5	1.3	1.0	1.0	1.3
JPN	0.2	0.2	0.1	0.0	-0.2	-0.3	0.0
LAT	1.7	1.5	1.4	1.3	1.2	1.1	1.3
MNA	2.6	2.4	2.4	2.2	2.0	1.8	2.1
NFT	1.2	1.0	0.9	0.9	0.9	0.8	0.9
NIS	0.3	0.0	0.0	0.1	0.1	0.0	0.1
RAS	2.1	2.2	2.2	2.1	1.9	1.6	2.0
ROW	1.9	2.0	1.5	1.3	1.2	1.2	1.4
SSA	2.8	2.8	2.7	2.6	2.5	2.4	2.6
Total	**1.5**	**1.4**	**1.3**	**1.2**	**1.1**	**1.0**	**1.2**
OECD	*0.6*	*0.5*	*0.4*	*0.4*	*0.3*	*0.3*	*0.4*
Non-OECD	*1.7*	*1.6*	*1.5*	*1.4*	*1.3*	*1.2*	*1.4*
Asia	*1.5*	*1.4*	*1.2*	*1.1*	*1.0*	*0.9*	*1.1*
Non-Asia	*1.5*	*1.4*	*1.4*	*1.3*	*1.3*	*1.2*	*1.3*

Source: UN Medium Variant population projections.

Table 4 provides the labour productivity growth rate assumptions. The world average over the period 1995 to 2020 is 2.3 per cent. The balanced-growth assumption implies that the labour to capital ratio (in efficiency units) is constant. Given the exogenous set of GDP growth rates for each region of the model, capital productivity is calibrated to the GDP targets and constrained by the balanced-growth assumption.

Several sectors are given special treatment. First, it is assumed that total factor productivity (TFP) in agriculture is given, and in the high growth scenario, it has been fixed at 1.5 per cent per annum in all regions. Second, the (autonomous) energy efficiency improvement factor (also called AEEI factor) is given. Due to the existing higher levels of efficiency in the OECD countries, the AEEI factor is assumed to grow by 1 per cent per annum in the OECD regions, and to grow by 2 per cent per annum in the non-OECD regions. Third, trade and transport margins are assumed to decline, thereby reinforcing further globalisation. Under the high growth scenario, the trade and transport margins decline by 1 per cent per annum (uniformly across regions and sectors).

Table 3. **Average Annual Growth Rate of Labour Supply**
(per cent)

	1992-1995	1995-2000	2000-2005	2005-2010	2010-2015	2015-2020	1995-2020
ANZ	1.1	1.2	1.2	1.0	0.6	0.5	0.9
CHN	1.3	1.1	1.4	1.0	0.5	0.0	0.8
DAE	2.0	1.8	1.5	1.4	1.1	0.8	1.3
ECE	0.4	0.3	0.3	0.0	-0.5	-0.6	-0.1
EUR	0.4	0.2	0.1	-0.1	-0.4	-0.5	-0.1
IDN	2.3	2.1	1.7	1.5	1.4	!.1	1.6
IND	2.2	2.2	2.1	1.8	1.5	1.3	1.8
JPN	0.2	-0.2	-0.4	-0.7	-1.0	-0.7	-0.6
LAT	2.3	2.2	1.9	1.6	1.3	1.1	1.6
MNA	3.1	3.0	3.1	2.8	2.5	2.2	2.7
NFT	1.3	1.3	1.3	1.1	0.6	0.4	0.9
NIS	0.2	0.6	0.4	0.5	0.0	-0.3	0.2
RAS	2.7	3.2	3.0	2.4	2.3	2.1	2.6
ROW	2.4	2.4	1.9	1.9	1.8	1.4	1.9
SSA	3.0	3.0	3.1	3.1	3.1	2.9	3.0
Total	**1.7**	**1.7**	**1.7**	**1.4**	**1.2**	**0.9**	**1.4**
OECD	*0.7*	*0.6*	*0.5*	*0.3*	*0.0*	*-0.1*	*0.3*
Non-OECD	*1.9*	*1.9*	*1.9*	*1.7*	*1.4*	*1.1*	*1.6*
Asia	*1.7*	*1.7*	*1.7*	*1.4*	*1.1*	*0.7*	*1.3*
Non-Asia	*1.6*	*1.6*	*1.6*	*1.5*	*1.3*	*1.2*	*1.5*

Note: Labour supply projections are based on overall population projections, projections of the working age population, and projections of labour force participation rates.

Source: UN Medium Variant population projections and OECD staff estimates.

Table 4. **Average Annual Growth Rate of Labour Productivity**
(per cent)

	1992-1995	1995-2000	2000-2005	2005-2010	2010-2015	2015-2020	1995-2020
ANZ	2.9	3.1	3.5	3.7	3.6	3.7	3.5
CHN	10.4	8.1	6.7	7.2	6.6	7.2	7.2
DAE	4.9	5.8	5.4	5.5	5.2	5.5	5.5
ECE	1.4	5.2	5.2	5.5	4.5	4.7	5.0
EUR	1.4	2.2	2.7	2.9	2.7	2.8	2.7
IDN	4.5	5.3	5.2	5.4	5.2	5.5	5.3
IND	2.3	4.2	5.0	5.3	5.0	5.3	4.9
JPN	1.0	3.5	3.4	3.7	3.4	3.0	3.4
LAT	1.5	2.1	3.9	4.2	3.7	3.9	3.6
MNA	-0.3	1.9	3.9	4.2	4.3	4.6	3.8
NFT	1.3	0.9	1.4	1.6	2.0	2.2	1.6
NIS	-4.1	2.9	5.6	5.5	6.9	7.2	5.6
RAS	3.2	3.1	3.5	4.1	4.1	4.3	3.8
ROW	3.5	4.0	4.6	4.6	4.7	5.0	4.6
SSA	-1.1	1.6	1.9	1.8	2.4	3.0	2.1

Note: The balanced growth assumption implies that labour productivity growth essentially equals the rate of growth of real GDP less the rate of growth of labour supply.

Source: OECD staff estimates.

The world oil market has a prominent role in the LINKAGE model. Supply of crude oil and natural gas is determined by resource depletion sub-models. Each region has an existing pool of proven resources, and a finite limit of unproven (or uneconomical resources). Regions which produce more oil (or natural gas), than they discover, will inevitably run out of fuel. This by and large determines trade patterns of oil and gas. Oil is treated somewhat differently from natural gas. The Middle East/North African region (MNA), is assumed to have some degree of market power over the crude oil market. In concrete terms, the price of oil (with respect to a basket of OECD export goods) is fixed in the model, and the MNA region is the supplier of last resort. Under the high growth scenario, the world price of oil is assumed to increase by 2 per cent per annum in real terms through the year 2010, and then to increase by only 1 per cent per annum afterwards. (The drop in the increase in the price of oil after 2010 is the outcome of two assumptions. The first is that exploration and production costs will drop, increasing potential supply after 2010. The second assumption is that alternative sources of oil will become competitive after 2010, lessening the market power of the large oil suppliers.)

Policy Assumptions

The key policy assumption in the high growth scenario is the elimination of all import tariffs and export subsidies/taxes by the year 2020. Reaching this target will require tremendous political will, but it has been a stated goal in several fora, including APEC, free trade in the Americas, and in a new trans-Atlantic partnership. These three regions encompass a major share of both world income and trade.

The model assumes that governments target their public sector borrowing requirements (PSBR). This is achieved in the model by having a shifting direct tax curve on household income. The PSBR is assumed to decline to zero in all regions by the year 2020. Coupled with the removal of tariffs, this could lead to rather significant increases in household taxation. However, economic growth can enhance government revenues from other sources. Government (real) expenditures grow at the same rate as GDP.

Model closure assumes that foreign investment flows are exogenous (implying the trade balance is fixed). They are constrained to sum to zero across regions. Given the difficulties in endogenising foreign investment flows and the constraints of achieving sustainable economic growth, foreign investment flows are fixed at their base year levels. (Any assumption which has the foreign flows declining with respect to national income would meet the sustainability requirement. The crucial assumption is the exogeneity of foreign investment flows. Changes in trade relations are reflected by changes in the real exchange rate.)

Aggregate Implications

This section will briefly describe the aggregate implications of the high growth scenario. It is a straightforward exercise to calculate the relative shift in economic weight across the regions. The rapid growth of the non-OECD Member economies leads to a shift in the distribution of income away from the OECD economies. At an aggregate level, the OECD region's share of world income drops from around 80 per cent in 1995 (at official exchange rates), to 62 per cent by the year 2020 (see Figure 1). The Asian region's share increases from 8.5 per cent to 19.5 per cent.

Figure 1. **Regional Distribution of GDP**
(Based on 1992 dollar official exchange rates, per cent)

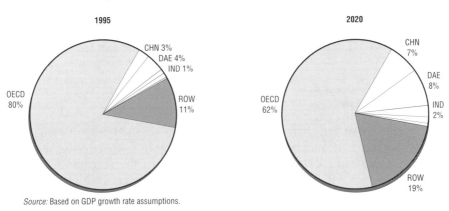

Source: Based on GDP growth rate assumptions.

While growth in aggregate income in the non-OECD regions is impressive, and the population growth rates are declining, there will continue to be a significant gap in income levels. Using PPP exchange rates, the OECD to non-OECD income differential in 1995 is 6 to 1. In the year 2020, the gap falls to 3 to 1, i.e. a halving of the average income gap in 25 years. Convergence of the Asian regions is even more impressive. The gap between the OECD and Asia is currently 7 to 1, and this ratio drops to less than 3 to 1 in 2020. Figure 2 shows the relevant figures for each of the individual regions. Under the high growth assumptions, the DAE region not only surpasses the 1995 level of OECD income, but there is an absolute convergence beyond the 2020 level of OECD income. The only other non-OECD region which converges beyond the 1995 level of OECD income is the rather heterogeneous ROW (rest of the world) region. One could anticipate significant reductions in the absolute level of poverty if these growth assumptions were to hold.

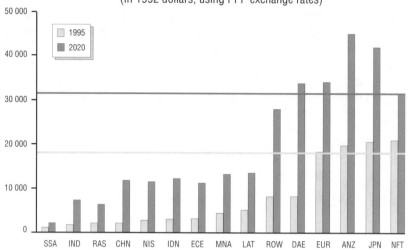

Figure 2. **Per Capita Income**
(in 1992 dollars, using PPP exchange rates)

Note: The two lines represent the average level of OECD per capita income in 1995 (the lower line), and 2020.
Source: Linkage model results.

The removal of trade barriers, the reduction in trade and transport costs, and the high growth rates, generate a boom in world trade. Exports from the Asian region may increase by a factor of 10, significantly more than exports from the non-Asian region on aggregate, which will grow by a factor of 3.3. Trade barriers are higher in the non-OECD countries, which partly explains the higher growth in trade to be expected in these countries. The regional patterns of trade also evolve. The growth in trade between the developing regions is more significant than either intra-OECD trade, or trade between the OECD and the non-OECD region. In 1995, intra-OECD trade represents 45 per cent of total world trade; by 2020, this share drops to 27 per cent (see Figure 3)[5]. Intra-Asian trade, on the other hand, increases from a 6 per cent share to a 12 per cent share, and the other non-Member economy trade share increases from 27 per cent to 37 per cent of total world trade.

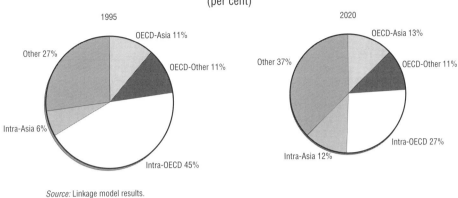

Figure 3. **Regional Trade Patterns**
(per cent)

Source: Linkage model results.

Structural Results

This section starts with a brief presentation of the trade and tariff structure of the OECD and Asian regions (see Table 5). By and large, the destination of the OECD exports is the other OECD regions, respectively 63 per cent for ANZ, 66 per cent for EUR, 56 per cent for JPN, and 75 per cent for NFT[6]. Japan is significantly different from the other OECD regions, since roughly one-third of its trade is with the Asian countries, though ANZ is not far behind. The NFT region has roughly balanced trade between Asia and the rest of the world. Europe exports roughly twice as much to the rest of the world as it does to the Asian countries[7].

The export trade shares for the Asian regions are not so different, with most exporting about two-thirds of the total to the OECD. Exports to other Asian countries range from 15 to 30 per cent of the total. India is the only Asian country with export shares to the rest of the world approaching 20 per cent.

OECD exporters typically face higher tariffs than they apply, and the tariffs they face in non-OECD countries are higher than in OECD countries. For example, Europe faces an average tariff of 8 per cent, but the average tariff on its exports to OECD countries is only 4 per cent, whereas it faces an average tariff of 16 per cent on its exports to non-OECD countries. On the other hand, the average import tariff in Europe is 6 per cent. The story is roughly similar for the NFT region. However, for exporters from ANZ and JPN the tariff structure is more uniform across trading partners. ANZ is a large exporter of agricultural and food products and faces high tariffs in all regions, particularly in the OECD regions. Japan on the other hand exports a significant volume of capital goods (including transportation equipment), and the tariffs faced by Japanese exporters of these goods are high and relatively uniform across all regions.

Table 5. **Tariff and Trade Structure in 1992**
(per cent)

	Tariffs faced by exporters to:				Export structure				Import tariffs Average	Import structure
	OECD	Asia	Other	Total	OECD	Asia	Other	Total		
ANZ										
LA	58.3	49.9	25.2	51.8	57.3	30.9	11.7	31.8	3.7	4.7
RE	0.7	4.0	20.4	2.2	69.5	27.5	3.0	22.4	0.2	3.8
CO	2.4	13.4	33.7	7.5	66.0	27.3	6.7	8.6	16.0	17.9
IM	1.0	7.2	10.8	4.7	45.9	46.5	7.7	10.9	6.3	6.9
KA	2.2	15.6	22.8	8.0	62.8	25.4	11.8	10.7	13.1	44.4
SH	0.0	0.0	0.0	0.0	77.3	16.2	6.5	15.6	0.0	22.1
Total	17.5	21.8	20.4	19.0	63.3	28.6	8.1		9.3	
EUR										
LA	30.6	40.5	23.1	28.8	55.8	8.8	35.4	6.1	31.7	8.0
RE	0.1	2.9	23.2	2.9	79.6	9.5	10.9	3.7	0.1	10.1
CO	5.0	19.9	24.3	10.8	67.7	10.1	22.2	16.8	8.6	16.0
IM	1.8	16.0	16.2	5.6	73.6	8.5	17.9	9.0	1.2	8.6
KA	3.9	20.0	20.6	9.8	64.4	11.7	23.9	39.5	5.1	35.7
SH	0.0	0.0	0.0	0.0	64.1	11.7	24.2	24.9	0.0	21.6
Total	4.2	14.8	15.9	8.1	65.7	10.9	23.4		5.8	
JPN										
LA	9.9	24.9	33.7	21.1	31.6	57.3	11.1	0.7	78.6	16.1
RE	0.4	6.1	5.2	3.0	52.5	39.9	7.6	0.3	2.1	18.0
CO	21.4	23.1	31.2	23.2	37.9	53.0	9.1	9.3	7.7	12.7
IM	7.4	12.2	15.6	11.4	23.2	66.0	10.8	5.7	1.4	6.5
KA	18.7	18.6	24.2	19.3	60.6	28.4	11.1	74.5	1.7	20.4
SH	0.0	0.0	0.0	0.0	55.5	30.8	13.8	9.5	0.0	26.4
Total	16.7	16.9	21.4	17.3	55.6	33.3	11.1		14.4	
NFT										
LA	49.3	67.9	16.5	46.3	66.3	15.6	18.1	10.0	15.9	6.1
RE	0.3	5.2	9.4	1.2	87.2	6.2	6.6	4.3	0.5	7.4
CO	7.7	16.5	18.8	10.7	69.8	15.2	15.0	11.5	11.5	15.4
IM	1.6	6.8	9.4	3.0	77.8	12.8	9.4	7.8	3.4	7.1
KA	3.7	13.0	18.5	6.6	75.9	12.6	11.5	46.1	9.4	50.5
SH	0.0	0.0	0.0	0.0	75.5	10.5	14.0	20.3	0.0	13.5
Total	7.1	17.4	13.4	9.2	74.8	12.5	12.7		7.8	
CHN										
LA	41.2	68.0	21.6	48.2	46.1	37.8	16.1	8.6	7.4	8.4
RE	2.5	2.6	22.5	4.3	68.7	22.8	8.5	3.1	1.7	3.3
CO	16.1	18.3	27.2	17.8	66.8	22.3	10.9	38.1	27.1	26.7
IM	3.1	9.1	16.3	7.9	31.0	60.2	8.8	3.4	9.5	10.9
KA	6.1	14.7	22.6	10.9	53.4	37.1	9.5	29.5	22.1	41.8
SH	0.0	0.2	0.0	0.0	73.5	15.4	11.1	17.3	0.1	8.9
Total	11.1	19.9	20.0	14.6	61.1	28.1	10.8		18.2	

Table 5 (end)

	Tariffs faced by exporters to:				Export structure				Import tariffs Average	Import structure
	OECD	Asia	Other	Total	OECD	Asia	Other	Total		
DAE										
LA	39.2	23.6	25.4	33.3	60.9	28.9	10.2	9.2	69.7	8.2
RE	0.8	9.2	18.3	5.4	48.4	49.1	2.5	2.3	4.3	8.0
CO	13.1	30.0	33.7	21.3	53.5	36.8	9.7	21.9	14.5	13.9
IM	3.5	6.4	9.2	5.8	29.9	61.1	9.1	6.6	6.7	10.7
KA	7.0	13.7	24.0	10.2	65.4	26.2	8.4	48.1	12.8	44.5
SH	0.0	0.0	0.0	0.0	77.9	13.8	8.3	11.9	0.0	14.6
Total	9.8	17.1	22.7	13.1	61.1	30.1	8.7		14.5	
IDN										
LA	21.5	25.3	37.7	23.2	68.2	27.5	4.3	13.8	27.3	7.4
RE	1.3	4.5	5.2	2.2	72.3	27.1	0.6	29.0	1.0	4.5
CO	12.3	11.0	39.9	15.7	59.9	26.5	13.6	25.7	13.2	17.6
IM	1.8	6.8	25.6	6.1	41.2	51.5	7.3	4.5	5.6	11.4
KA	7.5	13.1	24.0	10.7	57.9	34.7	7.4	20.8	16.8	42.3
SH	0.0	0.0	0.0	0.0	87.3	6.5	6.2	6.1	0.0	16.7
Total	7.9	11.2	32.0	10.4	65.1	28.4	6.5		12.2	
IND										
LA	23.5	34.2	21.1	24.9	50.2	20.0	29.8	15.9	19.5	6.4
RE	0.4	3.1	18.9	1.7	76.2	19.5	4.3	16.4	3.5	27.7
CO	12.3	23.6	20.4	14.9	72.1	11.7	16.3	37.0	68.5	15.6
IM	4.6	7.2	17.2	7.0	49.3	39.9	10.8	5.1	45.4	12.0
KA	6.0	14.0	22.3	12.8	48.4	19.7	31.9	12.0	58.4	22.3
SH	0.0	0.0	0.0	0.0	59.3	20.4	20.3	13.5	0.0	16.0
Total	8.9	15.0	17.8	11.7	63.5	17.9	18.6		31.4	
RAS										
LA	26.4	31.5	18.6	25.9	39.7	32.3	27.9	16.7	14.6	15.8
RE	0.1	3.9	21.6	2.2	64.1	31.9	4.0	1.6	34.5	7.7
CO	13.7	19.2	31.9	16.7	73.3	14.5	12.1	54.7	31.9	24.4
IM	0.9	10.3	14.4	7.9	33.9	47.8	18.4	0.5	9.7	10.7
KA	6.5	18.9	21.7	9.7	76.9	11.3	11.8	4.3	15.1	32.1
SH	0.0	0.0	0.0	0.0	87.8	6.9	5.3	22.3	0.0	9.3
Total	10.5	20.8	23.8	13.9	70.8	16.1	13.1		18.6	

Notes: The OECD aggregate region includes: ANZ, ECE, EUR, JPN and NFT. The Asia aggregate region includes: CHN, DAE, IDN, IND and RAS. Other aggregate region includes the remaining five regions: LAT, MNA, NIS, ROW and SSA.

The definition of the aggregate sectors is given in the Annex in the sectoral concordance table. They are respectively: agriculture and food (LA), energy and mining (RE), consumer goods (CO), intermediate goods (IM), capital goods (KA), and non-tradeable goods (SH).

Source: GTAP (Hertel, 1997).

A quick glance at the tariff structure clearly indicates that the most distorted markets are agriculture and food, consumer goods (particularly textiles and apparel), and to a lesser extent capital goods, particularly in the non-OECD countries. (Due to grossly deficient data, trade barriers in the service sectors are missing entirely. Clearly, these sectors will play a prominent role in the future, particularly for OECD countries. There has already been significant progress over the last few years in reducing barriers in the telecommunications and information technology sectors, and to a lesser extent in financial and transportation services.)

Changes in the patterns of output and trade in the high growth scenario will be the result of several factors: income growth, changing demand patterns, tariff elimination, and changing comparative advantage. As countries raise their income levels, the share of the budget allocated to basic necessities declines, and there is a rise in the consumption of luxury goods and services.

Under such a scenario there will be some significant shifts in the structure of output in all of the regions. On aggregate, the OECD regions will witness a larger concentration of economic output in the service sectors, where the sheltered sector's (construction plus services) share in total output could increase from 61.5 per cent to 66 per cent (see Figure 4 and Table 6). (This is probably an understatement since implicitly the scenario assumes no change in trade barriers in the service sectors.) There will also be a shift towards the capital goods sector, though not as pronounced. Growth will be slowest in agriculture and food and the consumer goods sector. This reflects both stagnant demand and changes in tariff structure. There is some variation across the OECD countries. Growth in food production will be brisk for ANZ, ECE, and NFT, reflecting their comparative advantage in producing competitively priced agricultural produce. Food production could actually decline in Japan, if it were to remove all trade restrictions completely, and would grow only very modestly in EUR.

The production structure in the Asia region will change quite substantially. Growth in all sectors will be high, reflecting the high GDP growth rate. Growth will be the highest in intermediate goods, capital goods, and services (over 8 per cent per annum). It will average only 3.6 per cent per annum in agriculture and food, therefore, this sector's share in total output will decline from 22 per cent to 8 per cent, converging towards the OECD average. The sheltered sector share will increase from 40 per cent to 48 per cent, in part because of the high income demand elasticity for services, but also because of the rapid pace of construction generated by high saving and infrastructure requirements.

The diversity of the Asian region is reflected in more disaggregated results. China, for example, sees relatively more rapid growth in the sheltered sector than Asia in general. Beyond the infrastructure needed for rapid growth, the integration of Hong Kong with the mainland Chinese economy provides a boost to the service industry. Agricultural and food output declines rapidly as a share of total output, from 24 per cent to 6 per cent. The DAE region benefits from rapid growth in the intermediate and capital goods sectors. The regions of South Asia (IND and RAS) also witness a large drop in the share of food and agriculture, but nonetheless these sectors continue to be relatively important, particularly in RAS.

Figure 4. **Production Structure**
(Index: 1992=100)

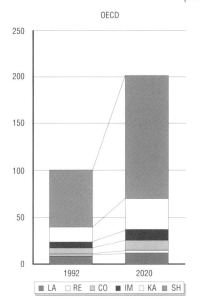
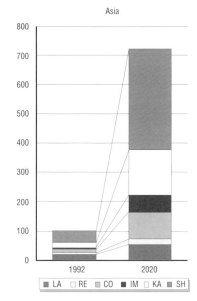

1. The OECD aggregate region includes ANZ, ECE, EUR, JPN and NFT. The Asia aggregate region includes CHN, DAE, IND and RAS.
2. The definition of the aggregate sectors is given in the Annex in the sectoral concordance table. They are respectively: agriculture and food (LA), energy and mining (RE), consumer goods (CO), intermediate goods (IM), capital goods (KA), and non-tradable goods (SH).

Source: Linkage model results.

In an alternative simulation, where all growth parameters (except for total GDP) are held fixed, but tariffs are not removed, there is no dramatic change in the structure of production between the OECD and the Asian region, with the exception of agriculture and food and the consumer goods sector. (The sub-regional differences are of course more important.) This would suggest that dynamic factors are a more important element in explaining the evolution of production and trade patterns than trade policies *per se*.

For the OECD as a whole, the major trade expansion occurs in agriculture and food, and intermediate and capital goods (see Figure 5 and Table 6)[8]. While trade increases in all sectors, there is a relative decline in the share of trade in resources, consumer goods, and the sheltered sector. Again there are significant regional variations reflecting different endowments and initial policy conditions. Exports in Asia expand at almost twice the rate of the OECD. The largest expansion is in the intermediate goods sector, followed by the capital goods sector. Exports of food also grow rapidly, particularly from India and RAS.

Table 6. **Output and Trade Structure**
(per cent)

	Exports		Imports		Output	
	1992	2020	1992	2020	1992	2020
ANZ						
LA	31.8	28.3	4.7	4.2	11.4	7.7
RE	22.4	22.1	3.8	9.2	4.0	3.3
CO	8.6	7.7	17.9	16.9	5.0	3.7
IM	10.9	15.9	6.9	7.0	6.2	6.4
KA	10.7	12.0	44.4	42.8	8.8	8.4
SH	15.6	13.9	22.1	19.9	64.6	70.5
Total	100.0	100.0	100.0	100.0	100.0	100.0
		4.5		4.5		4.3
ECE						
LA	11.6	11.6	10.0	11.4	21.0	12.0
RE	3.9	5.1	10.6	13.3	4.5	3.7
CO	21.7	18.0	20.5	17.2	11.1	10.6
IM	13.2	17.1	7.5	8.4	7.0	8.4
KA	28.4	31.3	36.0	36.5	13.2	16.8
SH	21.2	17.0	15.4	13.2	43.2	48.5
Total	100.0	100.0	100.0	100.0	100.0	100.0
		4.8		4.5		4.5
EUR						
LA	6.1	5.2	8.0	10.0	9.6	5.2
RE	3.7	2.8	10.1	9.8	1.4	1.1
CO	16.8	14.6	16.0	15.5	7.5	5.8
IM	9.0	10.9	8.6	7.7	6.3	6.1
KA	39.5	45.1	35.7	36.7	14.6	15.5
SH	24.9	21.4	21.6	20.2	60.5	66.2
Total	100.0	100.0	100.0	100.0	100.0	100.0
		3.4		3.5		2.4
JPN						
LA	0.7	0.7	16.1	16.5	8.7	3.8
RE	0.3	0.2	18.0	12.6	0.3	0.2
CO	9.3	8.5	12.7	13.8	7.8	6.5
IM	5.7	6.2	6.5	8.5	6.3	6.2
KA	74.5	78.3	20.4	24.1	19.9	23.1
SH	9.5	6.2	26.4	24.4	57.0	60.2
Total	100.0	100.0	100.0	100.0	100.0	100.0
		4.0		4.7		2.5
NFT						
LA	10.0	21.2	6.1	5.7	7.5	7.3
RE	4.3	2.2	7.4	5.2	2.0	1.2
CO	11.5	8.4	15.4	17.0	6.0	4.4
IM	7.8	6.6	7.1	8.4	5.5	4.6
KA	46.1	44.8	50.5	51.8	14.2	14.0
SH	20.3	16.7	13.5	12.1	64.8	68.6
Total	100.0	100.0	100.0	100.0	100.0	100.0
		3.5		3.5		2.5

106

Table 6 (end)

(per cent)

	Exports		Imports		Output	
	1992	2020	1992	2020	1992	2020
CHN						
LA	8.6	2.1	8.4	16.7	21.9	5.8
RE	3.1	0.8	3.3	7.2	5.8	3.0
CO	38.1	32.4	26.7	25.0	12.9	12.3
IM	3.4	5.4	10.9	11.3	5.7	6.9
KA	29.5	38.3	41.8	35.3	14.1	21.6
SH	17.3	20.9	8.9	4.5	39.5	50.3
Total	100.0	100.0	100.0	100.0	100.0	100.0
		7.6		7.3		8.3
DAE						
LA	9.2	10.2	8.2	11.2	16.0	7.3
RE	2.3	0.7	8.0	11.3	1.2	0.8
CO	21.9	22.7	13.9	13.5	12.7	14.0
IM	6.6	11.5	10.7	11.4	8.2	10.1
KA	48.1	46.1	44.5	41.6	20.1	23.6
SH	11.9	8.7	14.6	11.0	41.7	44.2
Total	100.0	100.0	100.0	100.0	100.0	100.0
		6.6		6.5		6.9
IDN						
LA	13.8	10.2	7.4	14.3	23.4	8.7
RE	29.0	11.5	4.5	15.0	8.9	3.6
CO	25.7	33.9	17.6	15.5	10.1	13.9
IM	4.5	8.5	11.4	12.3	5.8	6.7
KA	20.8	29.0	42.3	33.5	11.0	14.8
SH	6.1	6.9	16.7	9.5	40.7	52.3
Total	100.0	100.0	100.0	100.0	100.0	100.0
		6.2		6.6		7.1
IND						
LA	15.9	16.5	6.4	8.8	27.4	12.1
RE	16.4	13.4	27.7	15.9	3.8	3.2
CO	37.0	34.0	15.6	16.5	12.8	12.1
IM	5.1	6.8	12.0	29.3	6.6	6.2
KA	12.0	16.4	22.3	22.5	10.4	14.6
SH	13.5	12.9	16.0	7.1	39.0	51.8
Total	100.0	100.0	100.0	100.0	100.0	100.0
		7.5		7.3		6.5
RAS						
LA	16.7	31.6	15.8	10.1	32.3	18.7
RE	1.6	1.1	7.7	10.4	1.8	0.9
CO	54.7	44.2	24.4	27.5	16.1	15.8
IM	0.5	0.8	10.7	16.0	4.8	5.3
KA	4.3	4.1	32.1	30.8	8.6	11.3
SH	22.3	18.2	9.3	5.3	36.5	47.9
Total	100.0	100.0	100.0	100.0	100.0	100.0
		6.9		6.3		6.3

Notes: The definition of the aggregate sectors is given in the Annex in the sectoral concordance table. They are respectively: agriculture and food (LA), energy and mining (RE), consumer goods (CO), intermediate goods (IM), capital goods (KA), and non-tradeable goods (SH).

The aggregate (average per annum) growth rate, 1992-2020 is provided below the Total line.

Source: GTAP (Hertel, 1997) for 1992, and LINKAGE model results for 2020.

Figure 5. **Export Structure**
(Index: 1992=100)

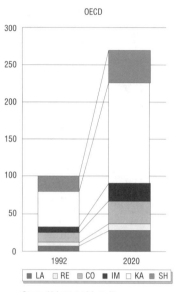

OECD

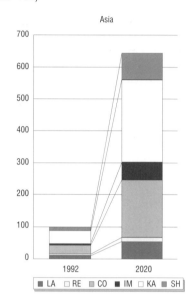

Asia

Source: Linkage model results.

Labour Markets

The composition of the labour force in OECD countries is already heavily skewed towards the service (and construction) sectors where over close to 70 per cent of the labour force is employed (see Figure 6). Agriculture employs about 11 per cent, with manufacturing (and resource extraction) taking up the remaining 19 per cent, mostly concentrated in the capital goods sector. The overall growth rate of labour supply is a modest 0.3 per cent on average through 2020, with the highest growth in the services sector. Agriculture, resource extraction, and consumer goods would shed labour on aggregate in the OECD. This story is somewhat different for ANZ which would see a pickup in employment growth in both agriculture and resource extraction, and in NFT which would also see a rise in agricultural employment, but a decline in resource extraction. Another notable feature is the decline in the labour force over the next 25 years in ECE (perhaps 1 million out of a base of 50 million), EUR (around 4 million out of a base of 176 million), and Japan (7 million out of a base of 63 million).

Figure 6. **Labour Structure**
(Index: 1992=100)

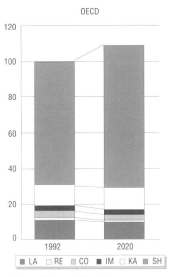

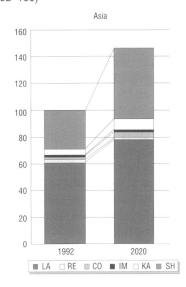

Source: Linkage model results.

The labour structure in Asia is quite different from the OECD's in the base year. Agricultural (and food) employment represents roughly 61 per cent of total employment, with employment in the sheltered sectors at about 29 per cent. Even in the rapidly emerging economies in DAE, agricultural and food employment is 45 per cent in the base year, with a 42 per cent share in the sheltered sector. Overall labour growth is projected to be 1.4 per cent per annum on average, considerably higher than the OECD, though declining towards the end of the period. Coupled with high productivity, the growth of labour in efficiency units is very rapid. China (and Hong Kong) account for about 55 per cent of the total labour force in the Asian region, with India representing an additional 26 per cent. By the year 2020, China's share will drop to 47 per cent, and India's will rise to 30 per cent.

The most rapid growth in employment will occur in the manufacturing sectors, particularly in intermediate and capital goods. Agriculture and food's share declines, from 61 per cent to 53 per cent, but perhaps less rapidly than one would anticipate from the high growth in this region. First, there are significant differences in development across the region. South Asia (India and RAS), and China have very sizeable rural populations, many living at best at subsistence levels. Second, labour productivity in the non-agricultural sectors is much higher than in agriculture, hence it is possible to have higher growth in non-agricultural production using relatively less labour. Third, the scenario assumes perfect labour mobility between rural and non-rural activities. An alternative specification would be to implement some labour market segmentation and have an explicit rural-to-urban labour migration function, thereby most likely increasing the relative supply of labour for manufacturing and services.

Is the scenario realistic? In the case of China, significant reform, particularly in the domain of property rights, will be needed to achieve significant modifications in the structure of production. It is also readily apparent that manufacturing productivity has ample scope for rapid increases. State-owned enterprises, which represent a considerable share of total manufacturing potential, are widely believed to be heavily overstaffed. There is significant concern about a large labour surplus in the cities, but it is not obvious that rapid growth in manufacturing and services will be able to absorb this surplus easily. In India, where manufacturing has been hiding behind closed borders for many years, the elimination of tariffs could have a dramatic impact on the productivity of manufacturing and could also lead to (relative) labour shedding, in a similar way to state enterprise reform in China. In both of these large countries, government expenditure on agricultural research has been declining, and investment in agricultural infrastructure has been lagging. Under these circumstances, it is hard to conceive of continued growth in agriculture without an increase in labour input.

Real wages increase significantly in all regions, ranging from a low of 1.8 per cent per annum 1995-2020 to 6.4 per cent per annum (see Table 7). There are a variety of factors which influence real wage growth: tightness of the labour market, terms of trade effects, and labour productivity. The OECD countries benefit from the first two. Labour supply growth is low, if not negative in some regions, creating tight labour market conditions. The combination of high embodied productivity and increased competition leads to a drop in the price of imports into the OECD, hence an improvement in the terms of trade. Therefore, real wages in the OECD region increase from 1.8 to 3.6 per cent on average per annum, with the slowest wage growth observed in NFT, which has a higher labour supply growth and lower base tariffs. Real wage growth tends to be higher in the non-OECD countries, reflecting the overall catch-up momentum towards OECD income levels.

Table 7. **Real Wage Index**
(1995 = 1)

	1995	2000	2005	2010	2015	2020	Change in real wage (average per cent per annum)1995-2020
ANZ	1.00	1.18	1.41	1.68	2.02	2.44	3.6
CHN	1.00	1.39	1.78	2.33	3.05	4.15	5.9
DAE	1.00	1.28	1.59	1.97	2.42	3.05	4.6
ECE	1.00	1.35	1.74	2.23	2.75	3.46	5.1
EUR	1.00	1.12	1.30	1.50	1.73	2.00	2.8
IDN	1.00	1.31	1.64	2.04	2.51	3.15	4.7
IND	1.00	1.23	1.52	1.86	2.27	2.87	4.3
JPN	1.00	1.19	1.41	1.76	2.09	2.41	3.6
LAT	1.00	1.13	1.40	1.72	2.06	2.51	3.7
MNA	1.00	1.17	1.30	1.42	1.72	2.14	3.1
NFT	1.00	1.05	1.14	1.24	1.39	1.58	1.8
NIS	1.00	1.25	1.79	2.38	3.37	4.74	6.4
RAS	1.00	1.17	1.36	1.61	1.92	2.31	3.4
ROW	1.00	1.24	1.53	1.86	2.27	2.87	4.3
SSA	1.00	1.13	1.28	1.42	1.60	1.83	2.5

Conclusion

The world economy could be on the brink of an age of global prosperity. The resolution of major regional conflicts, the determined opening up of many previously closed economies, and productivity growth engendered by a panoply of pro-competition policies and technological advances could put many economies on a virtuous cycle of growth. The recent past and the best guesses of many economists suggest that non-OECD economies, particularly those in Asia, are likely to grow at rates significantly higher than those likely to be feasible in the OECD economies, and for many countries better than historical rates.

The first impact of these high and different growth rates will be to shift the centre of economic weight away from the OECD countries. Depending on the choice of weighting schemes, in 2020 the non-OECD countries' share of total world income could range from 36 per cent (at official exchange rates) to 67 per cent (at PPP exchange rates) if these growth rates are achieved. Second, there will be a significant convergence in income levels, with the average non-OECD income rising to 30 per cent of the average OECD income from a level of only 15 per cent today (at PPP exchange rates). By the year 2020, many non-OECD countries could achieve a level of income on a par with that of the lower-income OECD countries, and some could even rank with the richest countries in the world. These GDP growth numbers will be surpassed by the growth in trade, both among non-OECD countries as well as between the OECD and the non-OECD.

Income growth, changing patterns of consumption, evolving comparative advantage, and changes in the policy environment will inevitably lead to changes in the structure of production, employment, and trade. To a significant extent, these changes have already occurred in the OECD economies, and we are simply likely to see a small reinforcement in the importance of the service sector. Changes in trade policies will force some rationalisation in agriculture, and textiles and apparel. High growth in the non-OECD countries will provide significant export opportunities for the OECD countries, particularly in intermediate and capital goods, and services. Labour income in the OECD will rise significantly, and assuming the OECD successfully resolves its employment and skill problems, it will provide a basis for equitable growth.

There will be significantly more structural adjustment in the non-OECD countries. Demand for higher quality manufactured goods and services, as well as derived demand for construction and capital goods, will lead to a significant shift in production and trade shares. In the poorer and larger countries, labour demand growth in agriculture and food processing could continue to be significant — though slower than overall labour supply growth.

Achieving these high levels of growth simultaneously in all regions will not be easy. Significant policy reforms need to be undertaken to tackle current and future bottlenecks. All regions need to provide adequate educational resources to ensure growth in a high quality labour force. In non-OECD countries, further progress must be made to liberalise trade in goods and services, as well improving the efficiency of financial systems. OECD countries need to implement policies to deal with the looming pension and medical needs of a rapidly ageing population. Further regulatory reforms in the OECD would also promote growth-enhancing competition, particularly in Europe and Japan. Internationally, significant progress needs to be achieved to lower remaining trade barriers and to provide a better environment for foreign investment flows.

While high growth is not guaranteed, there is a relatively broad consensus among policy analysts on the best practice policies which can improve the chances of success. If the right policies are implemented, global prosperity will provide the opportunity to deal with some pressing and acute problems, such as marginalisation of the poorest countries and environmental degradation.

Notes and References

1. The LINKAGE model used for this paper differs from the LINKAGE model used for the OECD's Linkages II study only in its regional definition. Otherwise, the model specification and underlying assumptions are identical. A detailed overview of the LINKAGE model is provided in OECD (1997*b*).

2. See OECD (1997*a*) for a full description of the assumptions underlying this high growth scenario.

3. The aggregate growth rates are weighted using the official 1992 exchange rates, not PPP exchange rates.

4. The population and labour statistics reflect UN projections on international migration (see United Nations). The model does not allow for international labour movements save through the initial projections.

5. The base data excludes most of intra-regional trade for the aggregate regions. For example, the EU region in the base data excludes intra-EU trade. The EUR region defined for the purposes of this paper includes trade between the three separate regions which compose the aggregate region. Therefore, intra-OECD trade is underestimated as a share of total world trade.

6. Note that the numbers understate the percentage for EUR, since as noted above they exclude to a large extent intra-EU trade.

7. It is worth noting that these numbers are based on 1992 statistics. Given the rapid growth in both GDP and trade, particularly in the Asian region, it is likely that these numbers have changed perceptibly over the last five years.

8. Note that the numbers in Figure 6 and in Table 6 include intra-regional trade.

Annex

Model Features

Summary Description of LINKAGE Model

The LINKAGE Model is an applied dynamic general equilibrium model. The regional and sectoral model definitions are provided below, including their correspondence with the GTAP data set[1]. The base year of the data is 1992, and the model is solved forward for the years 1995, 2000, 2005, 2010, 2015, and 2020.

The broad features of the model resemble fairly standard AGE models. Constant returns to scale are assumed in production in all sectors. Producers choose an optimal mix of intermediate goods, capital and labour to produce goods, subject to exogenous substitution elasticities. Production in the model differs in three ways from the standard model:

i) The production structure is differentiated by crops, livestock, and the remaining sectors. Land, chemicals (in crops), and feed (in livestock) are distinguished in the agricultural sectors.

ii) Energy plays a prominent role in the production structure in all sectors. It is possible to substitute energy for the other factors of production (for example labour), as well as to choose the optimal mix of fuels (as a function of relative fuel prices and existing technology).

iii) A distinction is made between old (or installed) capital, and new capital (i.e. a vintage capital model is assumed, also called a putty/semi-putty technology). Typically, the substitution possibilities with older capital are smaller than with new capital. Economies with higher rates of investment will have more flexibility since on average they will have a larger share of new capital.

There is a single representative household to which all factor income accrues. Households purchase an optimal bundle of goods, under a modified Stone-Geary demand system, known as the Extended Linear Expenditure System. The level of savings is directly integrated into the decision making of households.

Government receives tax revenues from households, and an assortment of indirect taxes (production, consumption, import tariffs, and export taxes/subsidies). Aggregate government expenditures are fixed as a proportion of GDP, and a fixed coefficient expenditure function is used to determine sectoral purchases. One of the closure rules is that the government deficit to GDP ratio is fixed. The household direct tax schedule is endogenous in order to achieve the given target.

Investment is savings driven, i.e. aggregate investment is equated to national savings (private and public) plus foreign inflows (or outflows). A fixed coefficient expenditure function is used to determine the allocation of investment expenditures on goods and services.

Trade in goods and services assumes that goods are differentiated by region of origin (this is the so-called Armington assumption). Typically, the more homogeneous the definition of a good, the higher will be the substitution elasticity between domestic and imported goods, though a low degree of substitution can also reflect high or prohibitive transportation costs (e.g. natural gas). The one exception to the Armington assumption is crude oil. It is both a relatively homogeneous commodity, as well as having low transportation costs relative to its value. Equilibrium on the oil market is achieved by equating world demand with world supply. All regions are assumed to be on their oil resource depletion profile, except for the Middle East/North Africa (MNA) region. Assuming the MNA region targets a given price for crude oil, it becomes the supplier of last resort (i.e. its extraction rate is endogenous).

The model distinguishes four different trading prices: pre-FOB (i.e. at producer prices), FOB (at border price), CIF (inclusive of international trade and transport margins), and post-CIF (i.e. inclusive of import tariffs). All price wedges are distinguished both by region of origin and destination. Unlike most standard models, there is no distinction between domestic output sold on domestic markets and exported, in other words, there is a single price for domestic production.

The final closure rule concerns the trade balance (or equivalently the capital balance). In each time period, and for each region, the trade balance is fixed. Equilibrium on the current account is achieved through an endogenous real exchange rate. For example, a reduction in tariffs typically leads to a real exchange rate depreciation as an increase in imports needs to be matched by an increase in exports.

Labour is assumed to be perfectly mobile across sectors, and the wage level is fully flexible and determined by the labour equilibrium condition. New capital is similarly perfectly mobile across sectors, and is allocated such that the rate of return is uniform across the economy. Sectors in decline, i.e. whose demand for capital is less than the initially installed capital, release capital according to a supply schedule. The released capital is added to the pool of new capital, i.e. released capital is assumed to be equivalent to new capital. The rate of return on old capital in declining sectors will be determined by equating the sectoral capital demand with the (remaining) sectoral capital supply.

Dynamics are captured through changes in factor supplies and changes in productivity. Population and labour growth are exogenous, based on the latest UN population projections. The capital stock in each period is equated to the previous period's depreciated stock plus new investment. Overall land supply is assumed to be available in fixed quantity, though actual demand may be less than the maximum available supply. (A logistic supply curve is implemented.) The other factors include energy resources: coal, oil and gas reserves, and non-fossil fuel generated electricity. Coal and the non-fossil fuel electric factor are assumed to follow a constant elasticity supply curve. Oil and gas resources are determined using a resource depletion module. Oil and gas reserves are split into two components — proven and unproven reserves. Production comes from proven reserves at a given extraction rate (except for the MNA region). Unproven reserves are converted to proven reserves according to a price sensitive discovery rate.

Productivity is calibrated in a reference scenario in order to achieve a given GDP growth rate. The basic assumption is that of balanced growth, i.e. the labour/capital ratio (in efficiency units) remains constant. Labour productivity is assigned exogenously so that labour in efficiency units grows at the same rate as GDP. Capital productivity is determined residually, consistent with GDP and labour projections. Energy efficiency improvement is exogenous. Finally, productivity in the agricultural sectors is also set exogenously.

Regional Concordance for the LINKAGE Model[2]

1	ANZ	Australia and New Zealand

Australia (AUS), New Zealand (NZL)

2	CHN	China including Hong Kong

The People's Republic of China (CHN), Hong Kong (HKG)

3	DAE	Dynamic Asian Economies

Republic of Korea (KOR), Malaysia (MYS), Philippines (PHL), Singapore (SGP), Thailand (THA), Chinese Taipei (TWN)

4	ECE	Eastern and Central Europe

Bulgaria, Czech Republic, Hungary, Poland, Romania, Slovakia, Slovenia (CEA)

5	EUR	European Union 15 plus EFTA countries

Belgium, Denmark, France, Germany, Greece, Ireland, Italy, Luxembourg, Netherlands, Portugal, Spain, United Kingdom (EU), Austria, Finland, Sweden (EU3), Iceland, Norway, Switzerland (EFT)

6	IDN	Indonesia (IDN)

| 7 | IND | India (IDI) |

| 8 | JPN | Japan (JPN) |

9   LAT   Central and South America

Argentina (ARG), Brazil (BRA), Antigua & Barbuda, Bahamas, Barbados, Belize, Costa Rica, Cuba, Dominica, Dominican Republic, El Salvador, Grenada, Guatemala, Haiti, Honduras, Jamaica, Nicaragua, Panama, St. Kitts & Nevis, St. Lucia, St. Vincent, Trinidad & Tobago (CAM), Chile (CHL), Bolivia, Colombia, Ecuador, Guyana, Paraguay, Peru, Suriname, Uruguay, Venezuela (RSM)

10   MNA   Middle East and Northern Africa

Algeria, Bahrain, Egypt, Iran, Iraq, Israel, Jordan, Kuwait, Lebanon, Libya, Morocco, Oman, Qatar, Saudi Arabia, Syrian Arab Republic, Tunisia, United Arab Emirates, Yemen Arab Republic (MEA)

11   NFT   North American Free Trade Area

Canada (CAN), Mexico (MEX), United States of America (USA)

12   NIS   Newly Independent States

Armenia, Azerbaijan, Belarus, Estonia, Georgia, Kazakhstan, Kyrgyz Republic, Latvia, Lithuania, Moldova, Russian Federation, Tajikistan, Turkmenistan, Ukraine, Uzbekistan (FSU)

13   RAS   Rest of South Asia

Bangladesh, Bhutan, Maldives, Nepal, Pakistan, Sri Lanka (RAS)

14   ROW   Rest of the World

Afghanistan, Albania, Andorra, Bosnia-Herzegovina, Brunei, Cambodia, Croatia, Cyprus, Fiji, Kiribati, Laos, Leichtenstein, Macedonia [former Yugoslav Republic of], Malta, Monaco, Mongolia, Myanmar, Nauru, North Korea, Papua New Guinea, San Marino, Solomon Islands, Tonga, Turkey, Tuvalu, Vanuatu, Vietnam, Western Samoa, Yugoslavia [Serbia and Montenegro]) (ROW)

15   SSA   Sub-Saharan Africa

Angola, Benin, Botswana, Burkina Faso, Burundi, Cameroon, Cape Verde, Central African Republic, Chad, Comoros, Republic of the Congo, Democratic Republic of the Congo (formerly Zaïre), Côte d'Ivoire, Djibouti, Equatorial Guinea, Eritrea, Ethiopia, Gabon, Gambia, Ghana, Guinea, Guinea-Bissau, Kenya, Lesotho, Liberia, Madagascar, Malawi, Mali, Mauritania, Mauritius, Mozambique, Namibia, Niger, Nigeria, Rwanda, Sao Tome & Principe, Senegal, Seychelles Islands, Sierra Leone, Somalia, South Africa, Sudan, Swaziland, Tanzania, Togo, Uganda, Zambia, Zimbabwe (SSA)

Aggregate Regions

1   OECD ANZ, ECE, EUR, JPN, and NFT

2   Asia   CHN, DAE, IDN, IND, and RAS

3   Other   LAT, MNA, NIS, ROW, and SSA

Sectoral Concordance for the LINKAGE Model[3]

1   Rice   Paddy rice

Agricultural & livestock production (paddy rice only): 1110, Agricultural services (servicing paddy rice production only): 1120 (PDR)

2   Wheat Wheat

Agricultural & livestock production (wheat only): 1110, Agricultural services (servicing wheat production only): 1120 (WHT)

3   OGrains Other grains

Agricultural & livestock production (grains except wheat & rice only): 1110, Agricultural services (servicing production of grains, except wheat & rice only):1120 (GRO)

4   Livst   Livestock products

Agricultural & livestock production (wool only): 1110, Agricultural services (servicing wool production only): 1120 (WOL), Agricultural & livestock production (other livestock production only): 1110, Agricultural services (servicing other livestock production only): 1120, Hunting, trapping & game propagation: 1130 (OLP)

5   OAgric Other agriculture

Agricultural & livestock production (non-grain crops only): 1110, Agricultural services (servicing non-grain crops production only): 1120 (NGC), Forestry: 1210, Logging: 1220 (FOR)

6   Coal   Coal

Coal mining: 2100, Manufacture of miscellaneous products of petroleum and coal (briquettes only): 3540 (COL)

7   Oil   Crude oil

Crude petroleum & natural gas production (oil only): 2200 (OIL)

8   Gas   Natural gas

Crude petroleum & natural gas production (gas only): 2200, Petroleum refineries (LPG only): 3530 (GAS)

9   OMining Other mining

>Iron ore mining: 2301, Non-ferrous ore mining: 2302, Stone quarrying, clay and pits: 2901, Chemical and fertilizer mineral mining:2902, Salt mining: 2903, Mining and quarrying n.e.c.: 2909 (OMN)

10   PrRice Processed Rice

>Grain mill products (processed rice only): 3116 (PCR)

11   MeatProd Meat Products

>Slaughtering, preparing and preserving meat: 3111 (MET)

12   Dairy   Dairy Products

>Manufacture of dairy products: 3112 (MIL)

13   BevTob Beverages and Tobacco

>Distilling, rectifying & blending spirits: 3131, Wine industries: 3132, Malt liquors and malt: 3133, Soft drinks & carbonated waters industries: 3134, Tobacco manufactures: 3140 (B_T)

14   OFdProc Other Food Processing

>Ocean and coastal fishing: 1301, Fishing n.e.c.: 1302 (FSH), Canning and preserving of fruits and vegetables: 3113, Canning, preserving & processing of fish, crustaceans and similar foods: 3114, Manufacture of vegetable and animal oils & fats: 3115, Grain mill products (except processed rice): 3116, Manufacture of bakery products: 3117, factories and refineries: 3118, Manufacture of cocoa, chocolate & sugar confectionery: 3119, Manufacture of food products n.e.c.: 3121, Manufacture of prepared animal feeds: 3122 (OFP)

15   Textile Textiles

>Spinning, weaving & finishing textiles: 3211, Manufacture of made-up textile goods excluding wearing apparel: 3212, Knitting mills: 3213, Manufacture of carpets & rugs: 3214, Cordage, rope & twine industries: 3215, Manufacture of textiles n.e.c.: 3219 (TEX)

16   Apparel Apparel, leather, and footwear

>Manufacture of wearing apparel, except footwear: 3220 (WAP), Tanneries & leather finishing: 3231, Fur dressing & dyeing industries: 3232, Manufacture of products of leather & leather substitutes, except footwear and wearing apparel: 3233, Manufacture of footwear, except vulcanised or moulded rubber or plastic footwear: 3240 (LEA)

17   PulpPa Pulp and Paper

>Manufacture of pulp, paper & paperboard: 3411, Manufacture of containers & boxes of paper and paperboard: 3412, Manufacture of pulp, paper & paperboard articles n.e.c.: 3419, Printing, publishing & allied industries: 3420, 3710 (PPP)

18   IronSteel Iron and Steel

Iron and steel basic industries: 3710 (I_S)

19   NFMet Non-ferrous basic metals

Non-ferrous metal basic industries: 3720 (NFM)

20   RefOil Refined oil

Petroleum refineries (except LPG): 2530, Manufacture of miscellaneous products of petroleum and coal (except briquettes): 3540 (P_C)

21   ChemPlast Chemical and plastics

Manufacture of basic industrial chemicals except fertilisers: 3511, Manufacture of fertilizers and pesticides: 3512, Manufacture of synthetic resins, plastic materials and man-made fibres except glass: 3513, Manufacture of paints, varnishes and lacquers: 3521, Manufacture of drugs and medicines: 3522, Manufacture of soap and cleaning preparations, perfumes and cosmetics: 3523, Manufacture of chemical products n.e.c.: 3529, Tyre and tube industries: 3551, Manufacture of rubber products n.e.c.: 3559, Manufacture of plastic products n.e.c.: 3560 (CRP)

22   TrpEqpt Transport equipment

Shipbuilding and shiprepairing: 3841, Manufacture of railroad equipment:3842,Manufacture of motor vehicles: 3843, Manufacture of motorcycles and bicycles: 3844, Manufacture of aircraft: 3745, Manufacture of transport equipment n.e.c.: 3849 (TRN)

23   OthManu Other manufacturing

Sawmills, planing & other wood mills, Manufacture of wooden & cane containers & small cane ware: 3312, Manufacture of wood & cork products n.e.c.: 3319, Manufacture of furniture & fixtures, except primarily of metal: 3320 (LUM), Manufacture of pottery, china and earthenware: 3610, Manufacture of glass and glass products: 3620, Manufacture of structural clay compounds: 3691, Manufacture of cement, lime and plaster:3692, Manufacture of non-metallic mineral products n.e.c.: 3699 (NMM), Manufacture of cutlery, hand tools and general hardware: 3811, Manufacture of furniture and fixtures primarily of metal: 3812, Manufacture of structural metal products: 3813, Manufacture of fabricated metal products except machinery & equipment n.e.c.: 3819 (FMP), Manufacture of engines and turbines: 3821, Manufacture of agricultural machinery and equipment: 3822, Manufacture of metal and wood working machinery: 3823, Manufacture of special industrial machinery and equipment except metal and wood working machinery: 3824, Manufacture of office, computing and accounting machinery: 3825, Machinery and equipment except electrical n.e.c.: 3829, Manufacture of electrical industrial machinery and apparatus: 3831, Manufacture of radio, television and communication equipment and apparatus: 3832, Manufacture of electrical appliances and housewares: 3833, Manufacture of electrical apparatus and supplies n.e.c.: 3839, Manufacture of professional and scientific, and measuring and controlling equipment, n.e.c.: 3851, Manufacture of photographic and optical goods: 3852, Manufacture of watches and clocks: 3853 (OME), Manufacture of jewellery and related articles: 3901, Manufacture of musical instruments: 3902, Manufacture of sporting and athletic goods: 3903, Manufacturing industries n.e.c.: 3909 (OMF)

| 24 | Elec | Electricity, gas distribution and water |

Electric light and power: 4101, Gas manufacture and distribution: 4102, Steam and hot water supply: 4103, Water works and supply: 4200 (EGW)

| 25 | Constr | Construction |

Construction: 5000 (CNS)

| 26 | NCA | All other goods and services |

Wholesale trade: 6100, Retail trade: 6200, Restaurants, cafes, and other eating and drinking places: 6310, Hotels, rooming houses, camps and other lodging places: 6320, Railway transport: 7111, Urban, suburban and inter-urban highway passenger transport: 7112, Other passenger land transport: 7113, Freight transport by road: 7114, Pipeline transport: 7115, Supporting services to land transport: 7116, Ocean and coastal transport: 7121, Inland water transport: 7122, Supporting services to water transport: 7123, Air transport carriers: 7131, Supporting services to air transport: 7132, Services incidental to transport: 7191, Storage and warehousing: 7192, Communication: 7200 (T_T), Activities not adequately defined: 0000, Monetary institutions: 8101, Other financial institutions: 8102, Financial services: 8103, Insurance: 8200, Real estate: 8310, Legal services: 8321, Accounting, auditing and bookkeeping services: 8322, Data processing and tabulating services: 8323, Engineering, architectural and technical services: 8324, Advertising services: 8325, Business services, except machinery and equipment rental and leasing, n.e.c.: 8329, Machinery and equipment rental and leasing: 8330, Motion picture production: 9411, Motion picture distribution and projection: 9412, Radio and television broadcasting: 9413, Theatrical producers and entertainment services: 9414, Authors, music composers and other independent artists n.e.c.: 9415, Libraries, museums, botanical and zoological gardens, and other cultural services, n.e.c.: 9420, Amusement and recreational services n.e.c.: 9490, Repair of footwear and other leather goods: 9511, Electrical repair shops: 9512, Repair of motor vehicles and motorcycles: 9513, Watch, clock and jewellery repair: 9514, Other repair shops n.e.c.: 9519, Laundries, laundry services, and cleaning and dyeing plants: 9520, Domestic services: 9530, Barber and beauty shops: 9591, Photographic studios, including commercial photography: 9592, Personal services n.e.c.: 9599 (OSP), Public administration and defence: 9100, Sanitary and similar services: 9200,Education services: 9310, Research and scientific institutes: 9320 Medical, dental and other health services: 9331, Veterinary services: 9332, Welfare institutions: 9340, Business, professional and labour associations: 9350,Religious organisations: 9391, Social and related community services n.e.c.: 9399, International and other extra-territorial bodies: 9600 (OSG), Dwellings (DWE).

Aggregate Sectors

1	LA	Rice, Wheat, OGrains, Livst, OAgric. PrRice, MeatProd, Dairy, BevTob, OFdProc
2	RE	Coal, Oil, Gas, OMining
3	CO	Textile, Apparel, ChemPlast,
4	IM	PulpPap, IronSteel, NFMet, RefOil
5	KA	TrpEqpt, OthManu
6	SH	Elec, Constr, NCA

Notes and References

1. For a more complete description of GTAP, see Hertel (1997).

2. GTAP acronym in parenthesis.

3. GTAP acronym in parenthesis, and ISIC sectors in detailed description.

Bibliography

ARMINGTON, P. (1969), "A Theory of Demand for Products Distinguished by Place of Production", *IMF Staff Papers*, Vol. 16.

BALLAD, C.L., D. FULLERTON, J.B. SHOVEN, AND J. WHALLEY (1985), *A General Equilibrium Model for Tax Policy Evaluation*, The University of Chicago Press, Chicago.

BRITISH PETROLEUM (various years), *BP Statistical Review of World Energy*, The British Petroleum Company, p.l.c., London.

BURNIAUX, J.-M., J.P. MARTIN, G. NICOLETTI, J. OLIVEIRA-MARTINS (1992), "GREEN — A Multi-Sector, Multi-Region Dynamic General Equilibrium Model for Quantifying the Costs of Curbing CO_2 Emissions: A Technical Manual", *OECD Economics Department Working Papers*, No. 116, OECD, Paris.

BURNIAUX, J.-M., AND D. VAN DER MENSBRUGGHE (1994), "The RUNS Global Trade Model", *Economic and Financial Modelling*, Autumn/Winter.

DRYSDALE, P. AND R. GARNAUT (1993), "The Pacific: An Application of a General Theory of Economic Integration", in C.F. BERGSTEN AND M. NOLAND (eds.), *Pacific Dynamism and the International Economic System*, Institute for International Economics, Washington, D.C.

EMF 14 (1995), "Second Round Study Design for EMF 14: Integrated Assessment of Climate Change", mimeo, Energy Modeling Forum, Stanford University, Stanford, CA.

FRANCOIS, J.F. AND K.A. REINERT (1997), *Applied Methods for Trade Policy Analysis: A Handbook*, Cambridge University Press, New York, NY.

FULLERTON, D. (1983), "Transition Losses of Partially Mobile Industry-specific Capital", *Quarterly Journal of Economics*, Vol. 98, February.

GUNNING, J.Q. AND M.A. KEYSER (1995), "Applied General Equilibrium Models for Policy Analysis", in T.N. SRINIVASAN AND J. BEHRMAN (eds.), *Handbook of Development Economics*, Vol. IIIA, North-Holland, Amsterdam.

HERTEL, T.W. (ed.) (1997), *Global Trade Analysis: Modeling and Applications*, Cambridge University Press, New York, NY.

HOWE, H. (1975), "Development of the Extended Linear Expenditure System from Simple Savings Assumptions", *European Economic Review*, Vol. 6.

INTERNATIONAL ENERGY AGENCY (1996), *Global Offshore Oil Prospects to 2000*, OECD/IEA, Paris.

LEE, H., J. OLIVEIRA-MARTINS, AND D. VAN DER MENSBRUGGHE (1994), "The OECD Green Model: An Updated Overview", *Technical Papers*, No. 97, OECD Development Centre, Paris.

LEE, H. AND D. ROLAND-HOLST (1995), "Trade Liberalization and Employment Linkages in the Pacific Basin", *Developing Economies*, No. 33.

LEE, H. AND D. ROLAND-HOLST (1996), "CGE Modelling of Trade and Employment in Pacific Rim Countries", in J.E. TAYLOR, editor, *Development Strategy, Employment, and Migration: Insights from Models*, OECD, Paris.

LEE, H., D. ROLAND-HOLST, AND D. VAN DER MENSBRUGGHE (1997), "APEC Trade Liberalization and Structural Adjustment: Policy Assessments", *APEC Discussion Paper Series*, No. 11, APEC Study Center, Graduate School of International Development, Nagoya University and the Institute of Developing Economies, Nagoya, Japan.

LLUCH, C. (1973), "The Extended Linear Expenditure System", *European Economic Review*, Vol. 4.

OECD (1997*a*), *The World in 2020: Towards a New Global Age*, Paris.

OECD (1997*b*), "The LINKAGE Model, A Technical Note", CD/R(97)2, Paris.

UNITED NATIONS (various editions), *World Population Prospects*, New York.

A Comment

Michel Fouquin

For several years there has been renewed interest in global economic projections after a period of disinterest going back to the 1970s. The skepticism of the 1970s was probably caused by the great, hitherto unknown, volatility of some strategic variables, of oil prices and exchange rates, to mention only the two most important. It was assumed that this volatility made it impossible to consider the long term, and it would be better to concentrate on the short term. Unfortunately, short-term projections also turned out to be disappointing, and all the analysts underestimated the 1991 crisis.

Why has interest in the long term revived? On the one hand it was realised the world is now integrated; on the other hand it was also recognised that there were major trends in the world economy besides short-term changes and that it was interesting to measure their possible impact. Little by little, the public also realised that economic projections contributed to understanding and they were not mere predictions.

The two long-term economic projections made using computable general equilibrium models presented in this volume are very impressive from the standpoint of the size of models and their expressed aims. Frank Harrigan's work was done for the Asian Development Bank. This economic projection was based on a world model of implicit conditional convergence: long-term growth profiles were deduced from the given initial conditions of growth for large regions. There is considerable recent literature on these themes. Researchers try to understand why some countries catch up to most advanced countries and others do not.

Harrigan does not discuss the quantitative link between structural conditions and growth profiles. More precisely, how did the Southeast Asian countries shift from low or average growth countries to the high-growth countries?

The best explanation for this hypothesis involves policy changes in Southeast Asia. Everyone wanted these policies to succeed but that is not certain. In any case, the link was not clearly explained. If it is not a normative hypothesis, it is unfortunate that it was not more explicit for this involves the exercise's credibility.

The Chinese and Vietnamese experience shows that agricultural liberalisation could be a key aspect of success in the very poor and mainly agricultural countries of South Asia. Is this region, whose rural society has some similarities with China and Vietnam, about to have sustained agricultural development? It is necessary to be explicit about the conditions of this success. Thus Harrigan's exercise should be interpreted as a simulation of the possible impact of accelerated development of Asia.

Dominique van der Mensbrugghe's presentation almost appears to be more ambitious than the former. It presents a large amount of exceedingly interesting statistical results which have been very clearly summarised. The work is remarkable and useful. However, the criticism of Harrigan's work also applies here. It is not very clear how the working hypotheses for the projection were constructed. It seems that they are mainly based on exogenous hypotheses of productivity growth. From this standpoint, the presentation has the merit of being more frank than the previous one, but it remains just as arbitrary. Once again, it is important to clarify the implicit model which made it possible to construct the exogenous hypotheses. That is practically not done, except for China.

The idea is that reform of the state enterprise sector is going to balance the development of the modern, competitive sector, which will lead to some stagnation of manufacturing employment in total employment. That is interesting but not necessarily convincing. It could also be argued that there will be a gradual fusion or absorption of part of the state sector with the private economy whose dynamism will then encompass everything.

What can be concluded from these two presentations? Above all, they are two possible pictures of the world and Asia in 2020. The statistical work is important. What should it be used for? In this respect, we note the work carried out at CEPII, even if it is much more modest than these presentations. We tried to simulate a shock of the emerging countries on European employment and wages via foreign trade[1]. For this purpose the world was divided into three parts: the European countries, Asia and the rest of the world. Obviously there is little geographic detail involved. But that enabled us to show that the impact of a doubling of the size of emerging countries on the world economy and on Europe, while having the expected sign, was not very large (wages and employment of unskilled workers decrease in developed countries and increase in the emerging countries, etc.). It seems that a variant of a computable general equilibrium model would be the best possible use for this type of model, whose central projection can be considered as making the hypotheses consistent with multiple interactions to determine plausible orders of magnitude.

Note

1.	See O. Cortes and S. Jean (CEPII), "Does Competition from Emerging Countries Threaten European Unskilled Labour?" EIAS Workshop, Macmillan (forthcoming).

Can the Ageing OECD Escape Demography through Capital Flows to Emerging Markets?

Helmut Reisen

Demographic Trends Inside and Outside the Ageing OECD Area

Despite some uncertainties in forecasting demographic trends over the next 50 or so years, uncertainties which are mostly due to assumed changes in fertility rates, some demographic trends can be predicted with a high degree of confidence. Three salient aspects deserve to be highlighted, because of their great importance for the future economic interdependence between the ageing OECD[1] and the non-OECD area:

— While population ageing is a global phenomenon, OECD populations are ageing from the "middle" of the age pyramid, in contrast to non-OECD which is ageing from the "bottom". In other words, the prospective demographic changes imply divergent trends in labour force growth across the two regions (Figure 1). Labour force growth rates will sharply decline in the ageing OECD area and turn negative after 2010. In strong contrast, ageing combined with rising participation is increasing the labour force in the non-OECD area; the proportion of the working-age group in the total non-OECD population will roughly remain constant.

— Ageing from the "middle", the ageing OECD area will face a strong drop in the support ratio of workers to retirees, in particular after 2010. Likewise, the support ratio will start to fall in the non-OECD area, but from much higher levels than in the OECD area (Figure 2).

— A much-neglected aspect of prospective demographic changes is that they will shift the balance between the age groups that may be characterised as net borrowers and net savers. Changes in the age composition of the population will have consequences for the rate of net financial asset accumulation and the rate of return on financial assets. The United States shows relatively high household savings in the high-income age cohorts (40-60), whereas net savings in the other age cohorts is low or negative (Attanasio, 1994). As the "baby boom" generation filters through its peak asset accumulation years, the ratio of prime savers to the working age population will rise until the year 2007 and then decline. For the entire ageing OECD, the prime savers ratio will peak somewhat later (2015), before it starts to drop. By contrast, the rise of the prime savers ratio in the rest of the world, which started around 1990, will not halt before the year 2050 (Figure 3).

129

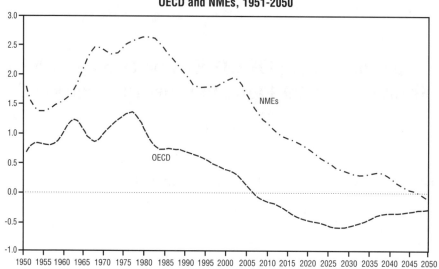

Figure 1. **Relative Change of Labour Force (= Age Group 15-60) OECD and NMEs, 1951-2050**

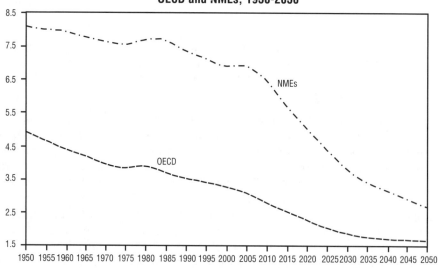

Figure 2. **Support Ratio = Age Group (15-60) / Age Group 60++ OECD and NMEs, 1950-2050**

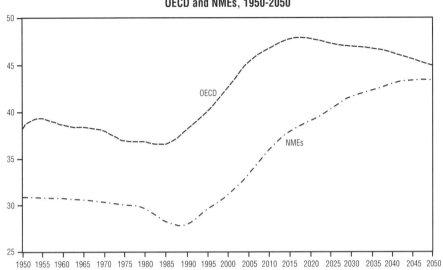

Figure 3. **Prime Savers Ratio = Age Group (40-60) / Age Group (15-60)**
OECD and NMEs, 1950-2050

To see how the ageing OECD can benefit from the delayed ageing process in the non-OECD area, the above three demographic aspects will be analysed for their implications as suggested by neoclassical growth theory, prospective asset developments and modern portfolio theory.

The Demographic Impact on Capital Returns in Neoclassical Growth Models

The arithmetic of unfunded, earnings-related pensions is largely governed by changes in the support ratio and by real wage growth (which in turn depends on labour productivity in the long run). These pension arrangements are essentially locked into the ageing economy, unable to escape the prospective demographic pressures resulting from the expected drop in support ratios.

It is little understood, however, that even fully funded pension schemes will not escape demographic pressures in the absence of considerable capital flows (retirement-related or other) between the ageing OECD and the younger part of the world. The arithmetic of funded pensions (that are fully dynamic with respect to growth in labour productivity) can be described by the intertemporal budget constraint:

$$\int_0^{(1-a)T} sy_0 e^{-(r-g)t}\,dt - \int_{(1-a)T}^{T} c_0 e^{-(r-g)t}\,dt = 0 \qquad (1)$$

where $(1-a)T$ = years of pension contribution

aT = years of pension receipt

$r-g = \delta$ = discount rate, equal to the real rate of return less labour productivity growth

s = yearly rate of pension contribution

y_0 = real per capita income in year 0

c_0 = yearly pension level in 0

$v = cy$ = pension benefit c as share of per capita income

Integration of (1) yields

$$s = v\,(e^{\delta aT} - 1)/(e^{\delta T} - e^{\delta aT}) \qquad (2)$$

which links the yearly level of pension savings for a given pension level v to the rate of return and to the length aT of pension benefits. While it is obvious that higher life expectancy will put pressure on the arithmetic of funded pensions, the demographic changes highlighted above may well add to that pressure by driving down the rate of return on pension investments. A variety of general equilibrium analyses that employ the standard optimal growth model predict a decline in the rate of return on capital as a result of the projected decline in the labour force and support ratios in the ageing OECD area (Cutler, Poterba, Sheiner and Summers, 1990; Börsch-Supan, 1996; MacKellar and Bird, 1997).

The autarkic effect of higher age dependency in the OECD area is to lower output per capita relative to the case of no ageing and, with a lag, consumption per capita. Slower and negative labour force growth will reduce investment requirements, because it lowers the capital-widening investment demand. With a fixed saving rate, lower labour force growth promotes capital deepening, that is a rise in the capital-labour ratio. That, in turn, will lower the marginal productivity of capital, relative both to the rate of time preference and to the marginal productivity of labour. Lower capital productivity results in lower returns on savings, both in absolute terms and relative to real wages.

While there is little debate on the validity of the neoclassical argument spelled out above, there is little empirical evidence on the quantitative effects of prospective population ageing in the OECD area. Simulating the autarkic response[2] of the ageing OECD to the prospective drop in the support ratio and labour force growth, Börsch-Supan (1996) and MacKellar and Bird (1997) arrive at very similar results for the prospective rate of return to capital. While these rates of return, proxied by the rate of return to physical capital, are around 6 per cent in the 1990s baseline, they drop in both simulations by more than 200 basis points to the year 2020. Note that savings, which equal investment for the closed OECD economy, fall as a result of the excess capital stock when the labour force shrinks. If a shift from pay-as-you-go (PAYG) to funded pension schemes would instead stimulate savings as is sometimes maintained (e.g. Feldstein, 1996), the rate of return might even decline more than in these simulations. Börsch-Supan (1996) notes, moreover, that reasonable changes in the rate of technical progress will not change the overall results of a substantial decline in savings, investment and the rate of return in the long run.

Opening the closed OECD-wide economy to the younger non-OECD area will not fully compensate for the ageing-induced drop in prospective capital returns; the drop, however, will be strongly attenuated. The neoclassical growth model predicts that ageing countries can partially offset the reduction in the rate of return by exporting capital (excess savings) to younger economies where the rising labour force leads to higher demand for capital-widening investment. Moreover, age-induced differences in the growth rates of labour and capital will cause growth differentials to widen in favour of the younger economies. The demand for capital from the younger economies drives up interest rates relative to the autarkic case.

For the arithmetic of funded pensions, presented above in equations (1) and (2), full capital mobility will thus imply higher pension benefits for retirees in OECD Member countries as a result of higher rates of return. Moreover, in the standard growth model, the discount rate will be raised as a result of slower labour productivity growth as part of the capital is shifted away from OECD labour. In turn, the extra capital which equips labour in the non-OECD area will foster labour productivity there, thus lowering the rate of return on funded pensions in the non-OECD world relative to autarky. However, higher non-OECD wages should translate into higher retirement savings in the non-OECD region.

As a matter of illustration, the benefits of full capital mobility for funded OECD pensions can be assessed by inserting Börsch-Supan's (1996) simulation results into equation (2). By adding Southeast Asia and a hypothetical country the size of India to the OECD, the simulated general-equilibrium rate of return is raised to 5 per cent compared to 3.5 per cent in the closed OECD. Assuming 45 years of pension contribution and 15 years of pension receipt and annual growth in labour productivity of 2 per cent, the required saving rate to finance a pension level worth half per-capita income would be 6.6 per cent for the open OECD economy compared to 10.8 per cent for the autarkic OECD.

The Demographic Impact on Pension Fund Performance

The rate of return is proxied in the neoclassical growth model by the rate of return to physical capital, but institutional pension assets tend to be held in equities, bonds and real estate. The ageing process can be expected to affect the relative return on these broad asset classes; research on this is virtually non-existent. It can be hypothesised, however, that real estate prices should be negatively affected by a shrinking population; bond yields by the decline in investment needs as analysed in the growth models, and by higher relative bond demand as pension funds mature; and equity prices as lower growth will translate into lower corporate profits.

This section will focus on the life cycle and cohort effects that the US "baby-boom" generation is expected to exert on financial asset accumulation and then decumulation (McKinsey Global Institute, 1994; Attanasio, 1994). The strong baby-boomer cohort (those born between 1950 and 1967) is now between 47 and 30 years old. A large part of this cohort has now entered the period in the life cycle (40-60 years) when their liabilities are decreasing on average, and they are saving at higher rates from an increasing income. While it seems that the United States is the only major OECD country that fits the hump-shaped life-cycle saving profile postulated by standard economic theory (Börsch-Supan, 1996), the US case will be of major importance for financial-asset developments and returns. First, in 1992, US citizens held more than 40 per cent of the financial stock in the OECD area. Second, financial market returns in OECD countries (except Japan) are highly correlated with and governed by the US financial markets.

Figure 4 shows a strong increase in the ratio of the prime-saving cohort relative to the working-age population for the United States, up to the year 2007. While the ratio peaked first around 1960 at 40 per cent, it fell continuously until 1984 (to 32 per cent). Since then, the ratio has steadily risen and will continue to rise until 2007, when it will peak at 46 per cent. From then on, the prime savers ratio is projected to decline gently. As the baby-boom generation enters its peak asset accumulation years, a strong increase in the rate of net financial asset accumulation can be expected (McKinsey Global Institute, 1994). Allowing for cohort effects should reinforce the result because the large baby boom cohort is saving at higher rates at every age than earlier cohorts and saving from higher income levels (Attanasio, 1994). Likewise, the combination of life cycle effects and cohort effects implies that the rapid phase of financial asset accumulation will, ten years from now, give way to financial asset stagnation or even decumulation. Then, not only will the prime savers ratio decline, but the large baby boom cohort will start to retire and to draw on the accumulated pension assets, while the subsequent prime savers cohorts will be much smaller. The support ratio in the United States will soon start a strong decline, as can be seen from Figure 5.

Multiplying the prime savers ratio (40-60 years old/15-60 years old) by the support ratio (15-60 years old/60+) yields another ratio that relates the prime-savers cohort in the United States with the age cohort of people 60 years and older. This demographic variable, which corresponds to the peak asset accumulation relative to the peak asset decumulation cohorts according to the life cycle hypothesis, can be expected to influence financial asset accumulation and stock market valuations, at least in the United States. Indeed, it does.

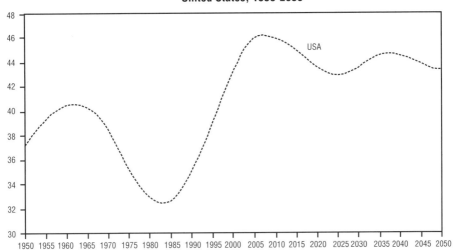

Figure 4. **Prime Savers Ratio = Age Group (40-60) / Age Group (15-60)**
United States, 1950-2050

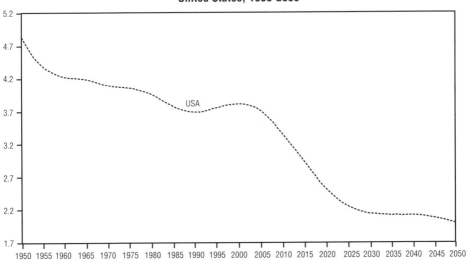

Figure 5. **Support Ratio = Age Group (15-60) / Age Group 60++**
United States, 1950-2050

Table 1 presents regression analysis for the determinants of Standard and Poor's 500 annual average price-earning ratio for the observation period 1977-96, based on 20 annual observations. The SP 500 P/E ratio is determined within a standard stock market valuation model, with the demographic variable (40-60 years old/60 years+), the (inverse of the) US Federal Reserve discount rate and the annual change in average hourly wages as explanatory variables. All these variables enter the regression with the expected sign and are significant at the 1 per cent level. The adjusted R^2 indicates model completeness, and the Durbin-Watson coefficient close to two indicates the absence of autocorrelation[3].

Table 1. **The S+P 500 Price/Earning Ratio and Demography**
(std. error in brackets)

Dependent variable	Explanatory variables		
SP 500 P/E ratio	Prime savers (40-60) as % of 60 years +	FRBNY Discount rate (inverse)	Change of hourly wages
	0.09***	46.1***	-1.5***
	(0.02)	(7.7)	(0.45)

Number of observations: 20
Period: 1977-96
Adjusted R^2: 0.88
Durbin-Watson: 1.98

*** =   significant at the 0.01 level

Sources: Own calculations based on data provided by Dresdner Bank (SP 500 P/E); UN Population data file; IMF, *International Financial Statistics* (items 60 and 65ey).

Beyond the importance of US interest rates in determining the price-earning ratio, the regression shows that US stock market valuations have been significantly supported by the rise in the prime savers ratio (since 1983). That favourable demographic support for valuations will not last long, however, as around the year 2000 the support ratio is projected to start a 30-year long decline, to be reinforced by the projected decline of the prime savers ratio from the year 2007. Figure 6 provides an out-of-sample forecast, assuming interest rates stay at the 1996 level and the hourly wage rises at the pace experienced over 1986-96. The out-of-sample scenario, which is fully driven by the ratio of prime savers to people older than 60, tells us that — other things being equal — the US stock market valuations will peak at a price-earning ratio of 20 and then start a long decline, before P/E ratios will stabilize at a level of around 14 around 2030. The prospective drop in the SP 500 P/E ratio would represent a decline of 30 per cent, on account of deteriorating demographic fundamentals.

While all this is highly speculative, it confirms earlier concerns (Schieber and Shoven, 1994) that, as US funded pensions cease to be a source of net savings, asset prices will be negatively affected[4]. This can reinforce the maturity-induced shift of pension portfolios from equities and long-term bonds into short-term securities or cash, as Schiefer and Shoven suggest, but it can also lead to a shift of equity portfolios into the younger economies where the prime savers ratio will continue to rise to the year 2050.

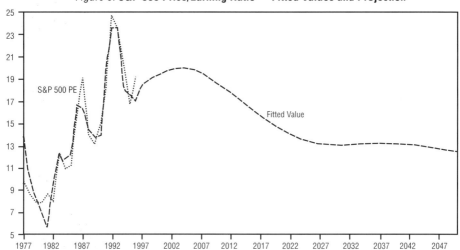

Figure 6. **S&P 500 Price/Earning Ratio — Fitted Values and Projection**

While the demographic trends (which can be anticipated well in advance) mean in the context of a closed OECD-wide economy prospective asset decumulation and lower financial returns, early asset diversification into the younger economies can change this gloomy outlook for funded pensions significantly. The effects of pension asset decumulation of the numerous baby boom cohort during their retirement years can be spread over emerging-market assets that still will benefit from net additions of the rising prime saver cohort in these younger economies. The diversification will also attenuate the retirement-induced run-down of OECD home assets and hence will help stabilize financial returns on OECD assets during the first half of the next century.

Global Diversification Benefits

Fully funded pension funds have so far been important (as a percentage of financial assets and GDP) in only a handful of OECD countries, such as the United States, the United Kingdom, the Netherlands and Switzerland. Nevertheless, at the end of 1990 funded pensions in the OECD area alone already had assets of more than $4 800 billion under their control. Taking into account country-specific demographic trends and the likely trends for asset appreciation and contributions, Davanzo and Kautz (1992) project an increase in OECD pension assets at an annual growth rate of over 10 per cent. US and British pensions are expected to grow at a slower rate because of their relative maturity. Continental Europe, still largely unfunded, and Japan, ageing most rapidly, will see their pension assets grow at higher speed. We can thus expect OECD pension funds to manage assets worth more than $12 000 billion by the year 2003. Pension assets will shape investment trends and capital flows around the world.

Table 2 documents the strong growth in OECD and non-OECD pension assets, the most important institutional vehicle for portfolio investments (equities and bonds). The table also shows that these are heavily invested into home assets (defined as assets held in the home country of the investor only) though the home bias in OECD assets has been reduced during the 1990s, including through investment into emerging markets. This latter trend should continue, because the emerging markets still offer much unexploited potential to improve the risk-adjusted returns of OECD pension assets or, put differently, to lower risk by eliminating non-systemic volatility without sacrificing expected return. It is less the superior growth performance of the non-OECD area than the low correlation of returns generated by the emerging stock markets with those of the OECD stock markets that governs this expectation (Reisen, 1994). The correlation between returns on OECD and emerging stock markets will remain low even when diversification gains are seriously exploited. Differences between the two areas with respect to the exposure to country-specific shocks, the stage of economic and demographic maturity and the (lack of) harmonization of economic policies suggest that the diversification gains for OECD pension assets will not disappear quickly. The benefits of global portfolio diversification also apply to emerging country pension assets as they could diversify away some of the risks stemming from high exposure to shocks in their own countries by investing some of their pension assets in OECD countries (Reisen, 1997).

Table 2. **The Home-Asset Preference in Funded Pension Assets**

	1990	1995[e]
Total Pension Assets, $ billion		
OECD	4 813	7 865
non-OECD	109	311
Home-Asset Share, percentage of Assets[a]		
OECD Pension Assets	92.8	88.9
non-OECD Pension Assets[b]	100.0	99.3

a.   Home assets share refers only to the share of assets invested in the home country of the investor.
b.   Excludes Hong Kong where the foreign asset share is 60 per cent.
c.   Estimate.
Source: InterSec Research Company

To be sure, emerging stock markets are risky — riskier as a group than the developed stock markets. What matters to the globally diversified investor, however, is not the local systemic risk but, rather, the contribution of the emerging markets to the riskiness of his total portfolio. The biggest diversification benefits that the emerging markets have offered in the past to the global investor have resided in the low (and at times negative) correlation of returns among the emerging stock markets themselves and *vis-à-vis* the developed stock markets (see, for example, Divecha *et al.*, 1992). By contrast, OECD stock markets are already highly integrated, with monthly returns displaying correlation coefficients on the order of 50 to 90 per cent. A key question for investors is whether stock markets in Asia and Latin America will continue to display low correlation with those in the industrialised countries (Mullin, 1993).

If anything, we observe a downward movement of the five-year averages of return correlations between the IFC Global Emerging Market Index, on the one hand, and the SP 500 and FT EuroPac indices on the other. Together they cover most of the OECD stock markets. The last published return correlation (for 1991 to 1996) between the IFC and the SP 500 index was 0.19, and for the FT EuroPac index it was 0.24. The evidence contradicts the hypothesis that the 1990s period of heavy equity flows to developing countries raised the correlation between OECD and non-OECD stock markets, and implies that the benefits from diversification of OECD pension assets into the emerging markets remain.

To the extent that average long-term returns in emerging markets are higher than in the mature OECD stock markets, OECD pension funds that put some of their assets (up to a fifth, see e.g. Reisen, 1994) into emerging markets will enjoy a "diversification free lunch", by both reducing overall portfolio volatility and by raising mean returns simultaneously. Only at a greater emerging-market share in the global portfolio does the proposition that higher returns can only be obtained at the price of higher volatility become operative.

Prospective Pension Flows

OECD pension funds are unlikely to abandon completely their preference for home assets, since that preference is not entirely explained by policy distortions (see below). First, investors who hold shares of domestic-based multinationals obtain some degree of global portfolio diversification. Second, pension fund managers bear more downside risk than the pension beneficiaries, since their contracts are fully exposed to shortfall risk while they do not fully capture the upside potential of their investment decisions; consequently, they prefer safe domestic assets. Third, pension funds have to align the mix of their asset holdings to the structure of their liabilities; mature pension funds, particularly if they are at risk of actuarial insolvency, will shy away from instruments that entail currency risk and potential capital loss, and instead will prefer domestic bonds. Fourth, and perhaps most importantly, to the extent that pensioners consume non-traded goods (such as health services) rather than traded goods, pension assets will be biased towards home securities. Pension fund managers may therefore seek a foreign exposure comparable to the traded-goods proportion of the basket of goods consumed by the typical pensioner. In countries where pension funds are not constrained by domestic regulation, we observe a fairly good correlation between the import ratio and the share of foreign assets held in institutional portfolios (see Figure 7). Foreign assets provide a hedge against imported inflation, and global diversification seems less governed by the principle of maximising risk-adjusted returns than by maintaining the future purchasing power of pension assets.

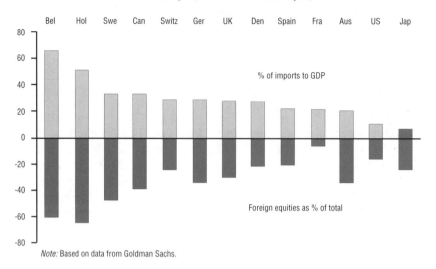

Figure 7. **Share of Foreign Equities in Total Equity Assets Held by OECD Pension Funds, Compared to the Share of Imports Relative to GDP**

Note: Based on data from Goldman Sachs.

For all these reasons, institutional investors have never held the world portfolio (with asset shares in accordance to country shares in world stock market capitalisation), as suggested by modern portfolio theory for fully integrated and efficient capital markets. They are unlikely to do so in the year 2020, either.

The OECD study, *The World in 2020: Towards A New Global Age* (OECD, 1997) provides back-of-the-envelope calculations to estimate future gross investment flows by OECD pension funds into non-Member economies. One scenario envisages a significant move towards a portfolio mix reflecting country shares in world stock market capitalisation (a world- portfolio-based strategy). In this scenario, there would be a substantial reduction in the home asset bias of OECD institutional investors (i.e. a halving by 2020) but some home asset bias would remain (as explained above). As an alternative scenario, pension fund managers would seek to maintain the future purchasing power of pension assets.

Based on these two diversification scenarios, it is estimated that by the year 2020, a minimum of 8.5 per cent of total OECD pension assets would be invested in the non-OECD area, implying an annual gross transfer — if unhedged — of $20 billion (in 2000) and $35 billion (in 2020) into emerging markets (see Box 1). The real rate of return of OECD pension assets would rise from 2.8 to 3 per cent (a 7.2 per cent rise). The increase in the rate of return would imply a rise in pension benefits of at least 2.5 per cent because of the gradual build-up of assets invested in emerging economies. Among OECD countries, the largest gains would accrue to countries that quickly build a sizeable stock of assets in emerging economies.

Box 1. **Alternative Scenarios for Future Pension Funds Investment**

There has been much speculation concerning the gains that could be expected from international diversification by OECD pension funds in emerging markets. Based on the following illustrative numerical exercise, we reach the following conclusions:

- Gross portfolio investments by OECD pension funds into emerging economies to 2020 would raise the average portfolio return by 0.19 per cent (when assuming a diversification strategy based on maintaining the future purchasing power of OECD pension assets) and by 0.54 per cent (when assuming a strategy based on world portfolio diversification and a home bias cut by half) over the next 25 years.

- The purchasing power strategy would require one-tenth of future new contributions to be invested in emerging markets. The net gain in total assets would amount at a minimum to $600 billion in 2020 (1.5 per cent of OECD GDP), thanks to higher capital returns in emerging markets. The increase in pension benefits would amount to 2.5 per cent in 2020.

Two scenarios for pension fund investments in emerging markets under a HG scenario
(per cent)

	Portfolio diversification strategy (determines the share of assets held in emerging markets in total pension fund assets in 2020)	
	Partial world portfolio diversification – fully-fledged liberalisation in NMEs and half-reduced home asset bias –	Purchasing power diversification – maintaining retirees' future consumption purchasing power –
	(25.5)	(8.5)
Share of new contributions to be invested in emerging markets (to move gradually to desired portfolio diversification by 2020)	46.9	9.6
Increase in the average rate of return on pension fund assets (due to international portfolio diversification)	+0.54	+0.19
Change in pension benefits (due to higher capital returns in emerging markets)	+7.7	+2.5

Note: In both cases, the rate of return differential is assumed to be equal to the future GDP growth differential between OECD and non-OECD, i.e. 3.7 per cent per annum. We assume that new contributions in OECD countries will amount to 1 per cent of GDP per annum until 2020.

Source: OECD, 1997.

In order to realise the mutual benefits of shifting OECD pension assets from ageing to emerging markets, policy makers will have to remove important regulatory and market barriers. The challenge for regulators in OECD countries is to free pension assets so that they will be able to seek the best mix of risk and return. The excessive home bias of OECD pension assets will only be corrected when policy makers, in particular in most of Continental Europe, remove localisation requirements and requirements of currency matching. A helpful step would be to proceed with an early application of the discipline of the OECD Codes of Liberalisation to portfolio investment abroad by insurance companies and private pension funds. An adequate representation of the emerging stock markets in the performance benchmarks relevant to the pension industry is also required.

In non-OECD economies, the agenda for reforms is much fuller. Many such economies still have excessive state intervention in the banking system, illiquid and poorly regulated stock-markets and over-regulated institutional investors. The challenge to policy makers in the non-OECD countries will be to remove discriminatory capital controls and restrictions to market access by foreign investors and institutions, to enact appropriate regulations and develop modern infrastructure for securities markets. Regulators in non-OECD countries also need to foster the deepening of domestic stock markets in order to deal with the illiquidity concern of institutional investors. Important ways to increase the supply of new stocks are the privatisation of public sector companies and bringing privately held companies to the market.

Notes and References

1. Some OECD member countries, notably Ireland, Korea, Mexico and Turkey, are excluded from the definition of "ageing OECD"since they tend to share the demographic features of the non-OECD world.

2. Under the premise that it is possible to suppress trade with and capital flows to countries outside the OECD area.

3. Since SP 500 price-earning ratios were only available from the year 1977 onwards, a similar regression for the consumer price index adjusted SP 500 index was performed for the period 1950-1996. After correcting for autocorrelation, the regression test statistics were very similar to the ones reported here, with a high adjusted R^2, a Durbin-Watson coefficient close to 2, and with all three explanatory variables highly significant.

4. While Schieber and Shoven's (1994) pension saving model predicts that pension benefits will first exceed contributions in 2006, they expect net asset decumulation at around 2030, thanks to annual investment income on accumulated pension assets.

Bibliography

ATTANASIO, O. (1994), "Household Saving in the US", in J. POTERBA (ed.), *International Comparisons of Household Savings*, University of Chicago Press, Chicago.

BÖRSCH-SUPAN, A. (1996), "The Impact of Population Ageing on Savings, Investment and Growth in the OECD Area", in OECD (1996) (ed.), *Future Global Capital Shortages: Real Threat or Pure Fiction?*, Paris.

CUTLER, D., J. POTERBA, L. SHEINER AND L. SUMMERS (1990), "An Ageing Society: Opportunity or Challenge?", *Brookings Papers on Economic Activity*, 1.

DAVANZO, L. AND L. KAUTZ, (1992), "Toward a Global Pension Market", *The Journal of Portfolio Management*, Summer.

DIVECHA, A, J. DRACH AND D. STEEK (1992), "Emerging Markets: A Quantitative Perspective", *The Journal of Portfolio Management*, Autumn.

FELDSTEIN, M. (1996), "The Missing Piece in Policy Analysis: Social Security Reform", *NBER Working Paper*, No. 5413.

MACKELLAR, L. AND R. BIRD (1997), "Global Population Ageing, Social Security and Economic Growth: Some Results from a 2-Region Model", mimeo.

MCKINSEY GLOBAL INSTITUTE (1994), *The Global Capital Market: Supply, Demand, Pricing and Allocation*, Washington, D.C.

MULLIN, J. (1993), "Emerging Equity Markets in the Global Economy", *FRBNY Quarterly Review*, Summer .

OECD (1997), *The World in 2020: Towards A New Global Age*, Paris.

REISEN, H. (1994), "On the Wealth of Nations and Retirees", in R. O'BRIEN (ed.), *Finance and the International Economy, 8*, The Amex Bank Review Prize Essays, Oxford University Press.

REISEN, H. (1997), "Liberalising Foreign Investments by Pension Funds: Positive and Normative Aspects", *World Development*, July.

SCHIEBER, S. AND J. SHOVEN (1994), "The Consequences of Population Ageing on Private Pension Fund Saving and Asset Markets", *NBER Working Paper*, No. 4665.

A Comment

Hans J. Blommestein

The answer to Helmut Reisen's question "Can the Ageing OECD Countries Escape Demography through Capital Flows to the Emerging Markets?" is that ageing-induced capital flows to emerging markets cannot solve the OECD countries' basic pension problem. The following arguments are based on both methodological and technical considerations.

Methodological Problems in Predicting Long-Term Trends

This thought-provoking paper focuses on key challenges facing OECD country policy makers in the coming decades in the area of the "economics of ageing populations". It is an excellent example of using economic analysis for peering into the future. Unfortunately, social scientists are almost always wrong when they try to predict future events and trends and economists are no exception. The epistemological reasons do not concern us here but they are important in explaining why the forecasting of long-term trends (demographic trends, labour force growth, the rate of net financial asset accumulation and the rate of return of financial assets over the next 50 years or so) is fraught with huge uncertainties. Enough to be careful in interpreting and accepting the simulation evidence presented in the paper. In this context, it is instructive to recall the fate of previous long-term projections such as the ones produced by the Club of Rome in the 1970s: they were dead wrong. Economists may be right about the direction of changing trends but they usually are completely wrong about the timing and size of these changes.

Funded Systems and Portfolio Diversification

In spite of these methodological problems in forecasting future trends, Helmut Reisen's study convincingly demonstrates:

i) Integration of financial markets of non-OECD countries into the OECD countries' financial area is beneficial for both the ageing OECD countries and the younger non-OECD economies.

ii) Asset diversification by OECD country pension funds into the younger non-OECD economies is a potentially sensible strategy. An interesting point in the paper is that it may also be sensible for non-OECD country pension funds to invest in the ageing OECD area.

iii) Fully funded systems probably cannot completely escape the demographic pressures of "baby boom bubbles". What has not been convincingly demonstrated is the seriousness of the problem.

The Basic Pension Problem

In order to comment on some of the issues raised in the paper, we begin with the "basic pension problem", regardless of the presence of pay-as-you-go (PAYG) or funded systems. The key issue in *all* retirement programmes is the availability of physical resources.

The financing of any pension system (funded, non-funded, public or private) merely facilitates the allocation of real resources that fund the consumption of goods and services during retirement. There is a pension problem when there is a (an expected) short-fall in resources needed for retirement consumption purposes.

Demographic Pressures on Funded Pension Systems

The paper focuses on the projected shortfall in real resources as a result of the demographic pressure of the "baby boom bubble" on funded pension systems in the OECD area. The paper presents two main arguments why it is beneficial for OECD pension funds to invest in the younger non-OECD economies.

The *first argument* is based on a simple neo-classical growth model. The paper notes that demographic pressures will drive down the rate of return on pension investments in the OECD area. It is not impossible that this will happen and it is perhaps even likely. However, the case for this scenario is not as strong as the author suggests. Ergo, the potentially beneficial effects of investing in the non-OECD area are less pronounced.

First, the quantitative evidence is weak since, by definition, it is based on crude projections about the distant future. On methodological grounds, for example, it is difficult to accept the paper's projected drop in the rate of return on capital of more than 200 basis points in the year 2020.

Second, an endogenous growth framework would allow a more optimistic perspective on productivity growth. But even in the neo-classical world, there is scope for higher capital productivity than suggested in the paper. The maturing of emerging technologies and further substantial deregulation of industry and finance, in themselves, will lead to an increase of the growth rate of productivity *without* large capital investment and savings. There are indications that years of heavy spending on new technology in many OECD countries is being translated into large productivity gains.

Indeed, savings and investment decisions are increasingly guided by market tests. It is likely that this will result in labour-saving investments (due to demographic developments) with improvements in productivity. (One could envisage growth based on scrapping older vintages of capital stock and replacing them by less labour-intensive, more productive vintages.)

Finally, in the emerging "knowledge economy", capital efficiency (and returns on physical capital) is becoming less of an engine of wealth creation. Investments in (and returns on) human capital are becoming progressively more important.

However, this line of argumentation weakens without necessarily invalidating the central point made in the paper: an ageing population is likely to reinforce the tendency for economic growth to slow gradually when the ratio of capital to labour rises and rates of return on new investment decline. Improvements in capital productivity from current rates sufficient to eliminate fully the ageing-induced funding gaps seem implausible. A solution to the "basic pension problem" requires not only an improvement in productivity but also an increase in domestic savings. In this respect, a switch from PAYG to a funded system leading to higher domestic savings, would be most welcome. This may, or may not, result in a decline in the rate of return on *physical* capital. (The paper states that the increased savings will result in a further decline in the rate of return.)

Assessing the Financial-Market Implications of Capital Exports to Emerging Markets

The paper's *second argument* is based on the consideration that demographic developments might make it sensible to export part of domestic OECD savings to younger non-OECD economies, in search of higher returns. However, the argument in favour of this portfolio reallocation process needs to be formulated very carefully.

First, as mentioned in the paper, many younger economies in the non-OECD area are not very attractive to invest in. Fragile banking systems, illiquid and poorly regulated stock markets, political risk, etc. may constitute a barrier for OECD pension funds and other institutional investors.

Second, it is not *a priori* clear that the portfolio reallocation process between OECD and non-OECD assets will improve the financial condition of OECD pension funds, even if the return on securities in the non-OECD area is higher. The portfolio reallocation process by itself does *not* induce new productive savings and investment. The reallocation could even induce great tensions on financial markets in the OECD area. (It could do the same in the emerging financial markets but this issue will not be analysed here.) If OECD pension funds are shifted from OECD securities (equity and debt instruments) to non-OECD securities, then holders of debt and equity instruments in the non-OECD area must be induced to exchange them, net, for OECD securities. (Current holders of non-OECD securities may include OECD pension funds!)

Moreover, if OECD pension funds achieved higher returns by investing in non-OECD securities than in lower-yielding OECD securities, OECD area incomes generated by their asset portfolios (including OECD pension funds) would *fall* by the same amount, potentially worsening the financial condition of OECD institutional investors. In order to induce a switch from OECD to non-OECD securities, the price of non-OECD securities must rise and OECD securities prices must fall. But, this could create considerable turbulence on financial markets. The total market value of OECD plus non-OECD securities is, to a first approximation, unlikely to be affected by a shift in the balance of paper claims.

One might speculate that the tension between the altered relative supply of non-OECD and OECD equities on the one hand, and unaltered overall economic value of companies in both the OECD and non-OECD areas on the other hand, would be resolved by an increase in the issuance of non-OECD securities relative to OECD securities. This could reverse much, if not all, of the price shift in favour of non-OECD securities.

This picture of changes in asset prices might become even more complex when the shift from government securities to private debt and equity instruments is taken into account, for example, in the context of the privatisation of social security systems. The negative impact of the portfolio reallocation process on OECD equity and bond prices reduces the potential diversification benefits for OECD pension funds to invest in non-OECD financial markets. Clearly, there is no easy ("free lunch") solution to the basic pension problem. Without an increase in productive OECD savings and an improvement in productivity, the shortfall in real resources needed for retirement consumption purposes is unlikely to be met by investing in younger economies.

Meeting the Human Capital Needs of Maturing Asian Economies

Sanjaya Lall*

Introduction

Many of the high-performing economies of Asia are "growing up", and maturity will bring its own set of problems. Further rapid growth may prove more difficult, growing prosperity may induce complacency, the unevenness of past development may create stresses, and the institutional framework may not keep up with emerging social and political structures. It is clear in the industrialised world that economic challenges do not cease with maturity — they merely take other forms. Driven by the relentless march of technology and globalisation and rising universal aspirations of economic development, hungry new competitors are constantly forcing richer countries to change the basis of their competitive advantage, something that needs difficult and often painful adjustment. Not that growth is a "zero sum game" — it is not, and all participants can benefit from economic exchange. But the benefits may not be distributed equally, and realising the benefits requires perpetual effort, however mature the economy. Like the Red Queen in *Alice in Wonderland*, any economy has to keep running, and often running faster, to stay in one place in the economic race.

This chapter deals with the challenges *for human capital development created by growing industrial maturity in Asia*. What does "maturing" mean in the industrial context? While there is no clear definition of this term, most analysts would agree that "maturing" involves industrial deepening (moving from simple to complex, more capital, skill and technology-intensive activities, raising the local content of inputs and undertaking locally more demanding technological tasks) and greater competitiveness in the whole range of production, management, innovation and marketing activities involved in industry. "Maturing" involves structural change in the industrial sector and in its base of competitive advantages; it should lead to growth on a sustainable basis in a liberalised world economy, not by staying in low-wage activities but by increasing value-added and incomes.

149

Maturing is thus a multifaceted process. Most developing countries in Asia started industrialisation with simple processing and assembly; if they were export-oriented, some of these activities also provided (in some cases under the aegis of multinational firms) a launching pad for manufactured exports in light industry where low wages for unskilled or semi-skilled labour provided the main competitive advantage. Most countries then moved into "heavier" industrial activity, often behind protective barriers, though in some countries export activities also deepened with rising wages and changing technologies. Those that "matured" industrially were able to deepen their industrial structures *efficiently* or to improve the competitiveness of protected activities. They increasingly competed in export markets in a diversifying, steadily more advanced, basket of products, using more skill- and technology-intensive processes in existing areas of competitiveness and relocating off-shore activities that could not be upgraded sufficiently at home. Their industries established strong local supply and technological linkages, and their enterprises developed the capability to keep up with world frontiers by importing, adapting and improving upon new technologies. Some even built up advanced design and development capabilities, and emerged as world-class multinationals in their own right.

Maturing is a process rather than a state, and there are many levels of maturity in Asia. Note, however, that an analogy with biological maturity may be misleading: industrial maturity is not a passive process of "growing up" with time. It generally requires *conscious and directed effort to develop national industrial capabilities* within manufacturing enterprises, along with supporting factor markets and institutions. This does not mean that extensive use is not made of foreign inputs — capital, technology and skills. On the contrary, the hallmark of maturity is a country's ability to draw fully upon world markets for all these factors and use them effectively, and to use them in activities where it has a genuine competitive advantage with respect to the rest of the world. What it does mean is that, regardless of the degree of reliance on imported inputs, a maturing country has to provide the complementary productive factors that are not movable or too costly to import: these include production, technical and management skills, physical infrastructure and inputs, a supplier base and supporting institutions. The ability, with rising incomes, to attract and utilise higher "quality" imported inputs, particularly direct investment, depends on the level and growth of local capabilities. The demands on these capabilities thus rise rather than fall with time, in a globalising world where economic space is rapidly shrinking and technologies constantly changing.

This does not mean that there is an optimal path to "maturity", to building industrial competitiveness and capabilities. There are many different feasible paths, each with its combination of domestic and foreign inputs, depending on each country's size, history, endowments and political economy. Each path entails different strategies and policy instruments. The high growth Asian economies embody a wide range of industrial development strategies; as a consequence, their "maturing" processes have different characteristics and create differing policy needs. These issues are taken up below.

Human Capital Needs

It is accepted almost as a truism that *human capital* is essential to gaining industrial maturity (even though this recognition is relatively recent to the development literature). The process of industrial deepening and upgrading requires higher levels of skill, know-how and organisation in almost every function, from the shop floor, via supervision and technical work to engineering, innovation, procurement, employee relations and marketing. The concept of "human capital" is, however, a very broad one, and can be considered under two headings: *skill development* and *technological capability formation*. "Skill development" is used here to refer mainly to industry-related education and training (both formal and informal, in educational institutions and firms). "Technological capability formation" is used to refer to the development of individual and institutional skills and knowledge derived from technological effort (again, both formal, in the form of R&D, and informal, in the form of a range of manufacturing activities, within manufacturing enterprises and in related institutions).

The requirements of both forms of human capital differ significantly according to the level of industrial development. Moreover, each level and strategy reflects and produces specific kinds of skills and capabilities. Figure 1 illustrates some of their main features at four levels or patterns of industrial development.

Figure 1. **Human Capital and Industrial Development Patterns**

Level/Pattern of Industrial Development	Human Capital Profile	
	Skills	**Technological Capabilities**
Low levels, mainly simple assembly and processing activity for domestic market	Literacy, simple technical and managerial training. Practically no in-firm training except informal on-job learning.	Ability to master assembly technologies, copy simple designs, repair machines, but many activities operate well below world best practice levels of technical efficiency.
Intermediate level, with export-oriented activities in light industry, some local linkages in low-tech products	Good secondary & technical schooling and management financial training. Low base of engineering and scientific skills. In-house training mainly by export-oriented enterprises. SMEs have low skill levels.	World-class assembly, layout, process engineering and maintenance in export oriented industries. In others, capability to undertake minor adaptations to processes and products. Little or no design/development capabilities. Technology institutions weak.
Deep industrial structure but mainly inward-oriented; technological lags in many activities	Broad but often low quality schooling, vocational and industrial training. Broad engineering base. In-house training lagging. Training institutes de-linked from industry. Management and marketing skills weak. SMEs have some modern skills.	Process mastery of capital and skill intensive technologies, but with inefficiencies. Considerable backward linkages, significant adaptation of imported technologies. Little innovation, low linkages with universities and technology institutions.
Advanced and deep industrial structure, with many world-class activities, own design & technology base	Excellent quality schooling and industrial training. High levels of university trained managers, engineers and scientists. Training institutes responsive to industrial needs. Large investments in formal and informal in-firm training. SMEs have high skill levels and competence.	Ability to monitor, import and adapt state of art advanced technologies. Good design and development capabilities in sophisticated technologies. Deep local linkages with suppliers, buyers, consultants, universities and technology institutions.

151

The figure is merely indicative, of course, and does not show in detail the characteristics of human capital for different patterns of industrial development in Asia. Nevertheless, it does illustrate that there is an intimate interaction between industrialisation and the kinds of skills and technological capabilities. The move from one level or strategic pattern to another requires changing both the skill creation-system and the way that the productive system uses it, contributes to it and interacts with it at all levels. The more "mature" the industrial economy, the greater and more diverse its human capital needs. Some important ways in which these will be needed follow:

— *The worker level*: Greater availability of better educated and trained workers, with higher quality of education (in particular numeracy and IT skills), more relevant to evolving technological needs. Greater flexibility in skills and work attitudes, leading to more efficient and co-operative team work and multi-skilling on the shop floor, more receptivity to and ability to manage new technologies, more willingness and ability to suggest improvements to products and processes. Continuous upgrading and retraining of employees. Greater range of specialised training institutes for particular technologies, operated by industry, associations, the government and international consortia.

— *At the technical and supervisory levels*: As above, plus more training for team-working, handling computer aided manufacturing methods, operating total quality management and continuous improvement systems, feeding back product and process improvements, liaising with engineering and development departments. The provision of proper incentives for implementing the best technologies and work practices.

— *At the engineering levels*: Larger supply of highly trained engineers with practical knowledge of industrial technologies and needs, spanning wider range of sub-disciplines, capable of undertaking more advanced functions in product and process design, quality management, reliability and cost in new activities, interacting with and helping vendors and subcontractors, using research results and drawing upon technology institutes for improvements.

— *At the management and marketing levels*: Highly trained managers able to launch and operate "flatter" systems with more intense interactions with suppliers and buyers, keep pace with globalisation, absorb and act upon increasing information flows and encourage investments in innovation and marketing. Most important, managers must be able to change traditional human resource management and development policies (to the extent that they have any) to take account of new demands on skills and teamworking, providing incentives for improvement and productivity, and give opportunities for continuous training and learning.

— *At the innovation levels:* Scientists and engineers of the quality, training and knowledge able to absorb and build upon the most advanced technologies, design and test new products and processes, interact with research laboratories and keep track of relevant developments in basic science. Science and technology support institutions have to be better equipped and staffed, and provide the motivation to conduct research relevant to industrial needs and to establish close linkages with the industrial sector.

Box 1. Findings of US Government's Competitiveness Policy Council on Training

"The economic vitality of nations will turn on the skills, ingenuity, flexibility and performance of their workforces. While policies to encourage investment in new technology are important, they must be coupled with a skilled, flexible workforce to promote market share, productivity and wage gains. The world's most competitive enterprises, those with peerless productivity and quality, have discovered that technology alone will not ensure competitiveness. Technology must be utilised by a workforce that gives "wisdom to the machine" — workers who have the kinds of skills that will allow powerful new technologies to be fully and effectively employed... Moreover, they must operate in an environment that encourages continuous improvement and advancement... Firms cannot design high performance work systems without the people and technology to power them. At the same time, new skills and cutting edge technology offer little advantage if they are not used.

Unfortunately, too many of America's workplaces still reflect turn-of-the-century production techniques. By some estimates, only five percent of our nation's businesses have replaced traditional production with high performance systems. We still break tasks into their smallest, most repetitive components and use status and bureaucracy to separate workers from management, or human resources departments from engineering. We reserve creativity and decision-making for specialists and managers. We replace workers with machines, and substitute foreign production for domestic. And we tend to emphasize cost over quality in addressing consumer demand.

Our nation's public policies and government programmes can be equally hidebound by traditions. We divide our commerce and labour functions as if the two were not integrally linked. We reward the processing forms rather than effective performance ... And we draw a bright line between our public and private sectors, encouraging an adversarial, not cooperative, relationship.

We propose, then, an economic strategy built upon a strong human resource policy, investing in the skills and work systems that command higher wages and promote greater productivity. The alternative — competition based on low wages — simply is unacceptable ...

Major Findings: "*1)* America's training needs are closely connected to reforming the workplace itself; new work practices, proven to promote competitiveness, will shift authority, responsibility and skill requirements to front-line workers. *2)* We substantially underinvest in training and high performance workplaces, with the price extracted in lower productivity and declining standards of living. *3)* Effective training policies today require attention both to the needs of the disadvantaged and to lifelong learning opportunities for all workers. *4)* Our present employment and training system fails to address these comprehensive needs and wastes precious resources through duplication and overlap. *5)* Public and private resources will be more efficiently and effectively deployed if we build real partnerships between business, labour and education. "

Source: Competitiveness Policy Council, *Building High Performance Workplaces,* Washington, D.C.,1993

As the industrial sector grows more complex and sophisticated, the challenge of providing a competitive edge through better human capital becomes more important (see Box 1). While the relevant institutions also develop and firms themselves become more conscious of the importance of skill development and training, they often fail to keep up with the evolving demands of competitiveness unless pro-active policies are launched. At low levels of industrial development, the way forward is in fact relatively clear and straightforward (if not easy to achieve in practice) — improving the quantity and quality of schooling and basic technical education, and encouraging all forms of in-firm training. In economies approaching maturity, it is far less obvious what the best use of education and training resources is. There are many improvements to be made, involving not just the educational institutions but also firms and the entire "culture" of training and management.

Even the most advanced economies can suffer from an under-provision of human resources. Let us return to some of the policy issues involved in the Asian context below; but first some background on the variations in industrial maturity in the region.

Different Levels of Industrial Maturity

There are very different levels of economic maturity in Asia. Some newly industrialising countries have just joined, or are about to join, the OECD; some are expanding at very rapid rates but without the internal sources of upgrading that the NIEs (Hong Kong, Korea, Singapore and Chinese Taipei) possess; some are just opening up and starting to realise some of the benefits of decades of industrial investment and technological learning; and some are lagging seriously in most important aspects of industrial and technological growth. Each group faces its own human capital challenges to cope with the next stage of development (for a broader analysis see ADB, 1997*a*).

This section looks at indicators of industrial maturity in selected Asian economies. There cannot be an unambiguous measure of "maturity" as conceived here, and a mixture of different indicators has to be used to capture the dynamism and complexity of the industrial sector, its competitiveness and technological prowess. To ease the exposition, we have focused on three groups of countries with relatively high degrees of industrial development, yet with different strategies and results. These are:

— *The Four Tiger Economies*: Hong Kong, Singapore, Korea and Chinese Taipei. These are, in their own ways, the industrial leaders within the region, and the most competitive countries in the developing world. Thus they represent the most mature of our economies.

— *Three New Tigers:* Indonesia, Malaysia and Thailand. These countries started on their export-oriented industrialisation later, but have recorded sustained expansion and deepening of their industrial sectors.

— *Three large inward-oriented economies:* China, India and Pakistan. These countries have large industrial sectors with some relatively advanced capabilities. China is already emerging as a dynamic exporter, while the other two are still performing relatively sluggishly.

There are important differences *within* each of these groups which also throw light on policy issues of human capital formation. In fact, each country has pursued different strategies with respect to industrialisation, technology and education, and these differences are showing up in interesting variations in their patterns of industrial competitiveness and success — and, by implication, in their evolving abilities to sustain growth in the future. The following sub-sections bring out some of the major differences.

Manufacturing Growth and Structure

Table 1 shows the growth, size and structure of the manufacturing sectors of the ten selected countries.

Table 1. **Manufacturing Growth and Structure**

Country	Annual growth rate (%)[a]			MVA[b]	MVA per employee[b]	% share of capital goods and chemicals in MVA[c]	
	1980-94	1980-90	1990-94	1994 ($ billion)	1994 ($)	1980	1994
Hong Kong	**2.5**	3.5	-0.2	13.1	26 448	20	24
Singapore	**7.1**	6.9	7.6	20.6	56 265	49	67
Korea	**10.5**	11.9	7.4	159.2	54 214	27	46
Chinese Taipei	**6.5**	7.4	4.4	73.3	33 777	36	46
Indonesia	**11.1**	11.8	9.3	28.6	7 526	24	22
Malaysia	**10.4**	9.3	13.0	18.6	15 339	25	46
Thailand	**10.2**	9.9	11.1	47.5	24 389	16	23
China	**11.4**	9.5	16.2	139.0	2 245	33	34
India	**6.1**	7.4	2.9	24.4	2 911	39	44
Pakistan	**7.2**	7.8	5.9	5.7	983	21	29

a.   Compound annual growth calculated from UNIDO data on manufacturing value added in constant 1990 dollars.
b.   UNIDO data for manufacturing value added, current 1994 dollars.
c.   World Bank data, except for UNIDO data for Chinese Taipei (both years) and Korea, Thailand and Pakistan (1994 only).

Sources: UNIDO, *Industrial Development: Global Report 1996*; World Bank, *World Development Indicators 1997.*

According to UNIDO data, the largest manufacturing sector in the sample, and the largest in the developing world, is in Korea, followed by China and Chinese Taipei (though World Bank data show that China is larger than Korea). The smallest is that of Pakistan. Among the Tigers, Singapore has a larger manufacturing sector than Hong Kong, though it has half its population size and about 10 per cent higher income (showing that "deindustrialisation" is not a necessary consequence of high wages).

Among the Tigers, the fastest growing manufacturing sector is in Korea. Chinese Taipei (its traditional competitor and comparator) has been growing distinctly more slowly since 1980. Singapore has not only maintained high growth rates, but is the only Tiger to accelerate in the 1990s. The other three countries distinctly slow down in the 1990s, perhaps a consequence of their growing "maturity" (ADB, 1997), but Korea continues to have a fairly high rate of growth, while Hong Kong goes into decline, the only country in the whole group to do so. The causes of this are taken up later.

The new Tigers have impressive and sustained growth performances, with Malaysia and Thailand accelerating in the latter period. Among the other three economies, China has by far the most impressive growth rate, with a sharp increase in the 1990s.

The value of manufacturing value added (MVA) per employee can serve as a rough indicator of the degree of sophistication of the industrial sector, since this value increases with capital, skill and technology intensity. The ranking is intuitively plausible and accords with what is known about the characteristics of the various countries (see below). Singapore and Korea have the most advanced sectors, with the former leading by virtue of its specialisation in a fairly narrow set of advanced electronics and chemical activities. Some way behind comes Chinese Taipei, and even further behind is Hong Kong, with average productivity levels under half those of Singapore or Korea. This suggests that it has a much "lighter" and less technologically advanced manufacturing sector than the other Tigers. Among the new Tigers, Thailand has the most advanced sector, followed by Malaysia and Indonesia. This may seem surprising at first sight: Malaysia has a more "advanced" structure in terms of the share of high-tech activities in electrical and electronic industries in production and exports, but is explained by the relatively low level of local integration of these industries, which remain largely at the assembly stage.

China and India have similar, and low, levels of MVA/employee, a reflection of their spread over a large number of low-technology and low-productivity manufacturing activities. Pakistan comes lowest in the list, with a shallow and rather backward structure.

The last two columns show the share of two advanced industries — capital goods and chemicals. The picture supports that shown by productivity figures, except that Singapore appears far more advanced than the other Tigers, while Chinese Taipei and Malaysia appear at the same level as Korea, with India fairly close behind. Pakistan has a more advanced structure by this criterion than several of the others.

Export Performance and Structure

Manufactured export performance offers another attractive way to gauge the competitiveness and sophistication of a country's manufacturing sector. This does have disadvantages: export data do not provide a good indicator of the technological competence of large economies with significant inward-oriented activities. Export data cannot distinguish between different levels of technology used in a country within a broad product group, so that a country undertaking only the assembly of a high-tech product appears as a very advanced exporter. Nor do they distinguish between exports by foreign and domestic firms; this distinction may be important if it reflects different local technological inputs. However, these deficiencies may be offset by looking at the local technological content of exports and the role of FDI in trade.

We start with aggregate figures, with the focus on the same ten Asian countries. Table 2 shows that in 1994 the largest exporters, both of merchandise and manufactures, were China, Korea, Chinese Taipei, Malaysia and Singapore[1].

Table 2. **Exports from Asian Countries**

Country	Merchandise Exports			Manufactured Exports
	1994 Value ($ million)	Growth rate (1980-90)	Growth rate (1990-94)	1994 Value ($ million)
Hong Kong (a)	28 739	11.5	-0.3	27 302
Singapore (a)	57 963	12.1	10.9	56 224
Korea	96 000	13.7	7.4	89 280
Chinese Taipei	92 847	11.6	5.9	86 348
Indonesia	40 054	5.3	21.3	21 229
Malaysia	58 756	11.5	17.8	41 129
Thailand	45 262	14.3	21.6	33 041
China	121 047	11.4	14.3	98 048
India	21 553	6.3	7.0	16 165
Pakistan	6 636	9.5	8.8	5 641

a.   Excluding re-exports.

Sources: World Bank (1996), *World Development Report;* Asian Development Bank (1994), *Key Indicators of Developing Asian and Pacific Countries; Hong Kong External Trade,* February, *1996 Singapore Trade Statistics.*

The figures support many of the trends shown earlier. The fastest rates of growth in 1990-94 were for Thailand, Indonesia, Malaysia, China, and Singapore. Hong Kong was the only country in the group that had declining exports (re-exports excluded), a dramatic deterioration on its earlier performance. Of the larger Tigers, Korea showed a stronger long-term performance than Chinese Taipei. China outperformed the other large economies, and by 1994 emerged as the largest single exporter of manufactures in the group (and in the whole developing world). The general export performance, higher than in other developing regions, suggests considerable technological dynamism.

However, these data reveal little about the sophistication or complexity of export activity. One way to compensate is to look at the *technological composition* of manufactured exports. There are numerous ways to do this. The most frequently used categorisation, between "high" and "low" technology products, is highly aggregated and may conceal interesting differences, especially between developing countries that are largely exporting simple products. A breakdown by the technological basis of production, derived from the OECD, is more useful (Table 3).

The categorisation is far from perfect. There are inevitable overlaps between the categories (resource-based industries can be very capital-intensive), and the groups are broad (for instance, many electronics exports are labour-intensive), but if carefully used the classification is helpful. Labour-intensive products tend to be at the low end of the technology spectrum, with low requirements of technical skills (though high fashion products may call for advanced design skills). Products in the scale-intensive group tend to use complex, capital-intensive technologies, but are generally not at the cutting edge of technology (this also applies to many resource-based exports). Within the scale-intensive group, process (e.g. chemicals) should be distinguished from engineering industries (e.g. automobiles). The latter tend to have more difficult learning requirements, be very linkage-intensive, and involve a larger variety of skills. "Differentiated" manufactures comprise more sophisticated engineering products, with advanced design, research and manufacturing skill requirements, while science-based products use leading edge technologies.

Table 3. **Technological Basis of Exports**

Activity Group	Major Competitive Factor	Examples	OECD Exports 1985 (%)
Resource-intensive	Access to natural resources	Aluminium smelting, oil refining	13.5
Labour-intensive	Costs of unskilled or semi-skilled labour	Garments, footwear, toys	9.8
Scale-intensive	Length of production runs	Steel, chemicals, automobiles, paper	33.8
Differentiated	Products tailored to varied demands	Machinery, power equipment	27.3
Science-based	Rapid application of science to technology	Electronics, biotechnology, medicines	15.5

Source: OECD, 1987.

In broad terms, we call the last three categories *"technologically advanced"*, and the last two *"high-tech"*, products. Resource-based products are not considered further here because their competitive edge is very specific and does not as such tell us much about industrial maturity.

Table 4 shows the technological breakdown of manufactured exports by the 10 countries since 1980[2]. The highest concentration on labour-intensive exports (primarily textiles and garments) is currently in Pakistan (94 per cent), followed at some distance by China (58 per cent), Hong Kong (54 per cent), India (50 per cent), Indonesia (49 per cent) and Thailand (38 per cent). There is some correlation between labour-intensity of exports and factor costs (i.e. low wages), but it is far from perfect: the lowest wages are probably in China and Indonesia, while Hong Kong is a very high-wage economy. The export structure also reflects the underlying industrial and technological structure, which in turn is determined by the industrial policies pursued (Lall, 1996). With industrial development there is a general tendency for the share of labour-intensive products to decline. But again there are exceptions: in Indonesia, Pakistan and Thailand the shares have risen over time.

Table 4. **Distribution of Manufactured Exports by Technological Categories (%)**

	China		Korea		Chinese Taipei		Singapore		Hong Kong	
	1985	1992	1980	1994	1980	1994	1980	1994	1980	1994
Resource-based	4.3	6.3	7.3	3.8	9.4	6.8	6.5	3.3	2.0	3.7
Labour-intensive	66.6	58.4	49.5	27.8	53.9	32.7	16.9	8.5	65.8	54.3
Scale-intensive	17.6	11.2	25.8	27.2	9.4	13.9	20.9	10.5	1.2	4.2
Differentiated	5.3	17.2	14.7	35.6	23.7	30.9	50.3	46.3	16.7	21.4
Science-based	0.0	1.1	2.7	5.6	3.6	15.8	5.4	31.4	14.3	16.4
	Indonesia		Malaysia		Thailand		India		Pakistan	
	1980	1992	1980	1992	1980	1992	1980	1992	1980	1992
Resource-based	14.7	29.5	11.0	5.4	53.9	20.1	26.5	28.7	15.5	4.5
Labour-intensive	28.9	48.7	18.4	17.4	28.4	38.3	55.4	49.6	84.5	93.8
Scale-intensive	20.2	7.6	4.9	5.3	4.3	5.6	11.2	17.1	0.0	0.0
Differentiated	19.0	7.6	60.1	29.6	13.4	15.7	4.1	1.2	0.0	0.0
Science-based	0.0	0.9	3.8	42.3	0.0	20.3	2.8	3.4	0.0	1.7

Notes: Figures for Singapore and Hong Kong are for total manufactured exports (including re-exports). No data for China are available for 1980, so the starting year is 1985.

Source: Calculated from UN trade data.

As for more technology-based products, the figures below show the shares of "technologically advanced" (Figure 2) and "high-tech" (Figure 3) products in total manufactured exports for these countries. These figures suggest the following:

Figure 2. **Shares of Technologically Advanced Products**
(per cent)

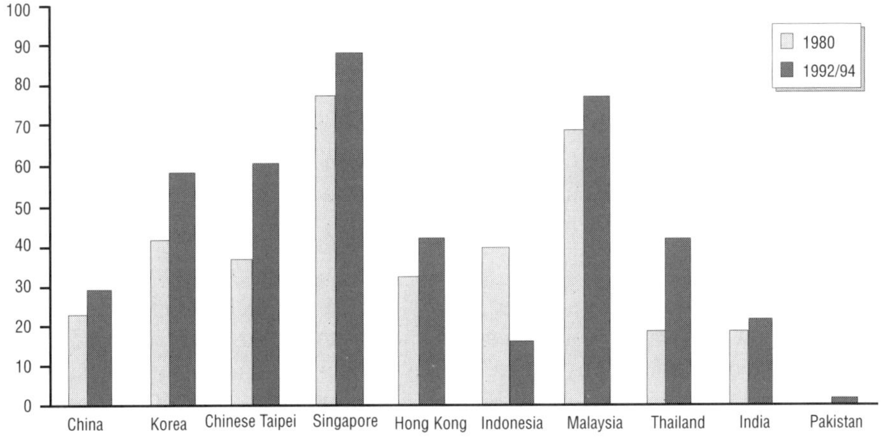

— The most technologically advanced exporters are Singapore, followed by Malaysia, Chinese Taipei and Korea. Hong Kong has the lowest technological content of exports of the Tigers. Pakistan is the least advanced overall; Indonesia is the next lowest, with India and China slightly ahead.

Figure 3. **Shares of High-Tech Products**
(per cent)

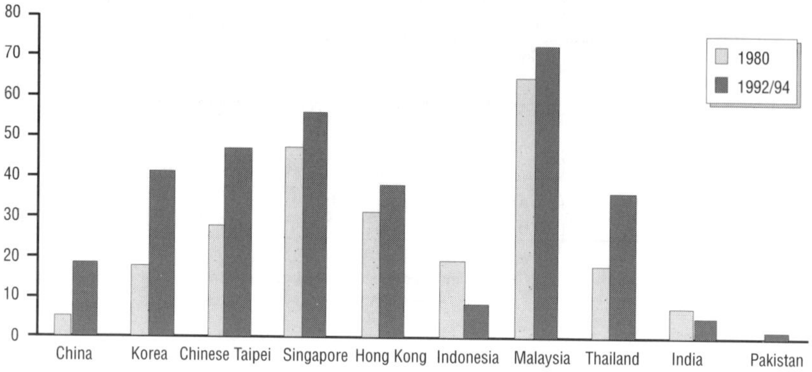

— In the narrower category of "high-tech" products, the leader is Malaysia, followed by Singapore, Chinese Taipei and Korea. The weakest is Pakistan, followed by India, Indonesia and China.

— The technology intensity of manufactured exports has been growing for all countries except for Indonesia, where the rapid growth of labour and resource-intensive exports has swamped other exports (though their growth has also been rapid, if from a small base, Lall and Rao, 1996).

We may also quantify the "*technological dynamism*" of manufactured exports, to capture *both* the share of advanced products in total exports *and* the change in this share over time. This index is obtained by multiplying the percentage points by which the relevant exports have increased their share by their share in the final year (Table 5): for instance, for Korea the share of technologically advanced products increased by 26.8 percentage points over 1980-94 and the share in 1994 was 68.4 per cent, giving an index of 1833.1. While the data in the previous table are for slightly different periods for different countries (and Chinese data could only be calculated from 1985), the index seems plausible in broad terms.

Korea and Chinese Taipei lead in dynamism for technologically advanced products, followed by Singapore, Thailand and Malaysia. In high-tech products, the leader is Singapore, followed by Korea, Chinese Taipei and Thailand (Malaysia suffers because it achieved a high share for high-tech exports at the start of the period, and had a decline in differentiated products). Thailand rapidly expands advanced exports, while Indonesia suffers a technological downgrading in both indices. Hong Kong comes well behind the other Tigers. China, while lagging the Tigers and two of the new Tigers, is more dynamic than the South Asians: India has a negative index for high-tech products; Pakistan does poorly in both.

Table 5. **Indices of Technological Dynamism**

Country	Technologically Advanced Products	High-Technology Products
Hong Kong	411.6	237.9
Singapore	1 023.1	1 709.4
Korea	1 833.1	980.6
Chinese Taipei	1 448.3	906.0
Indonesia	negative	negative
Malaysia	648.5	575.2
Thailand	994.2	813.6
China	194.7	237.9
India	78.1	negative
Pakistan	2.9	2.9

However, some qualifications have to be made to these indicators if they are to indicate the domestic technological base more accurately. In particular, we have to account for the *level of technology* involved in the export activity, and the *role of MNCs* in export and technological activity.

Level of Technology: The local technological content of similar exports can vary between countries, according to the level and extent of local inputs of components, equipment and technical knowledge. For instance, a "high-technology" export in one country may come from locally assembled imported components, with few local inputs, physical or technological; in another, it may be based on substantial local equipment, components, design, development and engineering. These clearly show different capabilities to deal with technological change. Asian countries differ greatly in this respect. Malaysia's high-tech exports are driven primarily by electronics and electrical assembly activity in export enclaves. While the activity has upgraded in process technology and product range, there are still few domestic linkages and little local technological input. Capabilities have certainly developed, but they are mainly in operating imported technologies. Singapore is also driven by MNC-based operations, but the processes and products are at a higher level of sophistication, use more advanced skills, and involve more local technological activity. However, there are still relatively low levels of design and development activity, which is done overseas by the MNCs involved.

By contrast, high-tech exports from Korea and Chinese Taipei have significant local linkages (both equipment and components), and far more local technological input up to basic design stages. Korea is ahead of Chinese Taipei, with a more diverse and "heavier" industrial structure and far greater R&D effort (below). Of the Tigers, Hong Kong has the lowest technological input, having remained specialised in light consumer goods (though within this there has been considerable upgrading); in addition, even its "high technology" exports are simpler than in the other Tigers (consisting largely of electronic items like games and watches). Thailand is also basically at the assembly stage in technologically advanced products, but its rate of growth in such activities is phenomenal, and in more traditional activities there is a lot of local "depth". China's high-tech exports have a mixture of assembled and manufactured items, the former largely off-loaded from the Tigers. India has a deep and backward integrated production structure, but one that past policies have burdened with high costs and technological lags.

Role of MNCs: A strong foreign presence has mixed implications for the local technological input in export activity and thus for the maturity of the industrial base underlying it. In industrially mature countries, MNC export activity generally has significant indigenous input and design, and interacts with and contributes to the local technological base. In less industrialised countries, MNC exports are usually driven by cheap labour, and have low local technological content. Between these two, there are innumerable combinations of MNC presence and technological activity. Asian countries show the whole range.

MNCs have played very different roles in economic activity in Asian countries (Table 6). In terms of the share of FDI in gross domestic investment, Singapore is the most FDI-intensive economy in the region (and probably in the world), followed by Malaysia. Then comes China, with a startling growth in its share of FDI in investment in the 1990s. At the other end of the spectrum, India and Korea have traditionally had very low levels of reliance on foreign investment. It is interesting to note the differences between the Tigers in FDI policies: Korea and Chinese Taipei, particularly the former, emphasized externalised technology transfer, while Singapore strongly targeted internalised modes and Hong Kong had a *laissez faire* attitude (Lall, 1996). The first two had selective policies on entry, restricting FDI where domestic capabilities were adequate (or were being protected). Once allowed in, investors were given incentives to diffuse technologies locally. Singapore also used selectivity, but to attract investors into targeted activities and, later, to induce upgrading of the technological content of manufacturing. Its FDI policies were finely honed to achieving the government's objectives; Singapore is the only country in the region which gives grants for firms engaging in designated activities (in this it is similar to many OECD countries). Only Hong Kong left FDI and technology transfer entirely to market forces.

Table 6. **Inward FDI**

Country	Annual FDI Inflows ($ million)							FDI as % GDI [a]	
	1984-89	1990	1991	1992	1993	1994	1995	1984-89	1990-94
Hong Kong	1 422	1 728	538	1 918	1 667	2 000	2 100	12.2	6.7
Singapore	2 239	5 575	4 879	2 351	5 016	5 588	5 302	28.3	28.4
Korea	592	788	1 180	727	588	809	1 500	1.4	0.7
Chinese Taipei	691	1 330	1 271	879	917	1 375	1 470	3.3	3.0
Indonesia	406	1 093	1 482	1 774	2 004	2 109	4 500	1.6	3.5
Malaysia	798	2 333	3 998	5 183	5 006	4 348	5 800	8.8	22.4
Thailand	676	2 444	2 014	2 116	1 726	640	2 300	4.4	4.3
China	2 282	3 487	4 366	11 156	27 515	33 787	37 500	1.8	11.6
India	133	162	141	151	273	620	1 750	0.2	0.5
Pakistan	136	244	257	335	354	422	639	2.0	3.6

a.   GDI stands for gross domestic investment. The figures are simple annual averages.

Source: UNCTAD, *World Investment Report 1996*, Geneva.

In terms of export contribution, MNCs account for around 25 per cent of manufactured exports from Hong Kong, 70 per cent from Malaysia, 90 per cent from Singapore and 17 per cent from Chinese Taipei. The figure for Korea is likely to be significantly lower than for Chinese Taipei, given the former's much lower reliance on inward FDI and the predominant role of its *chaebol* in export activity. Thailand and Indonesia depend heavily on MNCs in many export activities, but large parts of the industrial sector are in local hands. Chinese labour-intensive exports largely originate from investors from the other NIEs, mainly Hong Kong and Chinese Taipei, but a number of local firms are also becoming active exporters in a range of products. MNCs are not significant exporters from India and Pakistan.

Export activity may not be a good indicator of technological strength in large inward-oriented countries. China and India probably possess technological capabilities far in advance of that suggested by their export structures, though many may not currently be at "best practice" international levels. In the other countries, where trade plays a larger role in manufacturing, the patterns shown above may not be unrepresentative of the underlying technological structure.

Levels of Industrial Maturity

What may we conclude from the evidence presented above about the levels and types of industrial maturity achieved in Asia? The most striking thing is how different the countries are in their industrial structures and capabilities. The process of "maturing" has taken them in different directions and to different levels, the differences explained largely by the strategies adopted by their governments[3].

Of the Tiger economies (and arguably in the developing world as a whole), Korea stands out as the clear leader on almost every criterion, and Hong Kong the laggard. The Korean industrial sector has achieved considerable depth and integration, with competitive export capabilities over a very wide range of activities, including practically all skill- and technology-intensive industries. Its leading firms have established production facilities and their own brand names worldwide, and are able to negotiate and strike alliances with technological leaders on more or less equal terms. Korea is followed by Chinese Taipei, which has a narrower, less heavy, industrial base with a specialisation in skill-based products. Its preponderance of SMEs gives it more flexibility, but perhaps less depth in technology generation and production weaknesses in heavy industry. As its industrial sector approaches technological frontiers this may prove a disadvantage (and may account for the fact that Chinese Taipei manufacturing output and exports have been growing more slowly than Korea's over the past decade). Both these Tigers demonstrate a growing independent *innovative* capability and should be counted as nearly mature.

The smaller Tigers have narrower spheres of competence. Singapore's specialisation in advanced producer electronics and chemicals gives it a high-tech profile unmatched even by most OECD countries. Despite its smaller size and higher wages, Singapore has higher rates of industrial and export growth than its close "cousin" Hong Kong, which has undergone a rapid contraction of its manufacturing sector and decline in its own exports. Their industrial structures have also diverged over the past four decades, Singapore using targeting and incentives to upgrade its industrial base while Hong Kong, with its reluctance to use industrial policy, remains in activities with low technological content. The Hong Kong economy continues to grow by moving into services largely directed at the mainland, but its rate of growth has been lower than that of Singapore (which has also enlarged its service sector without running down industry). However, in comparison to Korea and Chinese Taipei, Singapore's technological edge is underdeveloped — it lies in providing an efficient, high skill and well-located base for MNC activity rather than in developing technologies. These countries have gained maturity of a sort, perhaps best suited to their size and special circumstances.

The new Tigers have relatively shallow, less mature, industrial structures. They have relied much more heavily on foreign investment to drive their export-oriented industrialisation than the larger Tigers (in fact, a very significant part of the foreign investment has come from the latter). Thailand appears the most advanced in terms of indigenous capabilities and Indonesia the least. Malaysia provides an interesting combination of a high-tech MNC sector which is gradually building up its (still small) local technological base; the domestic sector remains relatively weak in industry but has built up a range of capabilities in resource processing, services and infrastructure. Indonesia is the industrial latecomer in this group. Its base of skills and technology is low, and its specialisation in low technology industries holds back beneficial spillover effects. However, its huge domestic market, natural resource base and ability to attract the low end of electronics from Singapore and Malaysia may allow it to upgrade its capabilities more rapidly in the future.

On present trends, the new Tigers seem set to remain good *implementers* of new technology, as producers at low to medium levels of technological sophistication. Domestic firms will dominate in the simpler technologies, and MNCs in high-tech ones. This may allow them to sustain high rates of growth as in the past; on the other hand, with a strong competitive threat from lower cost economies or those with larger technological bases, they may lose momentum as these competitors offer similar incentives to foreign investors and improve their infrastructure. As their initial advantages erode, continued growth will depend on the success of their efforts to move up the technological ladder. Whether or not they have established the base to upgrade on a sustained basis remains to be seen. Thus, these are economies on the way to maturity.

Of the larger economies, China and India have deep and diverse industrial sectors, but with significant protected and inefficient sectors that suffer from technological and organisational lags, along with large traditional activities. At the same time, they have the size, production experience, supplier base and technological skills to move to high levels of production and innovation. In order to achieve this they need to reform further the trade and industrial incentive systems, and to improve considerably their human capital base (see below) and infrastructure. China is growing dynamically; this growth gives it the resources, momentum and access to information that should ensure further upgrading. India is a less dynamic performer, and faces a more difficult task. Pakistan has many weaknesses, with a shallow industrial structure, low ability to attract advanced FDI, a small human capital base, and minuscule technological activity. Unless these are improved, it seems poorly placed to participate in the dynamics of the region. These economies thus have some elements of maturity, but a lot of work and change is needed to realise the full potential.

Human Resource Levels and Needs in Asia

Educational Enrolment Data

This section provides data on human resource development in the ten Asian countries as measured by educational enrolments. This is far from an ideal measure. Formal education is only one way to create skills: on-the-job learning and training are often more important. Enrolment data may not be a sound indicator even of formal education: dropout rates differ across countries, as do the quality and relevance of the education. For these reasons, it is difficult to compare directly educational systems across countries. Nevertheless, these are the best data available on a comparable basis, and enrolment rates do say something about the base for industrial skill acquisition. Table 7 shows *general enrolments* at the three levels, as well as tertiary students abroad and the adult literacy rate.

Table 7. **Educational Enrolments and Literacy Rates**

Most recent available (per cent of age group)

Country	Primary	Secondary	Tertiary	Per cent Tertiary Abroad (a)	Adult Literacy Rate
Hong Kong	102	75	21	32	91
Singapore	107	78	19 (b)	25	90
Korea	101	93	48	2	97
Chinese Taipei	100	88	38	n.a.	n.a.
Indonesia	114	43	10	2	83
Malaysia	93	59	7	38	82
Thailand	98	37	19	1	94
China	109	52	6	3	79
India	105	45	6	1	50
Pakistan	65	17	3	9	36

a.   1987-88.
b.   Figure for 1995, referring to percentage or persons aged 18 that are university graduates. In addition to these, Singapore also has 27 per cent that are polytechnic graduates.

Sources: World Bank, *World Development Indicators 1997*; UNESCO, *Statistical Yearbook,* various; UNDP, *Human Development Report 1995*; Government of Chinese Taipei, *Chinese Taipei Statistical Yearbook,* 1994; data from Singapore Economic Development Board Website.

Secondary enrolment rates are very high in the Tigers, with Korea and Chinese Taipei at developed country levels. Hong Kong and Singapore are slightly behind, followed by Malaysia, Indonesia and Thailand. What of the quality? It is interesting, in this context, to report on the latest findings of the Third International Maths and Science Study (TIMSS) from *The Economist* (1997). This provides some indication of the quality of the technical teaching at secondary schools. Of the 41 countries in which half a million 13 year olds were tested, the position of three of the Tigers and one of the new Tigers tested (Chinese Taipei was not in the test) is shown in Table 8.

Table 8. **Ranks in TIMSS Tests for Science and Maths for 13 Year Olds**
(Total of 41 countries)

Country	Rank in Maths	Rank in Science
Hong Kong	4	24
Singapore	1	1
Korea	2	4
Thailand	20	21
Some OECD countries		
United States	28	17
Japan	3	3
United Kingdom	25	10
France	13	28
Germany	23	19
Other developing country		
Colombia	40	40

Source: The Economist (1997).

Singapore reaches first place in both maths and science; Korea comes second in maths and fourth in science; Hong Kong comes fourth in maths and 24th in science. Japan is the best of the developed countries, coming third in both. By contrast, the only new Tiger in the sample, Thailand, is about half way down the scale in both (but above the international average in terms of actual marks). The only other developing country in the sample, Colombia, is second from the bottom in both (the last place is held by South Africa). East European countries generally do well. These data support the presumption that the Tigers have good educational systems geared to technology.

Coming to tertiary enrolments, Korea, followed by Chinese Taipei, are both at developed country levels. Then come Hong Kong, Singapore and Thailand, with around 20 per cent. Indonesia and Malaysia have tertiary enrolments of 5-10 per cent. There are high proportions of students studying overseas from Hong Kong, Singapore and Malaysia. Singapore also has very large enrolments in polytechnics (see footnote (b) to Table 7). If we include these in the tertiary enrolment figures, Singapore's total enrolments (46 per cent) approach Korean levels. The emphasis on polytechnics rather than universities in Singapore reflects its strategy of concentrating on production-related skills that have provided its greatest strength[4].

The breakdown of tertiary enrolment *in technical subjects* is more relevant for our purposes (Table 9). This table includes some advanced industrial countries for comparison, and shows interesting differences, not just between the Asian Tigers, but also between them and the developed countries. It shows, in particular, that some Tigers, in particular Korea and Chinese Taipei, are now significantly ahead of the technological leaders in the OECD in investing in high-level technical skills. Note that the figures are expressed as percentages of the total population rather than of the relevant age group (as in the previous table). Take enrolments in *all technical subjects* (which includes medicine, architecture and so on). The norm in the European technological leaders is around 1 per cent; the United States is much higher, at 1.47 per cent. However, Korea has larger enrolments than all these countries, at 1.66 per cent. Chinese Taipei follows with 1.45 per cent, higher than Europe or Japan but just behind the United States. There is a large range among the other Asian countries. Among the new Tigers, the lowest figures are for Indonesia and Malaysia (under 0.2 per cent). The three larger countries come even lower. China and India are roughly equal at 0.15 per cent, while Pakistan reaches only 0.07 per cent.

Enrolments in *core technology subjects* (science, mathematics, computing and engineering) are probably the most relevant indicator of manufacturing-related technical skills. Korea has an impressive lead here over the whole group. Compare its 1.34 per cent with 0.73 per cent for the United States, 0.87 per cent for Germany and 0.46 per cent for Japan. While this figure has not been calculated for all countries, it would not be surprising if the Korean figure is the highest among *all* market economies. Chinese Taipei comes next with 1.09 per cent. Singapore has around half of this (0.56 per cent), Hong Kong less (0.47 per cent), followed by Thailand (0.32 per cent), Malaysia (0.15 per cent) and Indonesia (0.13 per cent). India is at the Malaysian level with 0.15 per cent, China slightly behind at 0.12 per cent and Pakistan much further at 0.07 per cent.

In *natural science*, the Asian countries lag behind the OECD countries, where France and Germany lead. Korea, again, has by far the highest proportion of science enrolments in Asia (0.17 per cent); Chinese Taipei has a relatively low figure (0.08 per cent), trailing Thailand, India and Hong Kong. Indonesia and Malaysia have relatively small enrolments in science. India performs well in this discipline with 0.10 per cent, while China lags badly (only 0.008 per cent), by far the worst in the group.

In *mathematics and computer science*, Korea leads both Asian and OECD countries. In relation to the size of the population, its enrolments are over twice that of United States and Japan (German and French data are not available separately) and 58 per cent higher than in the United States. The nearest Asian follower, Chinese Taipei, has less than half the proportion of its population in these disciplines, though it leads most European countries (but not the United States). Hong Kong performs better here than Singapore; this may seem surprising in view of their production structures, but the competitive edge of Singapore lies in production of electronic hardware rather than computing. Indonesia and Thailand are relatively weak in this discipline. India and Pakistan do not provide separate figures.

Table 9. **Tertiary Level Students in Technical Fields**
(numbers and per cent)

Country	Year	Natural Science		Maths & Computer Science		Engineering		All Technical Subjects[a]		Science + Maths & Computers + Engineering		Ratio of Engineering to Science Enrolees
		Numbers	% population	Numbers	% population	Numbers	% population	Numbers	% population	% total tertiary	% population	
Hong Kong	1992	5 503	0.095	6 661	0.115	14 788	0.256	35 068	0.607	30.3	0.47	2.69
Singapore	1994	1 281	0.046	1 420	0.051	13 029	0.465	16 767	0.599	20.4	0.56	10.17
Korea	1993	75 778	0.172	145 948	0.331	367 846	0.834	730 346	1.655	31.2	1.34	4.85
Chinese Taipei	1993	16 823	0.080	32 757	0.157	179 094	0.857	303 964	1.454	42.3	1.09	10.65
Indonesia	1992	22 394	0.012	13 117	0.007	205 086	0.109	315 325	0.167	13.4	0.13	9.16
Malaysia	1990	8 775	0.049	4 557	0.025	12 693	0.071	32 222	0.180	21.4	0.15	1.45
Thailand	1992	77 098	0.135	1 292	0.002	105 149	0.185	249 952	0.439	15.9	0.32	1.36
China	1993	95 492	0.008	174 862	0.015	1 156 735	0.098	1 831 966	0.155	31.7	0.12	12.11
India	1990	869 119	0.102	..	..	216 837	0.025	1 236 414	0.146	27.9	0.146	0.25
Pakistan	1991	29 433	0.025	..	..	41 244	0.035	75 168	0.065	34.0	0.065	2.55
Memo item: Some OECD Countries												
Japan	1991	59 030	0.048	20 891	0.017	488 699	0.394	730 637	0.590	19.6	0.46	8.28
France	1991	266 299	0.467	n.a.	n.a.	123 514	0.217	614 159	1.078	21.2	0.68	0.46
Germany	1993	310 435	0.384	n.a.	n.a.	389 182	0.481	805 801	0.997	37.3	0.87	1.25
Netherlands	1992	16 707	0.110	8 742	0.058	n.a.	n.a.	137 510	0.905	n.a.	0.17	n.a.
United Kingdom	1992	105 983	0.183	76 430	0.132	219 078	0.378	596 404	1.029	26.3	0.69	2.07
United States	1990	496 415	0.199	525 067	0.210	801 126	0.320	3 676 985	1.471	13.3	0.73	1.63

a. All technical subjects include the three categories earlier plus medical; architecture, trade & crafts; and transport & communications.

Sources: UNESCO, *Statistical Yearbook, 1995*; Government of Chinese Taipei, *Taiwan Statistical Yearbook, 1994*; data from Ministry of Education, Singapore.

Engineering is strongly emphasized in most, but not all, Asian countries. Korea has 0.83 per cent of its population enrolled in engineering and Chinese Taipei 0.86 per cent (it is worth noting that the *absolute* number of Korean engineering students is actually 70 per cent larger than India's). Singapore follows far behind with 0.47 per cent. China's figure is only 0.1 per cent, but its size means that its 1.2 million engineering enrolments are almost equal to the entire EU's 1.23 million. Indonesia is notable for the rapid expansion of enrolments in engineering; the percentage of the total population in this field is now four times higher than India's. The two large Tigers are well ahead of the OECD countries, where Germany leads with 0.48 per cent; they enrol over twice the proportion of their populations in engineering than the United States (0.32 per cent). The weakest performer here is India, which trails Pakistan at the bottom. This is surprising in view of the apparent oversupply of engineers in India, but is probably due to the fact that very large parts of manufacturing operate at low levels of technology where formal engineering is not used.

We may compare *relative enrolments in engineering and science*, an indicator of the emphasis on the practical versus the theoretical aspects of technology. In Asia, there is a clear bias towards engineering. Only India has more enrolments in science than engineering. China is at the other extreme, with a ratio of engineers to scientists of 12. Japan has a ratio of 8, Chinese Taipei 11, Singapore 10 and Korea 5. In Europe and the United States, the norm is 2 or below, with France having more enrolments in science than engineering. This may have implications for coping with new technologies, but it is difficult at this stage to discern this clearly: arguments may run both ways, depending on emerging skill and knowledge requirements.

Let us look now at enrolments in *vocational training* (at the secondary level) in Table 10, an indicator of investment in the basic technical skills that feed into industrial operations. Chinese Taipei is the strongest performer here, followed by Korea. Singapore is relatively weak among the Tigers, but this may be due to the fact that it uses the polytechnics rather than secondary schools to impart (relatively advanced) forms of technical skills, and also relies more than most countries on post-employment training. Among the new Tigers, Malaysia underperforms relative to Indonesia and Thailand. China lags these countries, but is well in advance of India and Pakistan; the latter, in particular, has minuscule numbers of trainees.

Finally, some remarks on *in-firm training*. Though it is widely accepted that it is a critical source of productivity improvement in developing as well as developed countries (Box 2), it is difficult to find comparable data on in-firm training expenses at the national level, even in the advanced industrial countries. What is known is that the leading enterprises in the advanced industrial countries spend *around 6-7 per cent of payroll* on employee training, and that "lifetime" learning is becoming an increasingly important preoccupation with governments in the OECD[5].

Most enterprises in developing countries spend little, if anything, on training programmes for their employees. As long as their activity involves simple technologies, learning on the job is probably sufficient to impart the basic operational skills. When, however, the technologies involved grow more complex, training has to be more

Table 10. Vocational Training Enrolments
Most recent year available

Country	Numbers (thousand)	% of Population
Hong Kong	45.9	0.78
Singapore	9.4	0.34
Korea	851.5	1.95
Chinese Taipei	513.7	2.45
Indonesia	1 430.5	0.78
Malaysia	40.9	0.22
Thailand	448.2	0.77
China	5 724.2	0.50
India	853.8	0.10
Pakistan	54.2	0.05

Source: UNESCO, *Statistical Yearbook,* 1995; Government of Chinese Taipei, *Chinese Taipei Statistical Data Book*, 1994.

structured and formal. Employers are reluctant to invest in expensive training when labour turnover rates are high, since they cannot recoup the returns to their investment. Many governments, in response, impose a training levy which is reimbursed to firms undertaking approved training courses for employees. The norm for such levies is 1 per cent of payroll, but it is often found that the levies are not collected or training implemented properly.

In the Asian sample, Korea stands out because its training levy on large firms was one of the highest in the world, *5 per cent of payroll.* Singapore records firm-level investments in training at *3.6 per cent of payroll* in 1995[6], very high even by developed country standards: the comparable figure for the United Kingdom in 1996 was 2.9 per cent (*The Economist,* 1997). Malaysia imposes a 1 per cent training levy on large firms and allows a 200 per cent tax deduction on SMEs; however, it is mainly the export-oriented MNCs that invest heavily in training there. Not much is known about training in the other countries in the sample (World Bank, 1996).

To sum up the enrolment data, it is clear that the larger Tigers and Singapore have gone the farthest in creating the broad educational base that human capital development requires. The Korean effort overall is impressive, but it is particularly remarkable in terms of the output of university-trained technical personnel: it is clearly this which provides the "brain-power" for its immense industrial machinery. Whether the effort is sufficient to drive it into the research and science base that Korea will need with further "maturity" is another matter. Chinese Taipei is not far behind Korea in formal education, but lags in the production of scientists. This may not have any direct implications for its industrial performance at this time, but over the longer term may inhibit its ability to keep up with emerging technologies. Singapore's education and training system is more geared to producing work-place rather than research skills, but there its output of industry-related skills is impressive. Its emphasis on middle-level training, which has served it well in the past, may not be as appropriate in the future, when it has to move into much more sophisticated activities. Hong Kong puts up a respectable performance but not at the level of the other Tigers.

Box 2. **Enterprise Training in Developing Countries**

A World Bank study of enterprise training, the largest and most comprehensive of its kind for developing countries, is based on data from large samples of firms in Taiwan, Malaysia, Indonesia, Colombia and Mexico. It finds that firm-level training has a significant and positive effect on productivity for all types of firms: large and small, domestic or export oriented, foreign and local and high or low tech. This evidence, supported by econometric analysis, provides a powerful case for the promotion of employee training at all levels of development.

The study finds that training and technology development tend to be closely related: the firms that invest in training also tend to invest in R&D, undertake quality control activities and use existing technology services. In contrast, the firms that do little training also tend to face technical problems and undertake little in-house technological activity. This supports the findings of the technological capability literature that training and technical effort are an intrinsic part of same set of capability building activities.

Despite its benefits, training is relatively neglected in most developing countries: the study finds that 50 to 80 per cent of SMEs, and 20 to 70 per cent of large firms, provide no training apart from informal on-the-job instruction that consists of watching and imitating experienced workers. This type of informal training is found to have *no significant effects* on firm productivity. It is *formal and structured training*, in-house or outside, that is important for efficiency.

Some of the important findings of the analysis with respect to formal training are:

— Training of skilled workers yields more productivity improvement than of unskilled workers

— In-house training has larger effects than training provided externally

— Lower income countries enjoy greater productivity benefits from training than high income countries

— SMEs have higher productivity benefits from training than larger firms, presumably because they start from a lower base

— High technology industries have larger productivity gains from training than low technology industries.

— Training leads to higher wages for all workers, but technological change tends to lead to greater inequality between skilled and unskilled workers.

On the incidence of formal training, the study finds that the following types of firms train more than others:

— Large firms

— Export-oriented firms

— Foreign-owned firms

— Technology-intensive firms

The types of training policies that work well are those that provide for skill development funds, financed by a levy on payroll and refunded for approved training efforts. Tax incentives for training are used mainly by large firms and MNCs, who would invest in training in any case — its effects on raising overall training levels are dubious. Non-trainer firms do not undertake training because of tax incentives.

The study finds that the majority of public training institutes are not very effective; they tend to be unresponsive to industrial needs, with outdated curricula and poor equipment and teachers. Private training institutions tend to be better received by industry. Institutions that are led by industry are the most responsive and effective.

Finally, the study notes that SMEs need special support to train. They face greater market failures than large firms in terms of information, access to credit and technology support services. It is critical to convince SMEs of the importance of training and to provide *packages* of training, credit, technical support and marketing assistance. The government has a large role to play because of the need to *subsidise* SME training for extended periods.

Source: Tan and Batra (1995).

The new Tigers have, in comparison, relatively weak performances in education and training, especially in view of the pace of their industrial expansion and export orientation. Thailand appears best in terms of enrolment figures, but account has to be taken of the quality and relevance of the training provided. Malaysia seems to have a better quality system but the base is narrow. Indonesia is trying hard to catch up in the sphere of higher education, but still has a long way to go both in terms of quantity and quality. Enlarging, broadening and improving the educational base thus has to be a top policy priority for these countries.

The larger inward-oriented countries have the weakest human capital bases for sustained industrial upgrading. This may be surprising because India and China appear to have ample skilled and technical manpower, but this is the effect of large absolute numbers rather than of skills in relation to the size of the population. The pockets of advanced industrial activity at present are probably amply supplied with skills, while the bulk of the low productivity industrial sector manages with largely unskilled workers. The "skills crunch" will come when the economies open up fully to international competition, particularly with the SME sector, when skills and operating practices have to be massively upgraded.

Examples of Skill Development

Let us look briefly at some of the skill development policies pursued by the Tiger economies, in particular by Singapore, Korea and Malaysia.

Singapore: Singapore already has a well-qualified labour force. In 1995, of a total work force of 1.75 million, 64 per cent had secondary or higher educational qualifications, and the schooling quality is among the best in the world (see the TIMMS results in Table 8 above). In addition, the government has set up an extensive system of encouraging and providing both pre- and post-employment training. Its labour force has consistently been rated the best in the world by the Business Risk Intelligence Service (BERI), a US firm. BERI's ranking of 15 countries between 1980 and 1996 is shown in Table 11; these countries include 7 of our 10 (but exclude Hong Kong, Korea and Pakistan). The ranking is based on four factors — relative productivity, workers' attitudes, technical skills and the legal framework.

While all such evaluations should be treated with a great deal of circumspection, they are suggestive and plausible. Note, for instance, that the rankings correspond roughly with our educational assessment, and also with the value added per worker calculation earlier. Chinese Taipei turns out to have a better workforce than the United States, Germany, France and the United Kingdom. India and China appear at the bottom of the rankings, reflecting the low levels of training and productivity, and perhaps also poor motivation.

Table 11. **Labour Force Evaluation Measure by Business Risk Intelligence Service**

Country	1980	1990	1995
Singapore	81	77	79
Switzerland	73	77	75
Japan	67	73	73
Chinese Taipei	73	69	69
United States	53	64	67
Germany	59	66	66
France	62	58	65
Philippines	60	58	57
United Kingdom	42	54	56
Canada	48	53	55
Malaysia	48	51	54
Thailand	39	49	52
Indonesia	47	42	44
India	37	43	42
China	-	32	39

Source: EDB Website, 1997.

Singapore's training system is impressive. The Vocational and Industrial Training Board (VITB) established an integrated training infrastructure which has trained and certified over 112 000 individuals, about 9 per cent of the existing workforce, between 1979 and 1993. The VITB administers several programmes. The Full-Time Institutional Training Programme provides broad-based pre-employment skills training for school leavers. The Continuing Skills Training Programme comprises part-time skills courses and customised courses. Customised courses are also offered to workers based on requests from companies and are specifically tailored to their needs. Continuing Education provides part-time classes to help working adults.

VITB's Training and Industry Programme offers apprenticeships to school leavers and ex-national servicemen to undergo technical skills training while earning a wage. The programme consists of both on-the-job and off-the-job training. On-the-job training is carried out at the workplace where apprentices, working under the supervision of experienced and qualified personnel, acquire skills needed for the job. Off-the-job training includes theoretical lessons conducted at VITB training institutes or industry/company training centres. Unusually, the government collaborated with MNCs (one Indian, one German and one Dutch) to jointly set up these centres, funding a large part of employee salaries while they are being trained (below) in state of the art complex manufacturing technologies. Later the Singapore government worked jointly with foreign governments (Japan, Germany and France) to provide technical training.

Under the Industry-Based Training Programme, employers conduct skills training courses matched to their specific needs with VITB assistance. VITB also provides testing and certification of its trainees and apprentices as well as trade tests for public candidates. The Board, in collaboration with industry, certifies service skills in retailing, health care, and travel services. Using various grant schemes, the National Productivity Board's Skills Development Fund (SDF) supports some 500 000 training places each year. The initial impact of the programme was found mostly in large firms; however, efforts to make small firms aware of the training courses and provide support for industry associations has increased SDF's impact on smaller organisations. SDF is responsible for various financial assistance schemes to help SMEs finance their training needs and to upgrade their operations. It has also introduced a Development Consultancy Scheme to provide grants to SMEs for short-term consultancy for management, technical know-how, business development and manpower training.

The Training Voucher Scheme supports employers with training fees. This Scheme enabled the SDF to reach more than 3 000 new companies in 1990, many of which had 50 or fewer employees. The Training Leave Scheme encourages companies to send their employees for training during office hours. It provides 100 per cent funding of the training costs for approved programmes, up to a maximum of $20 per participant hour. In 1990, over 5 000 workers benefited from this Scheme. The success of the Skills Development Fund is due in part to a strategy of incremental implementation. Initially, efforts focused on creating awareness among employers, with *ad hoc* reimbursement of courses. The policy was then refined to target in-plant training, and reimbursement increased to 90 per cent of costs as an additional incentive. Further modifications were made to encourage the development of corporate training programmes by paying grants in advance of expenses, thus reducing interest costs to firms.

In 1996, the Economic Development Board's Specialist Manpower Programme (SMP) implemented the following programmes: Precision Engineering Specialist Manpower Programme, to support the precision engineering cluster of industries; Press Tool Design Development Programme, to support the precision stamping industry; 3D Solid Technology Development Programme to help the local mould design and manufacturing industry to keep up with the latest developments in solid design methodology and so keep up with the needs of MNCs; MSc in Mechatronics to train engineers in automation of micro-precision handling, miniaturisation assembly equipment and advanced robotics; and others. A programme was also launched for Skills Redevelopment of middle-aged and under-educated workers.

Singapore is increasing grants under its Initiatives in New Technology (INTECH) scheme from $50 to $250 million, and will include specialist training in such areas as wafer fabrication, training manpower for the "Regionalisation" thrust of the EDB, and the setting up of an International Business Institute. The EDB has introduced a $15 million scholarship programme to send students abroad to meet the need for middle-level managers and engineers and to meet the skill needs of new critical technologies.

These examples illustrate the comprehensive, targeted and forward-looking nature of Singapore's human resource creation policies. It is worth noting that these policies are not "neutral" or "functional", but highly selective and geared to the government's industrial policy targets.

Korea: Korea has, as noted, among the highest levels of educational attainment relevant to industry of any developing country. Its secondary and tertiary level enrolments are at developed country levels. Dropout rates are very low and the quality of the education, as judged by international numeracy and science tests, is high. It has impressive levels of vocational training enrolments, and encourages significant in-firm training of employees. The government's manpower planning has been based explicitly on comparisons with high-level technical manpower in highly industrialised nations like Japan, Germany and the United States.

The education of high-level technical manpower was promoted by the setting up of institutions like KAIST (Korea Advanced Institute of Science and Technology) at the post-graduate level and KIT (Korea Institute of Technology) at the undergraduate level. These were aimed at exceptionally gifted students, while the normal university system catered to the normal run of science and engineering training. KAIST turned out a total of 6 652 graduates between 1975 and 1990, of whom 832 were PhDs., and the rest MScs. An example of educational targeting in support of industrial strategy is the strategy to upgrade electronics design skills. In 1988 the Korean government began funding the Seoul National University's semiconductor laboratory to train a new generation of chip designers. The laboratory mounted annual programmes for about 200 students and employees of private firms, and some of the work for Korea's highest profile electronics project, the development of a 64-megabit DRAM chip, has been conducted at this laboratory. The laboratory receives about 600 million won from the Education Ministry. About 70 per cent of the money is distributed to students and faculty at smaller universities for use in related research efforts. The laboratory, with about 10 billion won of equipment, is also involved in materials analysis.

Malaysia: We noted that Malaysia suffers severe shortages of high-level technical manpower, seriously constraining its upgrading into higher technology activities (World Bank, 1996). However, it provides an interesting example of industry-led training that other countries can emulate: the *Penang Skill Development Centre* (PSDC).

Penang has a concentration of high technology activities, with many major electronics MNCs engaged in export-oriented activities. The PSDC was launched in 1989 in response to the growing skill shortages. The initiative, land and some financial support came from the Penang State Development Corporation, which induced three leading US electronics MNCs to participate in the venture. The MNCs formed a steering committee, provided financing and full access to their own training programmes, materials and methods. Other MNCs and local firms then started to participate and private industry continued to play a leading role in the institution, developing a strong sense of "ownership" in its activities. The PSDC borrowed trainers from these companies, and devised a range of training programmes suited to their needs. Full cost was charged for its services, and the programmes were continually upgraded and adapted to evolving skill needs. The centre is nevertheless entirely autonomous in its operations and decision making.

The Malaysian government offered a 200 per cent tax deduction for training costs to firms that sent their personnel to the PSDC (and to other approved training centres) for training; this scheme has been recently replaced by the training levy mentioned above for large firms. It also allowed the centre to bring in, without formal work permits, high-level foreign trainers (however, 40 per cent of the PSDC's training is done by local staff, and the proportion is rising steadily). The equipment needed for training was often obtained for free from equipment manufacturers, hoping to increase sales of their products. Some firms in Penang moved their own training equipment to the PSDC, releasing space in their plants.

From employee training, the PSDC has recently moved into pre-employment training, also paid for by companies seeking skilled workers. The centre has started to give scholarships to school leavers and is now producing its own teaching materials. The PSDC has 58 member companies, 80 per cent of them foreign. Its annual budget (1994) was around $385 000, of which only $48 000 came from the state government. It has conducted around 6 300 courses, attended by about 9 500 participants. Salaries paid to trainers are on a par with the private sector, and they are hired on contract without tenure. The Board is dominated by private industry, with some representation by technology institutions but none from the central government. Industry continues to give grants to the centre and regards its contribution as extremely valuable. The Malaysian government is now emulating the PSDC model in every other state of the country, with some degree of success.

Policy Challenges

The analysis shows how the Asian countries face very different policy challenges in human capital formation. Many of these challenges have been hinted at already. To reiterate:

—   The most advanced countries, Singapore, Korea and Chinese Taipei, have to advance their strong educational sectors in new directions, particularly to create new, specialised skills at all levels. At the higher levels, as they reach the stage of industrial maturity where research, development and scientific advance start to take precedence over production and engineering, their educational systems have to be regeared to these needs[7]. At the lower levels, there has to be greater emphasis on spreading skills related to information technology, improving worker training (both pre- and post-employment), and raising the levels of middle-level technical and managerial skills. Hong Kong's skill and education needs will be increasingly related to its role as a service and trade centre for China rather than an industrial base.

—   The new Tigers have to achieve the broad and deep base of human capital that the Tigers have established — and this is still some distance away. The base of secondary and tertiary education remains small, and the industrial training system weak. Malaysia suffers from grave shortages of skills at most levels, felt most acutely in its high technology export-oriented industries (World Bank, 1996).

Malaysian firms are relieving high-level skill shortages by relying on expatriate personnel, but this is expensive and cannot be seen as a long-term solution to the problem of a lack of domestic educational facilities. The presence of large numbers of illegal workers in Malaysia also holds back skill upgrading and training investments in the labour force. Thailand and Indonesia are also constrained by skill shortages; in Thailand, in particular, the upgrading of the technological base is being held back by this factor.

— The large inward-looking economies need massive investments in the quantity and quality of human capital if they are to attain broad-based industrial competitiveness. In China, the main needs are at the tertiary level, while in South Asia they are also at the primary and secondary level. Worker training is probably very weak, and needs to be enhanced.

Technological Development

R&D Performance

This section uses R&D expenditures as an indicator of technological performance. Though Asian countries are, like developing countries generally, highly dependent on imported technologies, they undertake increasing amounts of formal R&D activity to absorb complex technologies, adapt and improve upon imported knowledge, and even to create new technologies. While R&D is a measure of technological inputs rather than outputs, it is a reasonable measure of inter-country technological differences in more mature economies. Admittedly, R&D figures do not capture the informal effort that is a vital part of industrial competitiveness and growth, but such effort is inherently very difficult to measure (Lall, 1996). In fact, the best measure of such informal effort is the "results" it produces in terms of industrial deepening and competitiveness, and this has been done already earlier in this paper. What is interesting is to see if formal R&D expenditures conform to the picture that the earlier data suggested.

Table 12 shows R&D as a proportion of GDP in these countries. The clear leader is Korea, which spent 2.7 per cent on this activity in 1995 (STEPI, 1997). Not only is this the highest figure in the developing world by far, it is also higher than most of the technological leaders in the OECD. Some 73 per cent of Korean R&D is financed by industry rather than the government, making its private R&D/GDP ratio (of 2 per cent) one of the world's highest, surpassing even Japan's: this may be regarded as a better indicator than total R&D of technological effort directly relevant to industrial competitiveness. The rate of growth of R&D/GDP is the highest in Korea — 24.2 per cent in 1981-91 — compared to 22.3 per cent for Singapore and 15.8 per cent for Chinese Taipei. These data point to the underlying policy differences on industrial and technology policies (Lall, 1996), and they support implications drawn earlier about relative capabilities. Countries that have promoted the most complex and deep industrial structures and the greatest level of local technological mastery have the highest expenditures on R&D.

Table 12. **R&D Expenditures**

Country	Year	As % of GDP		R&D per capita
		Total	By industry	
Hong Kong	1995	0.1	n.d.	19.8
Singapore	1992	1.0	0.6	153.6
Korea	1995	2.7	2.0	271.1
Chinese Taipei	1993	1.7	0.8	179.6
Malaysia	1992	0.4	0.17	11.2
Thailand	1991	0.2	0.04	3.1
Indonesia	1993	0.2	0.04	1.5
China	1992	0.5	n.a.	2.4
India	1992	1.0	0.22	3.1
Pakistan	1987	0.9	0.0	2.6
Memo Item: Some OECD Countries				
Japan	1995	3.0	1.9	1 225.6
France	1994	2.4	1.5	544.8
Germany	1991	2.3	1.5	674.8
United Kingdom	1994	2.2	1.4	383.6
United States	1995	2.4	1.7	655.2

Sources: UNESCO, *Statistical Yearbooks;* STEPI (1997); Chinese Taipei Government (1994).

In value terms, however, these figures remain low. In *per capita* value terms, Korean R&D is only one-fifth of the Japanese figure and about 40 per cent of that of Germany or the United States. Chinese Taipei comes next, with more than half its R&D from the government: its dominant SME sector is unable to undertake expensive research. The government compensates with an extensive infrastructure of public institutions that offer extension, contract R&D and productivity services (Lall, 1996).

Private industrial R&D is relatively weak in the other countries. Singapore's enterprise R&D has increased in recent years, a result of strong government incentives and targeting, but much of it is in foreign affiliates and does not reach the depth that has been achieved in Korea and Chinese Taipei. Hong Kong, in line with its specialisation in low-technology activities, lacks a significant R&D base. Of the new Tigers, only Malaysia has some R&D capability, but this is largely confined to the product engineering units of a few large MNCs (the bulk is in 25 electronics firms, World Bank, 1996).

Technology Development Policies in Some Leaders

Asian governments have undertaken several policies to promote technological activity in their manufacturing sectors.

Hong Kong: The deindustrialisation and low technological status of Hong Kong has recently provoked the launching of some schemes to finance and promote technological activity (Box 3). This reaction provides insights into the outcome of the *lack* of industrial and technology policies in an otherwise successful economy.

Box 3. **Hong Kong's Efforts to Upgrade Technology**

Some newspaper reports on Hong Kong's belated attempt to adopt industrial policy:

"The government isn't watching passively as Hong Kong's manufacturing sector withers. Instead, the traditionally *laissez-faire* colony is trying both to shore up what is left of the domestic manufacturing base and to bolster the colony's position as the gatekeeper of Chinese manufacturing...As part of the new interventionist tilt, the industry department on May 9 [1994] gave preliminary approval to spend HK$ 140 million ($18 million) on 39 projects designed to upgrade Hong Kong's industrial structure. These are the first projects approved under a scheme to spend some HK$ 200 million annually to improve technology. Though far short of the degree of intervention in regional powerhouses Singapore, Taiwan and South Korea, it marks a notable turn-around for the colony.... A typical project aims to make palladium-coating technology available for the colony's watch and jewellery makers. The two year HK$ 4 million project is being conducted by the Hong Kong Productivity Council in conjunction with the Hong Kong Watch Manufacturers Association. The arrangement — where projects are tied to trade associations or universities — is characteristic of the strategy to fund projects that would be too costly for individual firms to conduct, but essential to their survival...

"The Hong Kong Industrial Technology Centre represents one of the colony's most tangible commitments to supporting technology-oriented companies. The centre is intended to promote technology activities in the colony by nurturing small companies and providing relatively inexpensive state-of-the-art facilities for more established ones... The government package supporting the centre includes a one-time grant of HK$ 250 million, the ability to tap a HK$ 188 million credit line (at 7 per cent a year) and 5 700 square meters of land next to one of the colony's busiest train stations..." (a)

"In order to encourage this trend [investment in new equipment], the government has toned down its *laissez faire* inclinations to permit a new applied research and development scheme. This is a $HK 200 million fund, which will match the investment of any start-up company which fulfils certain criteria, in exchange for an equity stake. This represents the first step towards direct government funding for research and development, and by implication, the creation of a government industrial policy...

"The government ... has provided a $HK 250 million grant for an Industrial Technology Centre, a new University of Science and Technology was recently completed, and plans have been initiated for a $HK 2.8 billion science park (the government's contributions would be much lower). In addition, its industrial estates in Tai Po and Yuen Long provide land for high-tech industries at significantly below market rates." (b)

a.   Clifford, M. (1994), "Trading Up", *Far Eastern Economic Review*, 26 May 1994, pp.68-9.

b.   *The Financial Times*, London, "Survey of Hong Kong", 4 May, 1993, p. 6.

The Chinese government is also contemplating a more interventionist stance on R&D in Hong Kong. It wants to nurture high technology R&D, both to enhance its competitive advantage and to act as a channel for more advanced technology transfer to the mainland. Its policy makers intend to reverse its decline in manufacturing and its lack of an advanced technology base. Its enterprises are considering the advantages of Hong Kong as a base for developing and selling technology. For instance, China Aerospace International, a rocket manufacturer, plans to have (as yet unspecified) high technology products developed in Hong Kong research centres. Chinese universities are setting up commercial subsidiaries to seek listing in Hong Kong to widen their international reach.

Singapore: The Singapore government has a very pro-active stance to encourage local R&D activity as a competitive tool. In 1991 it set up the National Science and Technology Board (NSTB) to spearhead technological effort in five strategic areas: manufacturing and engineering systems; information technology and services; electronics components and systems; chemicals and environmental technology; and life sciences, including biotechnology, food and agrotechnology. The five-year National Science and Technology Plan, launched in 1996, allocates $2.8 billion to this purpose. It will finance the technology infrastructure, specialist manpower development, as well as $500 million under an Innovation Development Scheme to "defray 50 per cent of the costs involved when undertaking or developing capabilities for innovation projects in products, processes, applications and services" in both manufacturing and service activities[8]. This is, to my knowledge, one of the most generous schemes for subsidising private research expenditure anywhere in the world.

The Singapore government often takes the lead in identifying and supporting strategic technologies that will build up its dynamic comparative advantage. One such effort is to develop national information technology capability by launching a plan "IT2000 — A Vision of an Intelligent Island". Managed by the National Computer Board, the Intelligent Island plan was launched in 1991 to lay down a fibre optic network connecting all homes, offices and factories in the island to provide a high speed and high capacity information infrastructure. Thus, "In our vision, some 15 years from now, Singapore, the Intelligent Island, will be among the first countries in the world with an advanced nation-wide information infrastructure ... The realisation of this vision will bring about new national competitive advantages and enhancement in the quality of life of the people of Singapore"[9].

The government also acts directly as a catalyst for launching research activity. Box 4 describes, for example, its foray into *biotechnology* as an area of future comparative advantage.

Korea: The Korean government has promoted local R&D and other forms of technology development by a broad series of measures. The strongly nationalistic stance of the government led it to encourage the import of technology mainly by "externalised" means, not involving foreign ownership and control. Thus, the main forms of technology inflows were by capital goods, licensing, subcontracting and imitation (Rhee *et al.*, 1984). The government intervened in these transactions to ensure that local technological capabilities were well served[10]. In the early years, the emphasis was on building basic mastery of imported technologies, but R&D was promoted from the early years, first in public technology institutions and later in private firms (Kim, 1997*a* and *b*).

The main thrust of private R&D comes from the large conglomerate *chaebol*; in 1995, only 20 *chaebol* accounted for 80 per cent of total private R&D in the country (STEPI, 1997). The *chaebol* were forced to raise their technological effort to be internationally competitive and meet export targets in the high-tech areas the government had chalked out for them; however, these pressures were reinforced by a range of R&D incentives offered by the government[11]. By 1995, there were

59.3 thousand researchers in the private sector in Korea, 15.5 thousand in public institutions and 42.7 thousand in universities. The number of corporate laboratories reached 2 270 (Lee, 1997). Their achievements in mastering very complex new technologies, investing in R&D and launching their own branded products in world markets is now legendary (Hobday, 1995).

Box 4. Singapore's Programme to Promote Biotechnology

The Singapore government set up an Institute of Molecular and Cell Biology (IMCB) within the National Biotechnology Programme, which was started in 1988 to strengthen the national R&D base and fund biotechnology development. An important incentive under this programme is pioneer industry status, which gives tax exemption for 5-10 years, with the largest benefits directed at technology-intensive and export-oriented projects. In addition, funding is provided by the government if there is active research collaboration with the public sector, with no specified limit to the available funding for R&D. Supporting this effort is a strong push in basic research at the National University of Singapore (NUS), which houses the IMCB. The University conducts one-third of Singapore's R&D, and NUS scientists have made their mark in several areas including materials technology, microelectronics and information technology. Singapore's decision to spend S$ 13.8 million to build IMCB and to provide annual funding of S$ 17.5 million is part of a broader approach to develop biotechnology.

To nurture this industry, the EDB established Singapore Bio-Innovation (SBI) Private Ltd. which by 1991 had invested S$ 41 million in 12 local biotech start-up firms with 1 428 employees making health care, food, and agricultural products. SBI also invests in overseas companies that might be strategic allies. The investment in IMCB appears to be paying off scientifically. An IMCB group is at the forefront of research on tyrosine phosphates, a hot topic in cancer research. Another group is sequencing the genomes of several fish species, which could serve as a reference vertebrate genome for the human genome project. IMCB's innovative assay systems convinced Glaxo, the pharmaceutical MNC, to establish a S$ 31 million trust fund for a drug screening centre within IMCB. Glaxo also invested S$ 30 million for a neurobiology lab focusing on genes that are expressed only in the brain.

In July, 1995, IMCB entered into a $0.9 million agreement with Boehringer Mannheim, the German company, to develop diagnostic/prognostic indicators for colorectal cancer. In April, 1995, it entered a $2.7 million joint venture with a local orchid grower to double the company's productivity. The University has also entered into several agreements with foreign companies to develop and transfer technologies in this area.

ICMB has also spun off a number of companies since 1994: Gene Singapore Pte Ltd, working on human healthcare products for regional markets; Gene Singapore China Pte Ltd. to work with Chinese companies on rabies vaccines; MediPearl Private Ltd to screen herbs and identify proprietary drugs to enhance the immune status of patients following chemotherapy; and Tetgen Private Ltd to serve as a vehicle to commercialise IMCB technologies.

Source: Lall (1996), EDB Website, "Singapore's Biotechnology Industry Sees Good Growth", 5 January.

The government also set up a number of institutions to promote technology development. In 1966 it established KIST (Korea Institute of Science and Technology) to conduct applied research of various kinds for industry. In its early years, KIST focused on solving simple problems of technology transfer and absorption. In the 1970s the government set up other specialised research institutes (on machinery, metals, electronics, nuclear energy, resources, chemicals, telecommunications, standards, shipbuilding, marine sciences, and so on), largely spun off from KIST. By the end of the decade there were 16 R&D institutions; in 1981 the government decided to reduce their number and rationalise their operations. The existing institutes were merged into nine under the Ministry of Science and Technology. The total R&D expenditure of the research institutions has increased steadily over time, from $28 million in 1970 to $2 billion in 1994; and the share of industry financing in their research has increased from 13 to 36 per cent in this period (Kim, 1997a).

The Korean government launched a series of *National R&D Projects* in 1982, large-scale projects regarded too risky for industry to tackle alone but considered in the country's strategic industrial interest. These were conducted jointly by industry, public research institutes and the government, and covered activities like semiconductors, computers, fine chemicals, machinery, material science and plant system engineering. National Projects were a continuation of the strategy of identifying and developing the country's dynamic comparative advantage, orchestrating the different actors involved, underwriting a part of the risks, providing large financial grants, and directly filling in gaps that the market could not remedy. Total expenditure on these Projects came to $680 million over 1982-89. The sums involved increased steadily from $25 million in 1982 to $151 million in 1989. Strategic technological activities are still targeted and promoted today. The Korean government provides massive financial support for technological activity (Box 5), quite apart from the various national schemes.

Other technology policy measures include the setting up, in 1989, of *Science Research Centres* and *Engineering Research Centres* and *Regional Research Centres* at universities to support R&D activities, the *common utilisation* of advanced R&D facilities, and the construction of *science towns*. Collaboration between universities and industry has grown over time, and the share of university R&D financed by industry has risen from 50 per cent to 72 per cent over 1976-94 (Kim, 1997a). The number of joint research projects between universities and industry has grown from 24 in 1990 to 415 in 1994. Daeduk Science Town has been under construction since 1974, and a large number of research and educational institutions are already well established there. Others are under construction. Technology diffusion is advanced through efforts of the Korea Institute for Economics and Technology which collects, processes and disseminates technical information to industry.

Weaknesses remain, despite the size and intensity of the technological effort in Korea. It is still felt by the government to be insufficient to sustain its drive into higher technologies. Collaboration between the public sector and industry is, while growing, still weak. Public research institutes, while having made significant contributions to the import, absorption and development of technology, still suffer from weak linkages with industry and insufficient commercialisation of their research findings. They also tend to lose good researchers to the private sector. Universities suffer from similar low linkages and their approach to teaching does not encourage creativity and originality. Several lack the equipment and facilities to conduct state-of-the-art research and development (Kim, 1997a). Daeduk Science Town has not been able to attract sufficient numbers of well-qualified researchers and scientists (Lee, 1997). There may be still too much government direction of research activity, and the Ministry of Science and

Box 5. **Financing Technology in Korea**

Korea launched a number of schemes for financing technological activity, often with a substantial element of official subsidy. The main *direct technology finance* schemes in Korea are as follows:

1) The *Designated R&D Programme* has, since 1982, supported private firms undertaking research in core strategic technology development projects in the industrial area approved by the Ministry of Science and Technology. It funded up to 50 per cent of R&D costs of large firms and up to 80 per cent for SMEs. Between 1982 and 1993, this programme funded 2 412 projects, which employed around 25 000 researchers at a total cost of around $2 million, of which the government contributed 58 per cent. It resulted in 1 384 patent applications, 675 commercialised products and $33 million of direct exports of know-how. The value of grants under the programme in 1994 was $186 million, of which 42 per cent was directed at high technology products like new speciality chemicals.

2) The *Industrial Technology Development Programme*, started in 1987 to subsidise up to two-thirds of the R&D costs of joint projects of national interest (National Research Projects) between private firms and research institutes. Between 1987 and 1993 this programme sponsored 1 426 projects at the cost of $1.1 billion, of which the subsidy element from the government was 41 per cent. In 1994, the programme gave grants of $180 million (with 31 per cent going to high technology products), a significant increase from $69 million in 1990.

3) The *Highly Advanced National Project* (HAN) was launched in 1992 to support two activities: the development of specific high-technology products in which Korea could become competitive with advanced industrial countries in a decade or two (Product Technology Development Project), and the development of 'core' technologies considered essential for the economy in which Korea wanted to achieve an independent innovative base (Fundamental Technology Development Project). So far 11 HAN projects have been selected, and during 1992-94 the government provided $350 million of subsidies for them. In this brief period, the programme resulted in 1 634 patent applications and 298 registrations. The plan is to spend $5.7 billion by 2020, of which the private sector is to contribute about half.

In addition, the Korean government set up three *funds to provide loans*, usually at subsidised rates, for technology development. The *Industrial Development Fund* provided low interest loans for long-term productivity improvement and technology upgrading in high technology industries. Several banks were used to channel the funds, which could go up to 70 per cent of the approved projects for large companies and up to 100 per cent for SMEs. The loans are given for five years, with a two-year grace period, and an interest rate of 6.5 per cent. The total funds disbursed over 1990-94 came to around $618 million. The *Science and Technology Promotion Fund* started in 1993 to fund firms and research institutes undertaking HAN projects (noted above). Loans could go up to 80 per cent of the total value of the project, up to $1.3 million per project and $3.8 million per firm. The loans are for seven years, with a grace period of three years and an interest rate of 6 per cent. In its two years of operation the fund has disbursed $255 million. Finally, the *SME Foundation Formation Fund* was set up in 1994 to support technology development and environmental investment by smaller firms. The fund could finance 100 per cent of approved projects at an interest rate of 8.5 per cent over 10 years, with a grace period of three years. In 1994 this fund disbursed $400 million.

Korea also has the largest and most successful *venture capital industry* in the developing world. Starting with the launching of the Korea Technology Development Corporation (KTDC), a joint effort by the government and the *chaebol*, in the early 1980s, several private venture capital funds were set up. There are 58 venture capital companies in Korea today, which disbursed loans and investment funds amounting to $3.5 billion during 1990-94 (85 per cent of this was in the form of loans).

(continued)

Technology does not seem to have sufficient authority to co-ordinate the various line ministries that are concerned with different aspects of technology development. The financial sector still has to be fully liberalised.

On the other hand, in the private sector, the engines of technological development, the *chaebol*, suffer from a rigidly hierarchical and militaristic structure of management which may reduce the efficacy and creativity of their R&D. The high levels of concentration engendered by the creation of these giant conglomerates may have held back innovation in smaller enterprises and the emergence of high-tech SMEs (Kim, 1997*a*).

Chinese Taipei: Chinese Taipei's industrial sector is mainly populated by SMEs and there is a large and efficient structure of institutions, arguably one of the best in the world, to serve their technological needs (Box 6). In addition to this support system, the government has mounted several policies to raise domestic technological effort.

A series of Science Plans have been launched since 1959, each targeting technologies important for future industrial development. For instance, the 1979 programme targeted four areas for technology development: energy, production automation, information science and materials science, to which biotechnology, electro-optics, hepatitis control and food technology were added in 1982. The last S&T Development Plan (1986-95) continued the targeting of strategic areas of technology. Private sector R&D has been relatively weak in Chinese Taipei because of the preponderance of SMEs, though some firms have now grown sufficiently large to perform substantial R&D, and are induced to do so in order to maintain competitiveness in international markets. In the late 1980s, some 43 per cent of total R&D expenditures went into eight national strategic programs for R&D, of which the bulk (62 per cent) was carried out by private enterprises; engineering accounted for 73 per cent of this.

Box 6. **Chinese Taipei's Technology Infrastructure**

There are around 700 000 SMEs in Chinese Taipei, accounting for 70 per cent of employment, 55 per cent of GNP and 62 per cent of total manufactured exports. Its technology infrastructure for supporting these firms is perhaps one of the best anywhere. In 1981, the government set up the Medium and Small Business Administration to support SME development and co-ordinate the several agencies that provided financial, management, accounting, technological and marketing assistance to SMEs. Financial assistance was provided by the Taiwan Medium Business Bank, the Bank of Taiwan, the Small and Medium Business Credit Guarantee Fund, and the Small Business Integrated Assistance Centre. Management and technology assistance was provided by the China Productivity Centre, the Industrial Technology Research Institute (ITRI) and a number of industrial technology centres (for metal industry, textiles, biotechnology, food, and information technology). The government covered up to 50-70 per cent of consultation fees for management and technical consultancy services for SMEs. The Medium and Small Business Administration established a fund for SME promotion of NT$ 10 billion. The "Centre-Satellite Factory Promotion Programme" of the Ministry of Economic Affairs integrated smaller factories around a principal one, supported by vendor assistance and productivity-raising efforts. By 1989 there were 60 networks with 1 186 satellite factories in operation, mainly in the electronics industry.

Several technology research institutes supported R&D in the private sector. The *China Textile Research Centre,* set up in 1959 to inspect exports, expanded to include training, quality systems, technology development and directly acquiring foreign technology. The *Metal Industries Development Centre* was set up in 1963 to work on practical development, testing and quality control work in metal-working industries. It later established a CAD/CAM centre to provide training and software to firms in this industry. The *Precision Instrument Development Centre* fabricated instruments and promoted the instrument manufacturing industry, and later moved into advanced areas like vacuum and electro-optics technology. The most important was perhaps the ITRI.

ITRI conducted R&D for technology projects considered too risky by the private sector. It had seven laboratories, dealing with chemicals, mechanical industries, electronics, energy and mining, materials research, measurement standards and electro-optics, but electronics was the institute's principal focus, with its Electronics Research & Service (ERSO) division accounting for two-thirds of the Institute's $450 million budget. ERSO has spun off laboratories as private companies including United Microelectronics Corporation (UMC) in 1979 and Taiwan Semiconductor Manufacturing Company (TSMC) in 1986, Chinese Taipei's most successful integrated circuit makers. The Institute for the Information Industry (III) was set up to complement ITRI's work on hardware by developing and introducing software technology.

The government also on occasion played a direct lead role in importing very complex technologies. It entered into a joint venture with Philips of Holland to set up the Taiwan Semiconductor Manufacturing Company, the first wafer fabrication plant in the country. The government also strongly encouraged industry to contract research to universities, and half of the National Science Council's research grants (about $200 million per year) provided matching funds to industry for such contracts.

The Taiwan Handicraft Promotion Centre supported Chinese Taipei's handicraft industries, particularly those with export potential. Its main clients were small entrepreneurs, most with under twenty employees. In addition, the Programme for the Promotion of Technology Transfer maintained close contact with foreign firms with leading-edge technologies in order to facilitate the transfer of those technologies to Chinese Taipei.

The China Productivity Centre (CPC) promoted automation in industry to cope with rising wages and increasing needs for precision and quality. The CPC sent out teams of engineers to visit plants throughout the country and demonstrate the best means of automation and solve relevant technical problems. They made rate approximately 500 visits and some 2 000 suggestions per year. CPC also carried out more than 500 research projects on improving production efficiency and linked enterprises to research centres to solve more complex technical problems.

The government set up a science town in Hsinchu, with 13 000 researchers in two universities, six national laboratories (including ITRI) and a huge technology institute, as well as some 150 companies specialising in electronics. The science town makes a special effort to attract start-ups and provides them with prefabricated factory space, five-year tax holidays and generous grants. In the 1980s the government invested $500 million in Hsinchu.

Source: Lall (1996).

Finally, where private firms were reluctant to enter into exceptionally expensive or risky technology development, the Chinese Taipei government itself played the entrepreneurial role. For instance, in launching the manufacture of DRAM chips, the government entered into collaboration with Philips, and then orchestrated the relevant private design, manufacturing and downstream firms around this venture. It has also for a long time been trying to launch an aircraft manufacturing industry, but has failed to find a foreign collaborator.

Incentives for R&D offered by the Chinese Taipei government include: facilitation of funds for venture capital companies, including venture capital finance from the Bank of Communications in high risk, high technology projects up to 25 per cent of the equity; financing for enterprises developing "strategic" industrial products (151 were selected in 1982, raised to 214 in 1987; the government provided NT$20 billion in loans at preferential interest rates for buying equipment, up to 65 per cent of the investment); encouragement of product development, with matching grants for approved projects; tax incentives for R&D, with all R&D deductible and accelerated depreciation for equipment; special incentives for enterprises based in the Hsinchu Science Park, with government financial institutions able to invest up to 49 per cent of the capital, and the investor able to count patents and know-how as part of equity.

Less is known about the weaknesses of technology policies and challenges in Chinese Taipei, but there are likely to be several. The relative lack of large firms may handicap its entry into very demanding new technologies. The "graduation" of Chinese Taipei firms from OEM (original equipment manufacture) activity, where all the marketing of export products is done by foreign firms, to OBM (own brand manufacture), where the local firm provides most of the technological and marketing inputs, has been limited (Hobday, 1995).

It may also be of interest to look briefly at one case of technology policy in *Malaysia*, which is otherwise not an impressive performer in this area. The Malaysian government recently launched a scheme to enter into the high technology end of information technology and raise the technological base of the economy by the promotion of a "multimedia super corridor". For a country with a small and under-developed R&D base, primarily an assembly site for electronics and electrical MNCs, this is a bold and imaginative step in industrial policy. If it works, the government initiative will catalyse technological activity at the most dynamic end and have enormous beneficial spillovers. Box 7 describes its main features.

Policy Challenges

As with education and training, the promotion of technological activity and upgrading poses very different challenges to the different Asian economies. The technological leaders in the group have turned out very impressive performances in their own ways, each pursuing different national objectives with different sets of tools. Each has to keep improving its policies and the supporting skill and institutional base, since each is entering into the most difficult competitive areas of manufacturing where it is sheer technological and skill superiority, flexibility and speed that count rather than just manufacturing capability. It is here, especially in terms of innovation, that there are the greatest challenges. The base of innovation, both within firms and in their supporting environment, is patchy and often weak. The educational and training system, developed to meet the needs of competitive production, has to be readjusted to the needs of design, creativity and frontier innovation. Firms, however powerful, cannot do this on their own — they need the entire structure of factor markets, suppliers and institutions to move with them.

It is worth quoting Hobday's conclusion on the electronics industry in the four Tigers, since this applies to manufacturing as a whole.

The strategies of East Asia's latecomers also pinpointed their continuing weaknesses. Only in a small number of areas have major new product innovations been generated by local firms. In most fields, they are still dependent on their natural competitors for key components, capital goods and distribution channels. Latecomer firms suffer from weak R&D capabilities and poor brand images abroad. Without stronger product innovation capabilities they will continue to rely on a mixture of catch-up, imitation-based growth and incremental innovation. Lacking strong R&D capabilities and a thriving capital goods sector in electronics, the technological roots of the latecomers remain shallow.

The majority of latecomers are still distinct from followers and leaders. Although some have made the transition to follower and leader in some areas, most are highly dependent on OEM and sub-contracting for access to markets and technology. As more latecomers approach the innovation frontier, they will require new strategies to gain technology and to overcome remaining weaknesses ...

To continue their success, much will depend on whether East Asian firms can overcome their latecomer disadvantages in design, capital goods, R&D and marketing. The strategy of the larger companies is to invest heavily in R&D and brand awareness campaigns. However, the results of these strategies are still unfolding and so far the results are mixed... some firms retreated back into OEM/ODM in the early 1990s after sustaining heavy losses in own-brand investments. Others witnessed the cost and risk of directly challenging the US and Japanese leaders, choosing to rein back some of their ambitions for the time being...

It would be wrong to overemphasize the difficulties facing the latecomers in the future. Some of these appear minor when compared to those already overcome since the 1960s. From a starting position of poverty and backwardness the four countries have become fast-growing, highly respected international competitors. Latecomer companies have built up impressive technological competencies, finely tuned to the needs of the most demanding export markets ... While it is impossible to predict the future, it is likely that equally remarkable advances will be made as new dimensions of latecomer innovation unfold. (Hobday, 1995)

This is as far as the technological leaders go. The evidence considered here suggests that Korea is the best placed on the drive to maturity. Singapore and Chinese Taipei face different structural problems, which they are tackling vigorously. Their governments continue to play vigorous roles in meeting the needs for human capital that markets on their own cannot. However, as their industrial structures grow more complex and markets and the institutional support structure improve, the role of the government is moving increasingly from the direct targeting practised earlier to meeting failures in factor markets, in particular in human capital formation and information.

The new Tigers still have to traverse successfully the technological road that the Tigers have covered. They have to build up their base of indigenous technological capabilities, moving from simple assembly to greater depth, diversification and integration in their production systems. They have been quite successful in creating efficient production structures, at least in certain parts of their industrial economies — now they have to create an "innovation culture" in industry, changing the largely passive and dependent approach spawned by the era of export-oriented production. Their local firms, especially the SMEs, tend to be technologically backward. The technology support institutions are weak. None of these are going to be easy to change. There are growing infrastructure problems, especially in Indonesia and Thailand.

The two giants in the region, China and India, have pockets of technological depth and capability, but these are islands in largely outmoded and inefficient production structures, operating with limited human capital. Even the technological leaders work in an environment not conducive to genuine innovation. Too much technological activity in these countries occurs in public laboratories isolated from production and market needs. Access to foreign technologies has been liberalised, and FDI is increasing, dramatically so in China; however, the ability of many local enterprises to absorb modern technologies is still constrained. Many public enterprises remain drags on industrial modernisation and technological progress. The infrastructure remains weak, in the case of India abysmal. The immediate challenge in these countries is to tackle these fundamental problems of production and production-related efficiency rather than technological development.

There are many lessons that the countries in the region can draw from each other, though large differences in political, social and economic circumstances dictate that the appropriate role of policy in fostering human capital development must differ around the basic core of functions that each government has to perform. Much more work is needed to define just what role policy should now play to cope with emerging challenges.

Notes and References

*   I am grateful to David O'Connor for perceptive comments.

1.   Note that the data for Singapore and Hong Kong exclude re-exports, which account for 40 per cent of total merchandise exports for the former and 81 per cent for the latter.

2.   Data for the Tigers go up to 1994, the others to 1992. The calculations are at the 2-digit SITC level.

3.   The concept of industrial "maturity", based on technological competence, is different from conventional approaches based on total factor productivity (TFP) growth. In a recent article, Krugman (1994) argues that the Asian Tigers did not have exceptionally high rates of TFP growth, and so presumably had little technological improvement, grew mainly by factor accumulation and so are bound to slow down as returns from accumulation decline. Moreover, the data adduced by Young (1994), used by Krugman, suggest that TFP growth rates over 1960-93 were as follows: Hong Kong achieved 2.2 per cent, followed by Chinese Taipei (1.8 per cent), Korea (1.2 per cent) and Singapore (-0.4 per cent). The ranking of countries differs from the one derived here. The real issue is whether TFP is a better guide to technological achievement than the more structural measures used here. It is suggested here that it is not. The TFP approach suffers well-known methodological difficulties, with different analysts reaching very different results. Apart from problems in measuring the basic factors, in particular physical capital, TFP estimates capture a range of other influences than technology, such as capacity utilisation, increasing returns to scale and imperfect competition. Moreover, the estimates cover entire economies rather than just the manufacturing sector, which is our present concern. The real problem arises, however, at a more fundamental level. TFP estimation is based on an identity, and cannot, as such, distinguish the validity of different underlying *causal* relationships. The theory makes certain critical assumptions: perfect markets, no technological learning, equal access to information, and so on (Cappelen and Fagerberg, 1995, and Nelson and Pack, 1996). As far as technological effort is concerned, its assumptions make TFP exercises particularly ill-suited to assessing technological competence — learning, technological lags and market failures are simply ruled out by the model. It is taken as a premise that factor accumulation takes place along a given and known production function along which firms move smoothly, without any additional risk, effort or cost and in a world without externalities or market failures. There is therefore no interaction between accumulation (moving into more capital and skill-intensive technologies) and technological effort: technical change comes only from a shift of the function. In real life, this distinction between moves along and of the production function is untenable. The process of "simple" accumulation (if efficiently carried out) necessarily requires enormous technological effort as more complex technologies are used (Nelson and Pack, 1996). In the standard TFP model, these efforts may not show up in the residual, even when the economy is moving into far more difficult and demanding technologies. Thus, TFP results cannot serve as reliable guides to technological capabilities. The TFP model also does not provide a useful framework for assessing the role of government in promoting technology development. It appears only as the facilitator of accumulation, with no valid role in influencing resource allocation in efficient markets. Once the assumption of efficient markets is dropped, however, there appears a role for the government in creating markets, stimulating technological learning

in difficult and risky activities, coordinating linked investments and capturing externalities (Stiglitz, 1996). Thus, the TFP approach does not negate our ranking of national capabilities. The fact that Singapore, for instance, was able to master much more complex technologies at world best-practice levels than Hong Kong, does still imply that it has achieved much greater industrial and technological maturity than the latter.

4. According to data shown in Table 5 of ADB (1997*a*), in the late 1980s Singapore had the highest proportion (75 per cent) of government financing of higher education of the Tigers, as compared to 40 per cent in Korea and 50 per cent in Chinese Taipei (no data for Hong Kong available).

5. See, for instance, the UK Cabinet Office (1996).

6. Singapore Productivity and Standards Board, *Current Productivity Issues*, November, 1996.

7. Kim (1997*a*) notes a deterioration in the quality of education and research at many Korean universities, though a few elite institutions have maintained their research output. Korea's rank in terms of publications in the Science Citation Index was 24 in 1994, much lower than its GNP rank of 11. The scarcity of research-oriented universities may have retarded the emergence of technology-based entrepreneurs.

8. *Towards a Developed Economy: EDB Sets Bold Targets for the Year 2000*, EDB Website.

9. IT2000 — *A Vision of an Intelligent Island*, EDB Website.

10. In the field of plant and process engineering, for instance, the government stipulated that foreign contractors transfer their design knowledge to local firms, which quickly absorbed design technologies in some process industries. The government intervened in technology licensing to lower prices and strengthen the position of local buyers, but in a way that did not constrain access to know-how. Licensing policy was also liberalised over the 1980s as the need for advanced technologies increased. The *chaebol* soon developed sufficient international presence to manage their technology imports, but the SME sector had to be assisted in buying technologies overseas. Korea compiled a database on sources and prices of technology supply, linked to similar databases overseas and provided on-line in major industrial centres.

11. Incentive for private R&D in Korea included tax exempt Technology Development Reserve funds, tax credits for R&D as well as for upgrading human capital related to research, accelerated depreciation for investments in R&D facilities, a tax exemption for 10 per cent of cost of relevant equipment, reduced import duties for imported research equipment, and a reduced excise tax for technology-intensive products. The Korea Technology Advancement Corporation helps firms commercialise research results; a 6 per cent tax credit or special accelerated depreciation provides further incentives. The import of technology is promoted by tax-deductible costs of patent purchase and other technology import fees. Income from technology consulting is tax-exempt. Foreign engineers are exempt from income tax. Grants, long-term low-interest loans and tax privileges were granted to participants in National Projects. Technology finance was provided by the Korea Technology Development Corporation.

Bibliography

ABBOTT, T. R. McGUCKIN, P. HERRICK AND L. NORFOLK (1989), "Measuring the Trade Balance in Advanced Technology Products", Working Paper CES 89-1, Center for Economic Studies, US Bureau of the Census, Washington, D.C.

ADB (1997a), *Financing Human Development: Lessons from Advanced Asian Economies*, Asian Development Bank, ADB Theme Paper 5.

ADB (1997b), *Emerging Asia: Changes and Challenges*, Manila.

CHINESE TAIPEI GOVERNMENT (1994), *Chinese Taipei Statistical Yearbook*, Taipei.

CLIFFORD, M. (1994), "Trading Up", *Far Eastern Economic Review*, 26 May.

Economist, The (1997a), "The Margaret Thatcher of Training", London, 17 May.

Economist, The (1997b), "World Education League: Who's Top?", London, 29 March.

Financial Times, The (1993), "Survey of Hong Kong", London, 4 May.

Financial Times, The (1997), "Special Survey of Malaysia", London, 19 May, .

FREEMAN, C. AND C. PEREZ (1988), "Structural Crises of Adjustment, Business Cycles and Investment Behaviour", in G. DOSI *et al* (eds.), *Technical Change and Economic Theory*, Pinter, London.

HOBDAY, M. (1995), *Innovation in East Asia: The Challenge to Japan*, Elgar, London.

KIM, L. (1997a), "Korea's National Innovation System in Transition", Science and Technology Policy Institute (draft), Seoul.

KIM, L. (1997b), *Imitation to Innovation: The Dynamics of Korea's Technological Learning*, Harvard Business School Press, Boston.

KRUGMAN, P.R. (1994), "The Myth of Asia's Miracle", *Foreign Affairs*, 73, November-December.

LALL, S. (1990), *Building Industrial Competitiveness in Developing Countries*, OECD Development Centre, Paris.

LALL, S. (1996), *Learning from the Asian Tigers: Studies in Technology and Industrial Policy*, Macmillan, London.

LALL, S. AND RAO, K. (1996), *Indonesia: Sustaining Manufactured Export Growth*, Report prepared for the Asian Development Bank, Manila, and the Ministry for Industry and Trade, Indonesia.

LEE, W.-Y. (1997), "The Role of S&T Policy in Korea's Industrial Development", Science and Technology Policy Institute, (draft), Seoul.

OECD (1994), *Globalisation and Competitiveness: Relevant Indicators*, OECD Directorate for Science, Technology and Industry, DSTI/EAS/IND/WP9(94)19, Paris.

OFFICE OF TECHNOLOGY ASSESSMENT (1990), *Making Things Better: Competing in Manufacturing*, US Senate, Washington, D.C.

PORTER, M. (1990), *The Competitive Advantage of Nations*, Macmillan, London.

RHEE, Y. W., B. ROSS-LARSON AND G. PURSELL (1984), *Korea's Competitive Edge: Managing the Entry Into World Markets*, The Johns Hopkins Press for the World Bank, Baltimore.

SELVARATNAM, V. (1994), *Innovations in Higher Education: Singapore at the Competitive Edge,* Technical Paper No. 222, World Bank, Washington, D.C.

SINGAPORE PRODUCTIVITY AND STANDARDS BOARD (1996), *Current Productivity Issues*, November.

STEPI (1997), *STEPI Newsletter*, Vol. 1, No. 2, The Science and Technology Policy Institute, Seoul.

STIGLITZ, J.E. (1996), "Some Lessons from the East Asian Miracle", *World Bank Research Observer*, 11(2), August.

TAN, H. AND G. BATRA (1995), *Enterprise Training in Developing Countries*, World Bank, Private Sector Development Department, Occasional Monograph.

UK CABINET OFFICE (1996), *Competitiveness: Creating the Enterprise Centre of Europe*, London, HMSO.

UNCTAD (1996), *World Investment Report — Transnational Corporations and Competitiveness*, Geneva.

US COMPETITIVENESS POLICY COUNCIL (1993), *Building High Performance Workplaces: Report of the Training Subcouncil,* Competitiveness Policy Council, Washington, D.C., March.

WADE, R. (1990), *Governing the Market*, Princeton University Press, Princeton, NJ.

WESTPHAL, L.E. (1990), "Industrial Policy in an Export-Propelled Economy: Lessons from South Korea's Experience", *Journal of Economic Perspectives,* 4(3).

WORLD BANK (1993), *The East Asian Miracle*, Oxford University Press, Oxford.

WORLD BANK (1996), *Made in Malaysia: Technology Development for Vision 2020*, Study prepared for the Ministry of Science, Technology and the Environment, Government of Malaysia.

YOUNG, A. (1994), "The Tyranny of Numbers: Confronting the Statistical Realities of the East Asian Growth Experience", Working Paper No. 4680, National Bureau of Economic Research, New York.

A Comment

David O'Connor

Professor Lall has produced an interesting paper that seeks to explore the human capital requirements of maturing Asian economies. His presentation of a range of statistical measures of technology level makes clear the pitfalls facing empirical work in this field. Trade and industrial statistics are unable to provide useful measures of technology-intensity except of the crudest sort. For example, using a classification developed by the Science, Technology and Industry Directorate of the OECD, the author shows the breakdown for each of 10 Asian countries of their manufactured exports by "factor"-intensity. Malaysia rates the most technologically sophisticated export structure (i.e. the largest share of science-based industrial exports) in both 1980 and 1992. Yet, as Professor Lall correctly notes elsewhere in his paper, Malaysian industry is rather shallow in terms of technological capabilities compared with Korea and Chinese Taipei. While his own index of technological dynamism comes closer to what seems a plausible ranking of countries, in this case Malaysia's dynamism would appear to be underrated by virtue of its having started the period with a high share of "high tech" exports. All of which suggests there is still considerable work to be done in developing better cross-country empirical measures of technological capabilities.

Turning from measurement questions to analytical ones, there are a few issues raised by Professor Lall's paper on which specific focus is merited:

—   Lall notes that at an early stage of development the task of education and training policy is fairly straightforward — i.e., to improve the quantity and quality of schooling and basic technical education, and to encourage all forms of in-firm training. As economies mature, he continues, it is less obvious what the best use of education and training resources is. Arguably, the same logic could be applied to a country's technology and/or industrial policy, viz., that as an economy matures and becomes more complex, government has a higher probability of "getting it wrong" if it continues to favour specific ("strategic") industries or technologies. Does it still make sense for governments in advanced Asian economies like Korea, Singapore and Chinese Taipei to be trying to pick winners?

— The author's discussion of the East Asian experience with technology upgrading tends to favour the more interventionist approaches of the three countries just mentioned over the *laissez-faire* approach of Hong Kong, where allegedly technological capabilities remain weak and the manufacturing base has been migrating to mainland China. Data on the sources of economic growth in these four Asian Tigers suggests, however, that Hong Kong has not done badly in terms of overall productivity growth — indeed, a well-known comparison among them (Young, A., 1994, "The Tyranny of Numbers: Confronting the Statistical Realities of the East Asian Growth Experience", Working Paper No. 4680, NBER, New York) finds that Hong Kong outperformed the others during the period 1960-93. While it is correct that productivity growth is not identical to technology upgrading, there is certainly a relationship between the two. Moreover, even if the particular measure of productivity growth is imperfect, it is not clear why it should produce biased estimates across the four economies (say, exaggerating productivity growth for Hong Kong but not for Singapore).

— *R&D investments*: The discussion of R&D *performance* is in fact a discussion of R&D investment (in relation to GDP) without providing evidence on how effective such investments have been. If R&D expenditures rise from 1 to 2 per cent of GDP, is that necessarily a good thing? That clearly depends on the expected returns to R&D investment, which will depend in turn on the availability of human capital to complement the investment. A country whose government raises R&D spending beyond a level that can be supported by the human capital base is likely to face very low returns. As a greater share of R&D spending comes to be assumed by the private sector, the test of expected returns is likely to be applied more rigorously, but with a growing focus on private as opposed to social returns.

— Confounding *what is* and *what ought to be*: Throughout much of the discussion of technology policy in the Asian Tigers, there is a focus on what has been done — of necessity this focus is on the countries which have *done* something, so Hong Kong's non-interventionist approach gets short shrift. Yet, rarely is there an actual assessment of whether a particular policy has proven effective — e.g. Singapore's Skills Development Fund and other training schemes. The implicit argument seems to be that "the proof of the pudding is in the eating", but it is not the case that the countries where intervention has been common have outperformed Hong Kong in terms of long-run growth. So, in what sense exactly is their performance superior to Hong Kong's? In the end, the higher marks awarded the other three seem to be based on a rather subjective judgment by the author about "technological capabilities" in manufacturing. Is the implication that Hong Kong's high living standards are somehow unsustainable because they are not based on such capabilities? If so, this commentator for one remains to be convinced.

Asia's Environment: Challenges and Opportunities

Vishvanath V. Desai and Bindu Lohani

Asia's Present Environmental Condition

Rapid economic development has created dynamism and wealth in Asia during the past 30 years. At the same time, however, Asia's environment has suffered from air and water pollution, and the loss of land and forests which were the basis of the livelihood of many poor people. In the past 30 years Asia has lost one-half of its forests and fish stocks, and nearly one-third of its land has been degraded. Asia as a whole is the most environmentally degraded region in the world, though not all parts of Asia are equally polluted, nor is the region the worst in every environmental indicator.

Asia has many types of environmental problems of which the main ones are pollution and depletion of fresh water; air pollution in its cities; loss of soil fertility through erosion, salinisation, and desertification; loss of forest cover, wildlife, and biodiversity; generation of toxic waste by industries; large emissions of greenhouse gases; and depletion of fisheries. The region's policy makers consider that the most important environmental problems are, in order of priority: water pollution and fresh water depletion; deforestation and air pollution; and generation of solid waste. On the other hand, the major environmental concerns of local communities are poor sanitation and garbage disposal, followed by polluted water and air. Several aspects of Asia's environment issues are discussed below:

Air Pollution. The air in Asian cities is dirty. The levels of ambient particulates are generally twice the world average. They are more than five times the levels in industrialised countries or Latin America. Throughout Asia, lead emissions from transportation fuels are also well above safe levels. Ambient sulfur dioxide (SO_2) is 50 per cent greater in Asia than in either Africa or Latin America, but still only one-third that of industrialised countries (Table 1). Air pollution greatly exceeds the international standards for air quality set by the World Health Organization. The major sources of air pollution are the increasing use of coal to meet energy demand and the rapid rise in vehicles using leaded gasoline or diesel fuel.

197

Table 1. **Asia's Air Pollution Levels in International Perspective**
(average 1991-95)

Air Pollution	Asia	Africa	Latin America	OECD	World
Particulate (mg/m^3)	248	29	40	49	126
SO, (mg/m^3)	0.023	0.015	0.014	0.068	0.059

Sources: Global Environmental Monitoring System (GEMS) Air and Water Data Bases and World Bank *World Tables*

The extent of air pollution also varies considerably within Asia (Table 2). Particulate levels are highest in South Asia, and moderate but rising in Southeast Asia, while they remain fairly low in East Asia. Lead pollution of air is highest in Southeast Asia, moderate in South Asia, and low in China, with the exception of a few eastern cities where it is rising rapidly. Sulfur dioxide pollution is the most severe, and still rising, in East Asia although much of it originates from outside the region. It is moderate in China, India and Southeast Asia although some hot spots exist in eastern China, northeast India and Thailand. In short, efforts to improve air quality should focus on particulates in South Asia and China, lead in Southeast Asia, and sulphur dioxide in East Asia and eastern China (Box 1).

Table 2. **Air Pollution Across Asian Sub-Regions, 1991-95**

Air Pollution	East Asia	Southeast Asia	South Asia	China	India
Particulates (mg/m^3)	85	225	431[b]	309	330[c]
SO$_2$ (mg/m^3)	0.192[b]	0.004	0.017[d]	0.028	0.017[c]

a. East Asia does not include Japan and China; South Asia does not include India.
b. 1986-90.
c. 1981-85.
d. 1976-80.
Sources: Calculated from GEMS Air and Water Databases and from World Bank *World Tables*.

Water Pollution. Asia's rivers are far more polluted than those in many other parts of the world. According to the Global Environmental Monitoring System (GEMS), Asia's rivers typically have four times the world average of suspended solids, and 20 times the levels in OECD countries.

Biological oxygen demand (BOD), an indicator of pollution of water by organic matter, of Asia's rivers is 1.4 times the world average, 1.5 times the OECD levels, and many times greater than in Latin America (Table 3). Specifically, Asia's rivers have three times the world average fecal coliform contamination (a cause of gastrointestinal disease), and over ten times the levels in OECD. Finally, there is 30 times as much lead in Asia's surface water as in the OECD countries, mainly from industrial effluents. Only nitrate levels, which indicate human or farm animal waste, or the run-off from chemical fertilizers, are lower in Asia than in the rest of the world.

Box 1. Relative Severity of Environmental Problems in Asia Subregions

	East Asia	Southeast Asia	South Asia	Pacific	China	India
Air Pollution						
Sulphur dioxide (SO$_2$)	xxx	xx			xx	xx
Particulates		xx	xxx		xx	xx
Lead		xxx	xx			
Water pollution						
Suspended solids		xx	xx		xxx	
Fecal coliform		xxx	xx	xx	xx	xxx
BOD		xxx	xx			xxx
Dissolved oxygen		xx				
Nitrates	xx		xxx		xx	xxx
Lead	xx	xxx				
Deforestation						
Deforestation rate		xxx	xxx		xx	xx
Land degradation						
Soil erosion		xxx	xxx		xxx	xxx
Waterlogging		xx	xxx		xx	xxx
Desertification			xxx			xx
Imperata		xxx				xx
Energy consumption						
Annual growth rate	xxx	xxx	xxx		xx	xx
CO$_2$ emissions	xx				xxx	xxx

xxx = very severe; xx = severe

Table 3. Asia's Water Pollution Levels in International Perspective
(average 1991-95)

Water Pollution	Asia	Africa	Latin America	OECD	World
Suspended solids (mg/l)	638	224	97	20	151
BOD (mg/l)	4.8	4.3	1.6	3.2	3.5
Without access to safe water (% of population)[a]	33	46	20	2	27

a.　　　　1991 figures.

Sources:　　GEMS Air and Water Data Bases and World Bank World Tables.

The nature and severity of water pollution in not uniform throughout Asia. Suspended solid levels are highest in the China, while BOD levels are highest in India and Southeast Asia (Table 4). Moreover, their levels are increasing rather than declining. Nitrates are a more serious problem in South Asia, including India, while lead in surface waters is worst in Southeast Asia.

Table 4. **Water Pollution Across Asian Subregions, 1991-95**

Pollution	East Asia[a]	Southeast Asia	South Asia	China	India
Suspended solids (mg/l)	5	103	607	3 065	n.a.
BOD (mg/l)	1.3	6.9	3.0	1.5	4.5[b]

a.   East Asia does not include Japan and China, South Asia does not include India.
b.   1986-90.
Sources: Calculated from GEMS Air and Water Database and from World Bank Tables.

Much of the potential health threat from polluted surface water could be reduced by providing people with access to safe water through municipal water systems and sanitation services. Yet here, too, Asia's record is poor. A far smaller proportion of people in Asia have access to safe drinking water than in any other part of the world, except Africa. Access to safe drinking water is lowest in Southeast Asia and South Asia, including India. Access to sanitation services is generally even lower than access to safe water. Nearly one in two Asians has no access to sanitation services. Facilities for the treatment of waste water and sewage are even poorer.

Solid and Hazardous Waste. With rising levels of income and consumption, the quantity of solid waste also increases. One study suggests that a 1 per cent rise in income brings about a 0.3 per cent increase in municipal solid waste. In Asia this ratio is even higher.

More worrisome than ordinary municipal solid waste is the hazardous and toxic wastes that hospitals and some factories generate. Fortunately, however, the output of hazardous waste decreases as a country gets richer and its economic structure changes. The use of plastics and other non-biodegradable materials declines, while chemical and industrial plants adopt more environmentally friendly technologies. China and India, for instance, produce 10-50 times more hazardous waste per person than Korea or Japan.

Deforestation. Asia's forest cover is shrinking by 1 per cent a year. This is particularly serious as Asia has relatively less forest cover than the rest of the world. With 13 per cent of the world's land and half its population, forest resources are scant. Asia has one-third as much forest per person as the world average, and only one-tenth as much forest per person as Latin America.

A great deal of deforestation has already occurred in South Asia, where it is partly responsible for higher rates of desertification, soil erosion, flooding and loss of biodiversity (Table 5). Today deforestation is particularly acute in Southeast Asia, mainly due to unsatisfactory logging practices and conversion of agricultural land to industrial and residential uses.

Table 5. **Pressure on Natural Resources Across Asian Subregions**

	East Asia	Southeast Asia	South Asia	China	India
Forest per 1 000 people, 1990 (sq. km.)	2.2	4.8	0.5	1.1	0.6
Deforestation rate, 1980-90 (%)	0.1	1.4	1.4	0.7	0.6
Agricultural land per capita, 1992 (ha.)	0.06	0.21	0.28	0.20	0.21
Change in agricultural land per capita, 1970-92 (%)	-25	-22	-39	-7	-34

Sources: World Bank World Tables and World Resources Database 1996-97.

Land Degradation. Agricultural land is scarcer in Asia than in other parts of the world. In 1992 Asia had only 0.3 hectares of agricultural land per person, compared to 1.6 in the rest of the developing world, and 1.4 in the OECD countries. Asia's soil is also of poorer quality. Less than 4 per cent of Asian soil has no inherent soil deficiencies (i.e. can be used for growing almost anything) compared to 15 per cent in Africa, and 12 per cent in Latin America. Soil erosion is Asia's most widespread natural resource problem, and it is equally severe in Southeast Asia, South Asia, China and India.

Salinisation and waterlogging are also acute. One hundred and thirty million hectares of Asian cropland (most of it in the China, India, and Pakistan) have excess salinity and are waterlogged due to poor irrigation practices. In the arid and semi-arid areas of South Asia, desertification is another big problem. As many as 63 million hectares of rain-fed land and 16 million hectares of irrigated land have been lost to desertification.

Biodiversity Loss. Asia accounts for about 40 per cent of the world's species of flora and fauna. However, encroachment on wildlife habitats by agriculture and infrastructure, deforestation, land degradation and water pollution have taken a toll on these biological resources and reduced their diversity. It is believed that Asian countries have lost between 70 and 90 per cent of the area of their original wildlife habitats.

Asia's coastal and marine fisheries, mangrove swamps, and coral reef systems are among the most diverse in the world. Approximately two-thirds of the world's coral reefs are in Asia. More than 1 200 species of fish inhabit the waters surrounding the Maldives alone. Fresh water ecosystems in Southeast Asia are among the largest and best developed in the world. However, more than half of Asia's wetlands have been lost, and more than half of the mangroves in the Indo-Malayan realm have been cleared.

Present Cost of Environmental Degradation

Environmental degradation may result in significant costs to society such as damage to health, loss of productivity and reduced well-being. Estimates of such costs vary across Asian countries and range from 1 to 9 per cent of the GNP. In China in 1990, for example, annual costs of productivity losses from soil erosion, deforestation, water shortages, and loss of wetlands were estimated to be 3.8-7.3 per cent of the GNP; while those from health and productivity losses due to urban pollution were 1.7-2.5 per cent of the GNP. The annual health costs of air and water pollution and productivity losses from deforestation in Pakistan in the early 1990s were estimated at 3.3 per cent of the GNP. In the Philippines in 1989, the health and productivity losses from water and air pollution in Manila were estimated at 0.8-1 per cent of the GNP. Estimates of costs of traffic congestion in Bangkok range between $270 million and $1 billion a year.

Projected Levels of Environmental Degradation

There are many uncertainties in how Asia's environment will change by the year 2025. On the one hand, economic growth, population increase, and higher energy consumption will increase pollution and resource-depletion; on the other, shifts in economic structure to light industry and services, availability of clean production technologies, and changes in policies and institutions, may help partially reverse environmental damage. Given these uncertainties, there would have to be a range of projections for environmental indicators in 2025 compared, for example, to 1990 under various scenarios. For energy use, and air pollutants related to fossil fuel use, the upper and lower limits of estimated changes are given in Table 6. Higher levels of air pollution would cause increased respiratory illness in urban areas, acid rain, and soil degradation over a wide area; and enhance the risks of climate change. Climate change, in turn, could cause loss of fresh water supplies, increase the severity of droughts and floods, increase the population at risk from malaria by 30 per cent, and reduce wheat crop yields by 15 to 55 per cent in China and India, although there may be an increase in rice yields in north Asia. Finally, about 15 per cent of the region's forests could be converted to grasslands and croplands by 2025.

Table 6. **Range of Increase of Energy Use and Some Air Polluants**
in 2025 Compared to 1990 in Asia

	Ratio: 2025/ 1990 level	
	Lower Limit	Upper Limit
Energy	2.3	3.5
CO_2	1.7	3.2
SO_2	1.7	2.5
No_x	2.0	3.4

Source: ADB (1997), *Emerging Asia: Changes and Challenges*, Manila.

The sharp increase in air pollution from fossil fuel use is related to the continued heavy reliance of China and India on coal for power generation. It is also related to the explosive growth in the number of automobiles throughout Asia.

Causes of Asia's Environmental Problems

A number of factors affect the quality of the environment. As most of them interact with others, it is difficult to single out any individual factor as "the cause" of a particular environmental problem. Some of the more important factors and their direct effects, or effects in combination with one another, are discussed below.

Population Growth and the Environment. Rapid population growth is usually correlated with deforestation, soil erosion, damage to the local ecosystem and other forms of environmental degradation. However, slower population growth does not necessarily slow down the rate of environmental degradation. In Sri Lanka and Thailand, for instance, where the rate of population growth has declined rapidly, environmental degradation has continued as fast as in other countries with higher population growth rates.

Although population growth cannot be correlated with environmental degradation, it can cause environmental damage when combined with factors such as poverty, poorly defined property rights, lack of employment opportunities, and certain systemic and policy failures. Since the environment does not have an infinite carrying capacity, at some point population density will damage the environment. Asia may not have yet reached that point. However, a combination of high population density, poverty and institutional failures such as undefined property rights over natural resources is more likely to damage the environment than population growth alone.

Poverty and the Environment. Almost 1 billion people in Asia live in absolute poverty. The poor are concerned about the present and heavily discount the future. Daily survival is their most important concern. Moreover, their ability or willingness to pay for environmental protection is virtually nil. As a result, the poor often exploit common or openly accessible resources such as forests, fisheries, water, etc. at unsustainable rates. The poor also tend to have very limited access to sanitation, water and living space, especially in urban areas, which also aggravates environmental degradation. Moreover, they have little access to credit or to technology, and lack secure property rights. When forests, fodder, fish, water are openly accessible resources, the poor try to obtain as much as they can. In such a race, children are an asset and this leads to high fertility. But high fertility, in turn, creates a vicious spiral of further impoverishment and environmental degradation.

Thus poverty is a contributory factor to environmental degradation without being an independent cause of it. Like population growth, poverty seems to exacerbate environmental problems in the presence of market, institutional, and policy failures.

Institutional, Policy and Market Failures. Decisions of individuals which do not reflect the costs or benefits of environmental improvements are an important cause of environmental degradation. This can be the result of institutional, policy or market failures.

Market failures can occur in several ways. For example, markets fail to price resources for which there are no secure property rights. Asia's policy and institutional failures fall into several categories. First, the private sector has been traditionally excluded from the provision of environmentally related services such as water supply and sanitation, solid waste collection, watershed protection, and treatment of waste water. The private sector has accordingly been unable to respond to the demand for such services. Second, Asia's public sector has failed to meet the demand for environmental improvement. Governments have been unwilling to charge users the full cost of environmental services. Moreover, they have been unwilling to reallocate other public funds to the environment or to impose higher taxation. Without full cost recovery or adequate public funding, the quantity and quality of environmentally related services will be inadequate.

Asian governments have often implemented inappropriate environmental policies. For example, raw water resources remain "open access" goods. Governments have not established well-defined and secure property rights over water resources (whether state, municipal, communal or private), they also tend to subsidise water for irrigation and other uses, and in many cases supply it free of charge. In Bangladesh, Nepal and Thailand, for instance, the total costs of supplying water in urban areas are at least 10 times the revenue collected. This policy not only leads to wasteful use of water and adds to the problem of treatment of waste water, but also places heavy demands on public sector financial resources to expand water supply networks.

Methods of pollution control in Asia also reflect institutional failures. In Asia it is generally based on a command-and-control approach. End-of-the-pipe standards, licenses, fines and specific government orders to cease polluting are the most common policy tools. Many countries have set targets for reducing pollution and also imposed a detailed system of pollution levies. Unfortunately, this system has been ineffective in reducing pollution. In many cases, the effluent charges have been set below the marginal cost of reducing pollution, making it cheaper for factories to pay the charge than to stop polluting. Finally, the ability and efficiency of enforcement and monitoring bodies have been very limited.

Why Not Leave the Environment Alone?

A relationship between environmental quality and per capita incomes during economic growth has been observed across and within countries. That is, with rising incomes, environmental quality at first worsens, then levels off, and later still, improves. This is sometimes called the "environmental Kuznets curve" (EKC), named for a similar relationship noted by Kuznets between income distribution and per capita incomes. The typical turning point at which environmental improvement sets in is a per capita income of about \$5 000-\$7 000 on a PPP basis. The "explanation" of the EKC is as follows: Economic growth initially involves more intensive exploitation of natural resources by industry and agriculture, which leads to increased resource depletion and pollution. As societies become richer, however, their economic structure shifts towards less polluting light industry and services, and prosperity increases the demand for a cleaner environment. The environment finally improves as environmental regulation becomes more effective and more resources are spent on treatment of waste.

Research has shown, however, that *not all* environmental indicators follow such a relationship, for example, biological oxygen demand (BOD) and chemical oxygen demand (COD). Second, the precise pattern of correlation with income varies across environmental indicators, and in only a few cases does it closely correspond to the EKC hypothesis. Third, there are clear differences in the relationships between income and environment for given pollutants in Asia and other regions. These empirical results argue against a simplistic interpretation of the EKC. If the curves for different pollutants differ for a given rise in income, and also change in different ways across regions, this would point to a number of other possible factors that influence changes in environmental quality. Policies are certainly among them.

The EKC hypothesis has prompted suggestions that the environment is best left alone during economic growth, as it will improve anyway when incomes increase. This is a seductive but fallacious argument. Even if the EKC hypothesis were valid, what societies seek in development is not simply per capita income growth or an improved environment, but an overall increase in well-being, which covers other things in addition to increased incomes and environmental quality. This notion of development would allow some environmental degradation if its cost in terms of perceived loss of well-being were more than offset by higher income. However, unless there is good reason to assume that the observed EKC is optimal without environmental safeguards, that is, at every point it represents the greatest well-being that a society can afford with its current resources, there is reason to determine whether or not well-being could be improved. For instance suspended particulate matter (SPM) levels begin to decline when per capita income is about \$7 000. In the case of countries such as China and India where SPM levels are already too high, it would be unacceptable to do nothing until incomes rise from their current low levels to the required level.

As it happens, there are some measures which can enhance environmental quality in developing Asia that would not involve a trade-off between environmental improvement and income growth. Indeed, several measures would enhance both economic growth and environmental quality. These include clarifying rights over natural resources such as forests and water, which would induce people to conserve resources rather than competitively extract as much as possible while some resources still remain; abolishing energy subsidies, which would make people use fuels less wastefully; and making people bear the costs of their polluting activities experienced by others, which would help them think about ways of reducing such pollution.

What Policy Changes are Needed?

This discussion has pointed to a general need for changes in policies and institutions to improve Asia's environment. Now some specific policies are discussed.

First, environmental policy must be more flexible. Rigid regulations issued by fiat, which have high compliance costs (and hence widespread non-compliance) should yield to a system which gives greater freedom to industries to choose their own cost-effective means of pollution control, as long as overall environmental quality is maintained. A flexible regulatory system would employ an array of economic incentives, although it would be unrealistic to assume that command-and-control instruments can be completely avoided, particularly where even small quantities of pollutants may cause serious damage, as with hospital waste, or toxic chemicals and heavy metals from industrial processes.

Second, environmental policies must address the market failures caused by open access natural resources. Rights, preferably tradeable, must be clarified and enforced with respect to water, fisheries, and forest products such as timber and wood for fuel. This does not necessarily mean that such rights must be conferred on individuals or private firms. For example, it may be appropriate to vest rights over fresh water sources or forests with local governments, or state governments, or local communities. However, as long as these resources are open to all without limit, everybody will have an incentive to exploit them as much as possible, and no one will feel impelled to conserve them. When rights are tradeable, the use of resources will carry a price, and users will tend not to waste them.

Third, unnecessary subsidies must be eliminated, for example, on energy or irrigation water. Such subsidies spur wasteful use, leading to depletion of the resources and increased pollution. Most subsidies have outlived their original intent and now constitute major fiscal drains. Removal of these subsidies will not only benefit the environment but also allow financial reallocation to extend services such as electricity and water to other users.

Fourth, several types of investments may benefit the environment and yield attractive economic returns at the same time. For example, this is possible in forest conservation, improving energy efficiency and treatment of waste water. These avenues should be pursued by governments or private sector investment should be facilitated.

Fifth, the new approach must not remain imprisoned in Asia's environmental ministries, but should inform policy making in diverse sectors such as energy, urban infrastructure, agriculture, transportation and other domains. Cost-effective environmental protection must be identified as an objective in each sector, and the impact of policies on the environment must be evaluated and taken into account.

Finally, institutional capability for environmental management must be strengthened. Government involvement must shift to focused strategic intervention and get away from top-down, micro-management of industries and firms. Streamlined environment ministries should coordinate a decentralised approach. They must ensure that environmental concerns are reflected at all policy making levels, at the level of both macro and sectoral policies. To some extent, this will occur naturally under market-based regulatory approaches. For example, finance ministries already view instruments such as pollution taxes as additional revenue sources. Central governments will need to devolve responsibility for environmental concerns to local and regional levels. Environmental management should be based on partnerships with local communities, NGOs, and civil society generally. This will require making information available, giving people the opportunity to participate in decision making on environmental issues that affect them (for example, through an environmental impact assessment (EIA) process), and ensuring effective administrative and judicial remedy.

How Can the OECD Help?

The OECD can help Asia meet its environmental challenges in several ways, which would also promote mutually beneficial trade and investment.

There is a crucial need for facilitating increased flows of private investment into environment-related infrastructure. The amounts involved are staggering. For example, water supply and sanitation investments are likely to be $8.9 billion and $4.2 billion a year respectively in 2000, rising to $16 billion and $7.2 billion in 2025. Investment in treatment of industrial waste will rise from $9 billion a year in 2000 to $48 billion in 2025. Overall, such investments are expected to grow 7.2 per cent a year between 1991 and 2025. However, private funds will not flow into such projects without supporting legislation and transparent regulatory structures in the host countries. For the most part, these are still lacking in most of developing Asia. A clear need therefore exists for the OECD to provide technical assistance and policy advice to help countries establish appropriate regulatory institutions and mechanisms.

Second, the OECD could contribute to facilitating transfers of clean technologies for the next phase of Asia's industrialisation. The global market for environmental technologies is already $300 billion a year, and is expected to reach $600 billion by 2000. With increasing effectiveness of environmental regulation, the market for such technologies in developing Asia is expected to account for a significant fraction of the world total. The OECD could help raise awareness of such technologies in developing Asia. Most Asian developing countries have enacted, or are in the process of enacting, domestic legislation to implement WTO agreements on intellectual property rights. With such regimes in place, a major new avenue for private investment in industrial plant and equipment embodying environmental technologies would open up in Asia. Furthermore, several developing Asian countries may themselves undertake commercial research and development in such technologies. However, bodies insuring respect for intellectual property rights in most developing countries are weak. The OECD could help developing countries in Asia in strengthening such agencies.

Third, the OECD could contribute to use of ISO 14000 environmental management practices. Adoption of ISO 14000 by Asian trading partners would facilitate their inclusion in global sourcing systems by manufacturers. However, the accelerated adoption of ISO 14000 requires training facilities in developing countries, besides qualified certifying agencies. This is an area where concrete results of technical assistance by the OECD would be visible quickly.

Fourth, the OECD could participate in the "Activities Implemented Jointly" (AIJ) pilot phase of the Convention on Climate Change. Some developing countries fear that the AIJ mechanism will enable industrialised countries to meet their greenhouse gas abatement commitments at low cost, without commensurate advantages to developing country partners. If such fears are not allayed at the pilot stage itself, it is unlikely that major developing countries in Asia will be persuaded to accept this mechanism on a long-term basis. The OECD could provide guidance to AIJ partner firms from its Member countries on appropriate contracting and benefit-sharing arrangements under AIJ pilot phase projects.

Finally, the OECD could monitor environmental regulations in Member countries which constrain trade liberalisation by acting as non-tariff barriers. Domestic environmental regulations in some OECD countries discriminate against developing country exports, an example being the regulations on packaging materials in Germany which discourage jute packaging, a Bangladesh export item. Another example is the use of "voluntary" eco-labelling systems which do not have proper scientific justification, and discriminate against processes and products from developing countries. Trade liberalisation is a two-way street, and the suspicion that environmental protection is used as an excuse by rich, industrialised countries to discriminate against developing country exports runs deep in the latter. The OECD should be sensitive to such concerns.

Conclusion

While Asia's environment has deteriorated faster with economic growth than in other regions, there are grounds for optimism that its recovery will also be quicker. However, this will not happen by itself, and will require policy changes, strengthening institutions, training, increased awareness, technology transfer and investment inflows. The OECD has an important potential role as a partner in the immense undertaking for the greening of Asia.

A Comment

Anil Markandya

Asia's environmental problems are among the most severe in the world, and will continue to be for some time to come. But the structure of the problems is changing. The issues arising from environmental degradation that is associated with low levels of development (and high population growth) will decline in the next century relative to the environmental issues that arise as a consequence of economic growth. This paper shows the increasing problems of industrialisation, but says less about the decline in other problems as a result of the economic growth that is taking place across much of the continent, growth which is reducing dependence on open access to resources, and providing more funds for environmental protection. It would have been useful to know more about that side of the environmental picture.

However, the paper does discuss the linkages between social and economic changes and the environment that are related to the above issues. There are two key mechanisms by which such changes affect the environment: population growth and poverty. The paper notes that population growth is not simply related to environmental damage. Examples are cited of countries where population growth is low but there is continuing high environmental degradation. Although population growth, per se, is not necessary for a deteriorating environment, it is an important contributing factor, and a decline in population pressure will help reduce some of the environmental problems in countries with rapid population growth.

On the other hand, the link between poverty and environmental degradation is not necessarily as strong as the authors believe. There are many cases in which poor communities have used their natural resources sustainably and with respect for the environment. However, other poor communities, which lack appropriate institutions for resource management, have experienced a significant deterioration in environmental quality. This suggests that the problem is not poverty but poor institutional management. In the absence of proper organisations to manage the resources, reducing poverty probably will not reduce environmental degradation.

Linkages between economic growth and environmental quality are also explored through the so-called "environmental Kuznets curve". Any observed relationship between these two dimensions of the quality of life is, of course, not deterministic. It depends on what policies are pursued and should be pursued, as the paper recognises. But many policy makers do not understand this and treat the relationship as deterministic. They do not recognize that some individual countries should aim for a better performance than the Kuznets curve would suggest for their level of economic development. Others may need to aim for a lower environmental performance. Policies depend on country-specific circumstances and the Kuznets curve is not a guide to the correct policy. The literature has perhaps given too much attention to the environmental Kuznets curve.

The paper discusses what policy changes are needed and what the OECD can do to help reduce the environmental problems that are emerging. The proposals in the paper are relevant and sensible. However, the following points also need consideration:

— There is a need to recognise the importance of linkages between macroeconomic policies and the environment. Structural adjustment policies, fiscal reforms, removal of subsidies, etc. all have environmental implications which should be understood. The existence of such effects does not mean that the macroeconomic policies should be rejected, but reforms may have to be modified to take the environment into account. Additional instruments may be needed to deal with some of the effects of macroeconomic reform on the environment.

— The OECD can provide more technical assistance to emerging Asian economies for ranking investments for environmental protection according to priority. Careful use of the limited resources is important because needs far outweigh resources.

— Technical assistance will also be needed to make greater use of market-based instruments, something which is proposed in the paper.

— With respect to trade and the environment, the problem is less one of technology transfer than of setting the trade agenda in a way that is fair to both the OECD economies and the emerging Asian economies. This question needs more thought. The paper indicates the importance of help to implement ISO 14000 in the emerging countries but at the same time notes that environmental regulations in OECD countries could become "non-tariff barriers". ISO 14000 could also be seen in that light. Hence, more dialogue is needed in setting the agenda on trade and the environment.

Third International Forum on Asian Perspectives

PROGRAMME

Third International Forum on Asian Perspectives

Experts' Seminar

Monday, 23rd June 1997

Session I: Opening and Introduction

Co-Chair of the Forum   Jean Bonvin, President,
                                   OECD Development Centre

                                   Bong-Suh Lee, Vice President,
                                   Asian Development Bank

Co-Chair of the Seminar   Vishvanath V. Desai, Director and Chief Economist,
                                   Asian Development Bank

                                   Ulrich Hiemenz, Director for Co-ordination,
                                   OECD Development Centre

Session II: Asian and Global Economic Growth: Aspects of Structural Interdependence

                                   Frank Harrigan, Senior Economist,
                                   Asian Development Bank

                                   Comment

                                   Philip Turner, Head, Emerging Markets Department,
                                   Bank for International Settlements, Basle,
                                   Switzerland

Session III: Trade, Employment and Wages: What Impact from 20 More Years of Rapid Asian Growth?

                                   Dominique van der Mensbrugghe,
                                   OECD Development Centre

                                   Comment

                                   Michel Fouquin, Deputy Director,
                                   Centre d'Études Prospectives et d'Informations
                                   Internationales — CEPII, France

                                   Open discussion

Session IV: Can the Ageing OECD Escape Demography Through Capital Flows to the Emerging Markets?

Helmut Reisen, OECD Development Centre

Comments

Koen De Ryck,
European Federation for Retirement Provision,
Brussels

Hans Blommestein, OECD Directorate
for Financial, Fiscal and Enterprise Affairs

Open discussion

Session V: Meeting the Human Capital Needs of Maturing Asian Economies

Sanjaya Lall, Professor, Department of Economics,
Queen Elizabeth House, Oxford, United Kingdom

Comment

David O'Connor, OECD Development Centre

Open discussion

Session VI: Asia's Environment: Challenges and Opportunities

Vishvanath V. Desai,
Director and Chief Economist,
Asian Development Bank

Comment

Anil Markandya, Professor,
Department of Economics, University of Bath,
Bath, United Kingdom

Conclusions

Vishvanath V. Desai,
Director and Chief Economist,
Asian Development Bank

Ulrich Hiemenz, Director for Co-ordination,
OECD Development Centre

Public Conference

Tuesday, 24th June 1997

Inauguration Francis Mayer, Ministry of Economy, Finance
and Industry, France

Welcoming Remarks Jean Bonvin, President,
OECD Development Centre

Bong-Suh Lee, Vice President,
Asian Development Bank

Session I: Asia and World Trade to 2020: A Post-Singapore Assessment

Arthur Dunkel, former Director General of GATT

Long Yongtu, Vice-Minister,
Ministry of Foreign Trade and Economic Cooperation,
People's Republic of China

Rak-Yong Uhm, Deputy Minister
for International Affairs,
Ministry of Finance and Economy, Korea

Jacques de Lajugie, Director for External
Economic Relations, Ministry of Economy,
Finance and Industry, France

Open discussion

Session II: Financing the Future: Pension Fund Diversification and Asia's Emerging Markets

P.G. Kakodkar, Former President, State Bank
of India, Bombay, India

Norbert Walter, Chief Economist, Deutsche Bank,
Germany

Roberto De Ocampo, Secretary,
Department of Finance, Philippines

Open discussion and end of Conference

LIST OF AUTHORS AND PARTICIPANTS

Co-Chair of the Forum

Jean Bonvin — President, OECD Development Centre

Bong-Suh Lee — Vice President, Asian Development Bank

Authors, Experts and Discussants — Experts' Seminar (23 June 1997)

Robert U. Ayres — Sandoz Professor of Management and the Environment, INSEAD, Fontainebleau, France

Hans Blommestein — Senior Economist, OECD Directorate for Financial, Fiscal and Enterprise Affairs

Françoise Caillods — Senior Programme Specialist, Institute for Educational Planning, Paris

Roberto De Ocampo — Secretary, Department of Finance, The Philippines

Koen De Ryck — European Federation for Retirement Provision, Brussels, Belgium

Vishvanath V. Desai — Director and Chief Economist, Finance and Administration, Asian Development Bank

Michel Fouquin — Deputy Director, CEPII, Paris

Frank Harrigan — Senior Economist, Asian Development Bank

Ulrich Hiemenz — Director for Co-ordination, OECD Development Centre

Hyun Jung-Taik — Minister, Delegation of the Republic of Korea to the OECD, Paris

Tom Jones — Administrator, OECD Environment Directorate

P.G. Kakodkar — Former President, State Bank of India, Bombay, India

Sanjaya Lall — Professor, Department of Economics, Queen Elizabeth House, Oxford University, United Kingdom

Bindu Lohani — Manager, Environment Division, Office of Environment and Social Development, Asian Development Bank

Anil Markandya — Professor, Department of Economics, University of Bath, Bath, United Kingdom

Françoise Nicolas — Chargée de recherche, IFRI, Paris

David O'Connor — Principal Administrator, OECD Development Centre

Helmut Reisen — Head of Division, OECD Development Centre

Philip Turner	Head, Emerging Markets Department, Bank for International Settlements, Basle, Switzerland
Renate Schubert	Professor, Institut für Wirtschaftsforschung der ETHZ, Zürich, Switzerland
Rak-Yong Uhm	Deputy Minister for International Affairs, Ministry of Finance and Economy, Republic of Korea
D. van der Mensbrugghe	Principal Administrator, OECD Development Centre
Friedrich von Kirchbach	International Trade Centre, UNCTAD/GATT, Geneva, Switzerland
Long Yongtu	Vice-Minister of the Ministry of Foreign Trade and Economic Cooperation, People's Republic of China

High-Level Panel (24 June 1997)

Jacques de Lajugie	Directeur, Direction des Relations Économiques Extérieures, Ministère de l'Économie, des finances, et de l'industrie, Paris
Roberto De Ocampo	Secretary, Department of Finance, The Philippines
Arthur Dunkel	Former Director General of GATT, Geneva, Switzerland
P.G. Kakodkar	Former President, State Bank of India, Bombay, India
Francis Mayer	Chef de Service des relations internationales, Direction du Trésor, Ministère de l'Économie, des finances, et de l'industrie, Paris
Rak-Yong Uhm	Deputy Minister for International Affairs, Ministry of Finance and Economy, Republic of Korea
Norbert Walter	Chief Economist, Deutsche Bank Research, Frankfurt, Germany
Long Yongtu	Vice-Minister of the Ministry of Foreign Trade and Economic Cooperation, People's Republic of China
Michèle Bailly	Principal Counsellor, World Bank, Paris
Anna Carin Krokstäde	Desk Officer, ASEM Directorate General I, European Commission, Brussels

Andrea Mogni	Economist, European Commission, Brussels
Benny Bergy Sorensen	Deputy Permanent Representative, European Commission, Brussels
Robert Hagemann	Senior Economist, International Monetary Fund, Paris
Carlos S. Milani	Spécialiste adjoint de programme MOST – UNESCO Programme, Paris
Thai Quang-Nam	Evaluation Specialist, UNESCO, Paris

OECD Development Centre
(in addition to those mentioned in the programme)

Catherine Duport	Principal Administrator
Giulio Fossi	Head, External Co-operation Division
Colm Foy	Head of Publications/Communication Unit
Kiichiro Fukasaku	Principal Administrator
Henny Helmich	Administrator, External Co-operation Division
Jody Kaylor	Conference Secretariat

OECD PUBLICATIONS, 2, rue André-Pascal, 75775 PARIS CEDEX 16
PRINTED IN FRANCE
(41 98 04 1 P) ISBN 92-64-16069-8 – No. 50077 1998